How I Went to Asia for a Colonoscopy and Stayed for Love

A Memoir of Mischief and Romance

DAVID GILMORE

ISBN-13: 978-0692952542
ISBN-10: 0692952543

Keep some room in your heart for the unimaginable.
— Mary Oliver

For Andy & Zoe.

ACKNOWLEDGMENTS

Special thanks to Jean Sward
for her expert editing and proofing skills.

Thanks to Therese Bagshaw, January Handl,
Trish Haines, Elizabeth Sparks, David Henry Sterry,
and Rob Zonfrelli for their encouragement to turn this story
into a book. Thank you to Thom Plasse for his promotional
help. Thanks to Larry Hermsen for his design advice.

Thank you to my husband, Chuan Choy, for his gentle
kindness, loyalty, and generosity of heart.
And thank you for feeding me
while I wrote.

INTRODUCTION

You know what people think when you tell them you're going to Thailand, don't you? You're either going for ping pong pussy or a facelift, lady boys or a laser vaginal tightening — vice or vanity. What drew *me* to visit Thailand for the first time, at age 42, was something far more mundane — a colonoscopy. I come from a long line of intestinal malcontents, and being that I was an uninsured American, such a procedure was going to come out of my own pocket. Facing the cost of several thousand dollars to ram a camera up my ass, I chose instead to take that money, fly to Bangkok, and get it done for 1/5ᵗʰ the price and enjoy a little beach time in Thailand before the procedure.

I boarded my flight bound for Bangkok poor and ugly, and 23 hours later I arrived rich and beautiful. That's the *other* reason people go to Southeast Asia — to be magically transported from dumpy, middle-age invisibility to the center of attention upon arrival. Thai people either don't have the same judgments we in the West do about age or they are savvy enough to recognize the pecuniary possibilities of lonely old white people. Add to that a hopelessly devalued currency, and the power of the US dollar instantly bootstraps you into an economic stature you as an ordinary American may never have seen. Thai people don't know you live in a trailer or clip coupons in America. To them, you're exotic, rich, and ginormous in size. You feel special for the first time since you won that honorable mention back in high school. You're an American in Asia — prepare yourself for untold attention and a thoroughly good fleecing.

There's really nothing you can do to prepare yourself for your first trip to Thailand. Coming from a Western country that is, by most world standards, considered sanitized and orderly, traveling to Southeast Asia is stepping through a portal into a world that immediately assaults your senses. Or tickles them depending on your willingness to shed your sheltered Western propriety and embrace the intensity of everything the moment you exit the airport. Forget all you've previously learned about cleanliness, forthright communication, and order. Those rules mean nothing in Southeast Asia.

Remember, though, you did this to yourself — you dreamed of a relaxing holiday with friendly locals, eating curry, and getting foot massages. You booked that flight, you ironed your shirts, and packed your bags, neatly tucking your espadrilles beneath your sun dress. You might as well just dump it all on the street, run it over with a car, and pour sewage on it. Welcome to Southeast Asia. You have no one to blame but yourself and nothing to do but surrender yourself wholly.

I entered Asia my first time through the mother of all brothels — a steamy pleasure palace called Babylon, tucked in the heart of Bangkok. I booked myself for a few nights in the hotel part of the notorious sauna. My wide-eyed taxi ride into Bangkok took me through the outer edges of the metropolis, arriving just past midnight. The air was thick and breeze-less and smelled of diesel fumes and fish. I was amazed at the ubiquitous sight of the King of Thailand — billboards, banners, photos — all adorned with royal yellow fabric. My taxi turned down a tree- and garbage-lined alley with mansions and embassies set behind spirals of razor wire fencing. I pulled up at Babylon which looks like a beige concrete fortress mildewing at the corners, with uniformed security guards to greet and usher me to the check-in desk. Southeast Asian cities are full of uniformed security guards who provide you with little more than a salute and the illusion of safety and security. Still, the salute contributes to that feeling of being special. When in my life heretofore has *anyone* ever saluted me?

I got to my room and settled in on my characteristically rock-hard Thai mattress for a long night of sleeplessness. The 14-hour time difference and the girlish cackling of money boys in the hallway kept me awake. A few times there were gentle taps at my door with more giggles and then phone calls to my room offering me companionship — for a price I was certain. At this late hour, I wasn't ready to negotiate such activities and figure out how to convert 1 US dollar to 1 Thai baht at a rate of .029. It was more than my tired brain could calculate. So, I pushed in some greasy earplugs and downed a Xanax for some much-needed shut eye.

I woke the next afternoon to find out that my first day at Babylon was indeed my lucky day. The notorious foam party would be happening in the sauna downstairs that evening. I got my ticket to it and descended into the bowels (ahem) of the bath house which is on the first few floors of the hotel. The name Babylon is perfectly apt as you enter an exotic kingdom when you pass through the giant wooden doors. Adorned with oversized fake stone statuary of naked men and lions cast in an ersatz art deco style, the place is larger than life. Smells of steam, eucalyptus, camphor, and pine oil cleanser overwhelm you as you enter. Upbeat lounge music is piped into every humid corner of the dimly lit caverns that seem to be designed by M.C. Escher. Staircases undulate in, over, and around each other. Hallways of dim blue lights spiral into completely dark dungeons and stone steps descend into a nautilus of warm water full of men. Thai men. Singaporean men. Japanese men. European and Australian men. Babylon is an intersection of East and West where everyone seems to find someone, *something* to play with.

I made my way to the upstairs locker room where I stashed my glasses and clothes in my locker and set forth in my towel and flip flops and proceeded to get hopelessly, wonderfully lost. I went around and around in circles past rooms full of panting men, past group showers behind walls of hanging chains, through passages with holes at waist height with hands reaching out to me like begging lepers. Mildly panicked that I might never find my way back to my locker and glasses, I finally just let myself enjoy the mystery

3

of being lost in this fascinating labyrinth of hedonism. I felt like Alice falling into a rabbit hole.

I eventually came to a door at the bottom of a staircase I had not yet encountered in my aimless wanderings. I heard music on the other side, which I thought might lead me back to civilization and my locker. I threw the door open and found myself right in the middle of the foam party. Hundreds of men were dancing in an open-air courtyard up to their necks in a layer of fluffy soap foam. It was like being caught in a warm snowstorm. Being a head or two taller than most men in Asia, I was able to glide into the foam without losing sight of the exit should I need it. But I didn't need it. I didn't want it. I dropped my towel which I later came to realize was terribly outré for the modest Thai people who are never seen naked in public. Suddenly I felt all eyes in the foam on me. There was a little parting of the foam as a few Thai men made a b-line toward me.

I was enjoying my first sensual encounter with a group of men surrounding me when all of a sudden, the heavens opened up and a monsoon cut loose on the foam party. Everyone scrambled to the side until the foam machine was kicked up to high, and the foam began flowing back into its corral in the center of this lush courtyard. There I stood, the only head above the foam surrounded by smooth little brown guys from all over Asia. I was indeed feeling like a rock star.

Never had I felt so welcomed and appreciated. This is the aphrodisiac of Asia. At age 42 I got to be the hot stud I've always been too skinny, hairy, and geeky for in America. And this was how Asia dug its hooks into me. Who can walk away from that? Who can turn their backs on feeling special? After my 3 weeks in Thailand were up, I went back to the US to save money for my return. So it went for 7 years — I carried out a lusty affair with a sensual, colorful, delicious place. I kept leaving my middle age doldrums in America to return to the place where I came alive — to a place where my all my senses crackled.

In those years of travel, I graduated from Thailand to Laos

and then Cambodia. I went on to advanced Asian travel in Myanmar and then Malaysia. It would seem in retrospect that I was searching for something and often getting a taste of it but not the real deal. Empty calorie encounters with people were intriguing enough to keep returning for, but in the end, they left me feeling unfulfilled and distracted...still the outsider. Determined to break through that thick skin of otherness, I continued to return, racking up countless miles, stories, and photos. Caves, temples, night markets, tuk tuks on hot nights, horse drawn carts in the desert, buck-toothed monks, money boys, lady boys, and crown princesses — Asia became a blur of rich experiences far from what I once called home.

Time spent back in the United States began to feel like I was just doing time waiting for my next big adventure in Asia. I felt more like a foreigner at home than I did in Asia. Maneuvering about there had become easy for me — kind of second nature.

Then one day on a bus in Kuala Lumpur, a strange and intriguing message foretelling of a great opportunity arrived as if borne by little Asian cherubs descending from the clouds. I heeded the message, packed up my life in America and moved to Malaysia. It was there that I finally found something deeper and more meaningful that made me feel wanted in a way that a foam party, or a money boy could never make me feel.

And that's when Asia ceased being my pleasure playground. Kuala Lumpur chewed me up like Burmese betel nut and spit me out. I ended up back where I started but with something completely unexpected and a changed man. I was as they say in Thailand, "Same same, but different."

In the end, I did go to see ping pong pussy, and I did get the colonoscopy but I got a whole lot more from my years of traveling in Southeast Asia — I got my life back. This book is a kaleidoscope of my adventures over 7 years through 6 countries, loosely tied together by my longing.

CHAPTER 1
PUSSY CHECK EMAIL

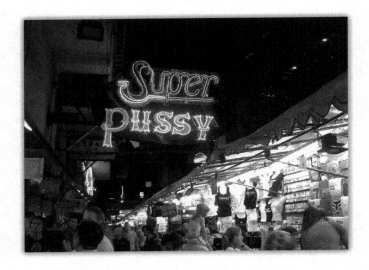

*A*ny trip to Asia begins with a monstrously long flight that most people dread the minute they book it. For me it's a chance to mix benzodiazepines and alcohol and watch movies while slumping into my seat. Slumping may not really be the word — more like melting in a *Fear and Loathing in Las Vegas* sort of way. I parcel out my flight time into the number of Xanax I will need to gobble in order to get through the trip. For example, a 14-hour flight from Los Angeles to Seoul, Korea, is divided by 4, the number of hours a Xanax will provide blissful relief from having my knees pushed up against the back of a seat while an autistic kid is repeatedly banging it. So, 14 divided by 4 is 3½...let's call it 4 doses of benzos and bourbon. Now before you yourself take any drug advice from *me,* be aware that this sort of dilettante pharmacist calculation can land you in the good company of Judy Garland, Whitney Houston, and Amy Winehouse.

While I have yet to actually meet any of these lovely celebrities in the hereafter who departed this earthly world on benzos and booze, I did have the pleasure of going to my own private hereafter aboard my first flight to Asia. First I was here — after I don't know what happened. All I know is that I awoke strapped to my seat, drooling onto myself with my toothpaste-covered backpack at my feet. In my desire to preserve my record of perfect dental hygiene, I must have set forth to the lavatory to brush my teeth and ended up brushing my backpack instead. It did occur to me that perhaps I might throttle back the dosage of my Xanax on my next flight. However, wisdom gained in a benzo stupor doesn't lend itself well to transference into the long-term memory portion of one's pickled brain.

My next most memorable moment of infamy on a long-haul flight was when on the above mixture of sedatives, I somehow managed to slide off my seat in the bulkhead section of the jumbo jet onto the floor. There I lay contentedly curled up in a ball like a package bundled up and shipped to Asia via airmail. I was awakened by the rustle of petite flight attendants in nylon skirts.

"Sorry sir, cannot sleep here!"

"Oh, yes I can. No problem," I replied. *No problem* is the fix-all for everything in Asia. It is pan-lingual. Find yourself in any country anywhere in the world trying to relieve yourself of any embarrassment or get yourself out of an awkward situation, and all you have to do is deploy those 2 words.

"Sorry sir, cannot sleep on floor," they repeated kneeling down and surrounding me.

I felt nails digging into my arms as I was I was politely but firmly lifted back into my seat for the duration of the flight. What happens on a long-haul flight stays on the long-haul flight. I would never see any of these people again and so why concern myself with the trivial matter of dignity? I put on my noise cancellation earphones, dialed up a James

Bond movie, and soothed my in-flight embarrassment with some bibimbap and hot green tea.

I've since switched from benzodiazepine to diphen-hydramine as a complement to the free-flowing cocktails on long-haul flights. While I may be achieving my dream of early onset dementia with Benadryl, at least I won't be meeting Judy and Whitney somewhere over the mid-Pacific.

My first trip to Asia was a dual-purpose trip. It was to hang out with my friend Darren who was hired to accompany a lady friend of his for her first facelift. The other was of course to get that colonoscopy. First the fun part.

Darren and I met up in Bangkok, a hot and humid, densely populated patchwork of Thai villages shot through with choking traffic jams. Cars, motorcycles, and growling tuk tuks zoom in every direction regardless of signage, and the presumed existence of traffic law. That is the way of the East in stark contrast to those of us who appreciate the meaning of a red light and a crosswalk. A red light in Asia is only a suggestion. A crosswalk is where the motorcycles sit waiting for a clearing to zoom through that red light that so inconveniently stopped them. A sidewalk is the overflow lane for traffic jams. And everyone is in a big hurry in Asia, and you dear tourist with your wide eyes and your camera are in the way.

Darren had already been there a week and was acclimated to the chaos. He showed me how to cross a road, something you'd think I would know how to do at my age, but crossing a road in Asia is considerably different than crossing a road in America. Darren took me by the hand and led me to the corner of a busy intersection. "First you have to remember that as a pedestrian, you're considered a loser and worthy of being run over, even if you're white. So, don't look. Start walking. Come on!" and he dragged me.

"I can't, there are motorbikes coming," I protested pulling back to the sidewalk.

"Just do it! They will go around you. But don't stop. Keep moving," he assured me grabbing my hand again. And they *did* magically go around us as if we were walking through a school of fish.

Darren then took me on a tour of Patpong, ground zero of the sex trade of Bangkok. You might think it's a large area from the highly-inflated media portrayals, but Patpong is in fact only a couple of blocks of highly concentrated, pink neon-bathed, hanky-panky on speed. We walked past thumping bars with abnormally skinny Thai women doing pole dances. Their faces seemed empty and lifeless while their bodies inched up and around poles mounted to the ceiling. If we gave more than a half-second glance at a bar's offerings, a hawker would come after us, "Hello my friend. Cheap drink. Ping pong pussy tonight, my friend!"

"Let's go see ping pong pussy!" Darren begged.

"We're gay guys, why would we want to do *that?*" I lightly protested spending money to see something I would likely find boring if not purely gross.

"See that sandwich board there, it says, 'Pussy Check Email! Pussy Smoke Cigarette! Ping Pong Pussy! Drinks 100 baht.' We can go and see ping pong pussy for about $3."

Yeah, but...but...I thought to myself. I saw ping pong pussy in the movies, *I* want to see pussy check email. I'm trying to imagine how a vagina is going to hit the command button and the letter "k" to poll her email program.

"Only $3, how could we go wrong? OK, let's do it." Always open for an adventure, I agreed and so we nodded to the bar hawkers that were swarming the streets. The nod meant, yes, take us into your lair and fleece us so we can lay our virginal eyes on your spectacle of filth. A group of scantily clad and highly made up Thai women immediately assembled around us beckoning us up the neon lighted stairs while jamming their nails into our arms. The nails seemed to portend some sort of warning that we better be generous with them or be shredded.

We were ushered to a noisy bar that surrounded a stage ringed with a bunch of other pale-faced suckers from the West. The bar tender impatiently demanded our drink orders. We each timidly asked for a beer — better to be safe than to try to negotiate a Manhattan in Thai. Beer bottles were plunked down and pried open in front of us while the girls continued to swarm around giving us painful neck massages. The bartender demanded 300 baht. The price had tripled since the street and there was no ping pong pussy and no pussy checking email or writing postcards. In fact, I'm not sure there was any pussy in this bar at all as the women were quite possibly all transgender.

"Not 300 for drinks. It's 100 baht for drinks!" I yelled over the noise of the girls behind me cawing like a murder of crows.

"You pay 300 baht!" the bartender demanded.

"No, 100 baht!" I countered again realizing my protestation was going to be futile.

The girls all joined in demanding 300 baht. I felt the first nails digging into my neck, dangerously close to my jugular veins. I knew there would be blood if we didn't get out quickly. Darren ponied up his 300 baht but I stuck to my principles and pulled out only 100 and slapped it on the bar and carefully replaced my wallet in my front pocket keeping my hand tightly on it. This enraged the girls who all began yelling in my face. I could see the ugliness and the desperation appearing beneath layers of makeup and fake smiles.

"Darren, we have to get outta here or we're gonna get killed." I was sounding desperate myself.

"Yeah, but *how?* I'm surrounded!"

"On the count of 3 let's just run for the door," I said.

"Ok you first."

"One…two…three…go!" I bolted for the stairs shrugging off 3 women who were clinging to me while pretending to call the police. Darren was fast behind me. We scampered down the stairs as fast as we could and out into the street where we immediately cloaked ourselves in the crushing crowd. We kept looking back to see if we were being tailed.

We made it out alive with only a few claw marks on our arms and necks but we never got to see pussy doing anything. Probably just as well that we gay boys stick to our own kind, I rationalized. In the name of desire, I can deal with some things that would horrify straight guys and I'm sure *they* can deal with razor-sharp fingernails if in the end, it gets them what they really want. I felt busted as an interloper in heterosexuality.

That was the closest I got to rubbing the dark underbelly of Bangkok's sex trade. I was forever put off by that underworld sex scene — completely and forever...that is until 3 days later when Darren and I went south to Patong, a honky-tonk beach town near Phuket.

Does anyone ever admit to being a "rice queen?" It's a term that makes those of us lovers of Asians wince. We get accused of racism, fetishism, exoticism, you name it. I personally happen to be fond of little guys and simply put, Asia is the place to find them. Say what you will, but I am a proud, card-carrying rice queen who also happens to like any other race as long as they're little. Besides, there is some credibility to the notion of opposites attracting. Caucasians of any stripe seem to have no problems picking up Asian men and as such there is absolutely no need to hire for sex unless you truly enjoy the sport of procuring and paying for a prostitute.

Being poor and un-fabulous in the US and rich and beautiful in Thailand, I thought it would be interesting to see what kind of flesh a little money can buy. After all, I had paid $3 for a sip of beer at the ping pong pussy show and didn't get my full view of the Thai sex trade. Besides, that show was for straight men — I wondered what it would be like if I crossed over to my home turf where I felt more confident. More biologically compelled.

Darren and I arrived by plane in Patong, a beach town

in the south of Thailand, where I decided to try the sex trade in a place a little less amped-up than Bangkok. We strolled the empty streets of the gay section of town on a weekday afternoon. We walked past a couple of quiet bars and a few guys came out to greet us enthusiastically. This was my first sight of Thai money boys. (Point of clarification: They are technically not boys. They are men.)

Most of the sex trade one finds on the street is not appealing to me — they look too street-tough and saucy and at the same time are aggressively flirty.

"Hey Mistah, you go wit me! Massa. Massa. Give you happy end!" they called out from the bar to passersby. "Massa" means massage, not master, lest you be thinking *Gone with the Wind*.

I'm attracted to refined little guys – shy, intellectual elves and was fairly certain I was not going to find anyone like that selling his ass on the streets of Patong. I figured I'd have to lower my standards or go without. These guys wouldn't take no for an answer and surrounded us, walked with us, and even stood directly in our way as if we were tanks rolling toward them in Tiananmen Square. The desperation level was starting to make me sad. But we smiled and laughed and shook our heads, "No thank you…sorry. NO!" I had to actually pick one guy up and move him out of my way and give him a friendly spank for being in my way. He enjoyed the pat and giggled as he took off.

I mentioned to Darren that if I saw someone who sparked my interest, I might go for it, but had little idea how to make a smooth transaction happen. Sealing the deal is a complex move — you have to face your own issues of money, power, shame, and illegality. Then, you have to negotiate the particulars of what you intend to do with someone who is likely not going to be speaking your language, finally agreeing on a price in a foreign currency. You are expected to do this with relaxed aplomb, smiling all the while, or they'll know you're a beginner and take advantage of you.

We walked up a side road and out came another group of boys to solicit us. I stopped in my tracks as one would when being pursued by a pack of wild animals. Hold your ground, I told myself, don't run...just back away slowly. One guy appeared from behind the crowd who caught my attention. He was not one of the aggressive guys. Looking over the top of his buddies, I smiled at him and he smiled back at me revealing a mouthful of braces. Oh no, *braces*, he's too young! It is particularly challenging to judge ages in Thailand. Their creamy, smooth skin seems to age so well in the tropical humidity such that someone in their 40s can look like their 20s. I beckoned him with a backward nod of my head and asked him his age. He said, "Twenty-two." Taking him for his word, I put him back in the running for my maiden voyage, braces and all.

In Thailand, the money boys are the "property" of the bar they hang out in. They sit at the bar waiting for customers to approach. The bartender or the bar owner makes the "sale" and keeps track of them and, offers some consumer protection that they are healthy and of legal age. It's all quite informal but nonetheless a functional business model. At the very least, the bar provides witnesses should anything untoward happen to the boy.

The other boys could see that I was focused on the one behind them. I felt strangely as if I were at a seafood restaurant picking out a lobster from a tank. The others backed away out of respect for the boy who might have a sale — a professional courtesy that thankfully didn't result in a territorial bitch fight. I was left standing alone with the boy in the street — Darren stood about 500 feet away watching with his arms folded. The boy came closer and I asked his name. Day-Arh was the best I could make of what he said. I told him I thought he was very cute and that later I would come back after my friend went to bed. He smiled and nodded and we said goodbye.

After dinner and a glittering drag show at a nightclub

called Tangmo — I walked Darren back to the hotel as he was feeling sick. He got into bed with a 101 fever. I, however, had a fever of another kind. I wanted to go out and hire my first money boy! I said goodnight to Darren, packed a condom into my shorts and set off.

I stopped by the lobby of our rundown gay hotel to talk to the owner, Phytoon, to ask him about money boys. I was amused that an anagram of his name spelled typhoon. He seemed like he either had been a money boy once or would have likely been part of that syndication that keeps track of them — there was a certain friendly netherworld quality to him. I approached him and told him I wanted to hire a money boy. He shot back a knowing smile that revealed some silver teeth — clearly, I wasn't the only one who had ever approached him about this. His English was excellent, and so I barraged him with questions.

"Typhoon…I mean Phytoon, I want to do this but I'm not sure how. What do you pay them, how long do you get and what are you allowed to do?"

Feeling the power of being the one with all the information, he had me sit at the bar and laid it out for me in long form.

"Well, this is how you do it," he said tapping his cigarette in the ashtray. "First you choose the boy you like and then you go to him and negotiate with him about what he is willing to do. You can ask him anything about the details. Then you ask him how much. He'll tell you. You can negotiate with him but around here it's usually about $1,000 baht. Then you have to pay the bar owner. He will pay the boy."

He gave me a few more pointers and then like a coach, he patted me on the shoulder and sent me into the alley to go get Day-Arh. The conversation with Phytoon was getting me excited. How easy and forthright. What a great opportunity to be able to negotiate exactly what I want, the price, and then actually do it. No skulking around smoky bars with drunken guys. No hours in front of the computer trying to bring a hookup to fruition.

Adrenaline was now coursing through my veins and my pace quickened as I turned up the now deserted street where I last saw Day-Arh. The boys all saw me coming. But this time they stayed seated and I heard one yell into the bar in English, "DAY-ARH! He's HERE!" The smiley boy with braces came bouncing out of the murky disco bar with a cigarette in his hand. My excitement was dashed seeing that he was a smoker. I hate the taste and smell of cigarettes on someone. He came right up to me and saw the smile fall off my face.

I frowned, "You smoke." He quickly hid the cigarette behind his back and flashed a big smile at me as if to say, *"Who, me? I don't smoke."* We both laughed. He immediately dropped the cigarette and mashed it out with his shoe and popped a breath mint in his mouth.

I leaned closer to him and said, "Are you free?" Oops — that was not the right phrasing.

"You want go with me?" he asked.

"Yes," I replied nodding with excitement.

"You pay bar. Not free," he told me with an indignant frown. I laughed and corrected myself.

"You are *available?"*

"Yes, available." he said.

"Now?" I asked. He nodded and smiled, swishing the breath mints around more rapidly.

"What do you like to do?" I inquired of the boy. Dammit — another wrong question. Phytoon was going to kick my butt. Deep breath, start over. Remember now, *I'm* the paying client — he's here to please *me.* I have to tell him what I want to do and then he will agree to it or not. Thus began my confusion over who the sex worker was and who the client was. It seemed I wanted to make him happy — to please *him.* Although it was a noble thought, it was confusing the guy and cheating him out of his services.

He starts back at me: "What *you* want?"

This time I got it right, "I want kiss you," I told him,

remembering to keep the sentences short and simple and in the present tense, maybe leaving out the prepositions. He gave me a definitive nod and smile. I leaned in to kiss him like one would try a sample of the salted caramel ice cream. He gave me a nice freebie kiss. Soft, wet lips, and gentle tongue. Excellent. I was all flush with excitement standing across from this beautiful young man with rosy lips, black hair, brown eyes, and gorgeous, thick eyebrows that almost met in the middle. He was clearly not pure-Thai — some Malaysian or Cambodian blood, I was guessing.

Just then one of the other boys came running out from the bar on a mission for something and swooped in past us. "Day-Arh you got good one. Handsome!" and he grabbed the crotch of my pants. Sheesh — was my arousal *that* obvious such that it could be spotted from the bar by his colleagues? Thai people are not known for their tactful discretion. Day-Arh seemed unfazed by this aggressive drive-by groping. I was now flying high on the dopamine and adrenaline that a man gets when he's got a live one on the line. I could have picked him up and carried him to the bar for payment.

I continued feeling him out a bit. I asked how much for his services and he said, 1,000 baht, which is about $29. I nodded my agreement and we basically moved on to the checkout counter. All the boys sat around the bar watching as I pulled out my wallet and thumbed through the notes as the bespectacled King's emotionless face looked at me from the bills.

Then came the extras...oh yes, the extras. It is after all the underground. Nothing is written and so you don't get a contract, receipt, warranty, and waiver to sign like you might in America.

Day-Arh says to me, "You have loom?"

"No have room. We go your place?" I asked him.

"Loom 200 baht."

I was not aware of this detail. I started to back away from the bar and put my wallet away to think for a moment. Hmm.

Could I bring him back to the hotel room with Darren sleeping next to us? Uh, not a good idea. I would have to go to *his* place — I assumed that's where we'd go anyway. I got assertive.

"You say 1,000. I pay 1,000. No more."

They all started squawking, "Loom 200! Loom 200 baht!"

"Nope, sorry." And I started to walk away thinking I'd been burned by the system *again* — no ping pong pussy in Bangkok, no money boy in Patong.

Day-Ahr followed me out to the street and grabbed my hand, blinked his big curly eyelashes pleadingly and said, "You pay 800 to me and pay bar 200."

"Total 1,000 for everything?" I asked.

"Yes. 1,000 total. No problem."

I turned and went to the bar, he said a few things to his comrades to quiet them down and I handed the bartender a 1,000 baht note. They gave Day-Ahr 800 and kept the 200 and Day-Ahr led me off down the street.

The momentary stress of that transaction began to fade as I focused on the back of Day-Ahr walking a few paces ahead of me. Everyone on that street knew Day-Ahr, so by association they knew what *I* was up to. All eyes were watching us not in disapproval so much as curiosity and gathering material for the gossip session they would undoubtedly be having later on. I may very well have been the only client for anyone that day.

On the way to the room, I found out a little more information about Day-Ahr. He is in school and lives with his boyfriend in Phuket. And in fact, the next morning I saw him drive by on the back of a motorbike holding fast to another young Thai man who I assumed was his boyfriend. He said his boyfriend knows that he is a money boy and gives his approval.

Day-Ahr didn't really look like a sex worker American-style, but the jeans he wore were undoubtedly chosen for the way they presented his ass, his shirttail riding just slightly above the waist. We went up three flights of a very rundown concrete building and into his room with only 1 tube of fluorescent lighting overhead and mattresses on the floor amid piles and piles of clothes. It appeared to be the crash pad of several guys — friends he said who loaned him the place for an hour. The building itself was crumbling. The apartment had no running water, just a toilet down the hall with a bucket of water used to spoon into the toilet — which was nothing more than a porcelain hole in the floor.

We settled in on a dirty mattress up against a wall, undressing each other and kissing. I couldn't decide whether I wanted the light on or off. Making love under the ghoulish glow of a fluorescent shop light was not exactly appealing, but the visuals of Day-Ahr were half the joy. We did a little lights-off and a little lights-on. I discovered to my delight that he had hairy legs and forearms and a little patch of hair in the middle of his chest — something very unusual in Thai men.

The rest of what happened with this beautiful young man is probably more interesting to me than to you. He was a great kisser and very easy to be with sexually — virtuosic in his profession. Interestingly, at first he wanted to only have sex facing me. I think that may be part of the unwritten code of safety — never turn your back on a client. But after a while he trusted me and didn't insist on this.

We wrestled back and forth with who was the client and who was the sex worker. I kept trying to do things that would please him and he would lose his desire. When I let him please me, he would get turned on. After a while I just stuck to my role as a paying customer.

Seeing Day-Ahr lying spread out before me, both of us smiling in the darkness, his body inviting and sensual as Thailand itself, I felt privileged that he shared himself with me. His body and his attention for an hour cost me so little. For him it was good money, an honest living (one could eat in restaurants for a week in Thailand for $29). For me it was money well spent, a chance to see into a world that is so shrouded in mystery and laced with shame.

Not being Day-Ahr's first, I'm certain that he forgot about me in some days or weeks. I could never say the same.

I returned to Bangkok for that colonoscopy that brought me to Thailand in the first place. On the morning of my procedure, I rang the front desk of the hotel at Babylon to tell them a hospital transport would be coming to pick me up. "Mister David, it is already here," they told me. Considering I wasn't allowed to eat or drink anything before the procedure, I rushed into my clothes and headed down in a flash.

The driver spoke no English and I spoke only about 3 phrases of Thai: "Food so spicy I have to put the toilet paper in the freezer," "Stop, that tickles," and "No, I'm not interested in your sister but how about your brother?" After I ran through those to break the ice, we were left to just smile in silence as we navigated through the sunrise traffic to the hospital, swatting mosquitoes on the windshield and giving the thumbs up with each victorious splat.

We neared the hospital and the driver radioed ahead as we pulled up the big circular driveway of what looked more like a luxury hotel than a hospital. An impeccably dressed and lightly perfumed woman in a tight beige pant suit and corsage approached the van and opened the door for me. I couldn't help notice how Thailand puts its most beautiful women in front-line positions. It reminded me a bit of the James Bond film I saw on the flight: *Goldfinger.* Bangkok Hospital's version of Pussy Galore escorted me to the revolving door where a security guard and 3 concierges saluted me. I could get used to *this*. Not knowing exactly what to do with a salute, I returned it with a smile and a nod.

Clacking over the highly-polished marble floor in her high heels, my escort walked me past the grand piano, water feature, and giant portrait of the Thai King and Queen and up an escalator to the receiving desk. Unlike American hospitals, there was no smell of death or announcements of 'code blue.' There was an eerie hush in the practically empty lobby. At receiving, I was the only patient — it was as if I had the whole hospital to myself. I filled out some paperwork, struggled with whom to call in an emergency (My mother in Florida? What is *she* going to do if a Thai doctor ruptures my colon?), and smiled for a picture.

I was issued an ID card, banded, and then escorted across the street to the GI and Liver Center — another quiet and immaculate building. I was turned over to the endoscopy unit and their team of beautiful nurses in high heels all resembling the flight crew in *Goldfinger* and all wearing the classic white nurse's caps that look like folded napkins. I sat and waited for my technician to escort me to the colonoscopy ward. The first and only ball was dropped — after sitting in the lobby for 10 minutes watching a Bangkok local news story of traffic cops delivering a baby while the mother was stuck in traffic — a nurse approached and asked me if I had an appointment. I explained that I did and then she immediately scrambled and returned in a couple minutes apologizing and explaining that the doctor would see me as soon as my bowels were ready. I wanted to protest and tell them I've been staying at a gay bathhouse, honey my bowels are ready for anything you've got. I inquired about doing the procedure without anesthesia to save a few bucks and get a better story for my blog. She seemed slightly taken aback. "Oh, no. This would be too 'discomfortable.'" I dropped the issue. Some things just don't translate.

Next, I was led by an adorable technician to the "bowel preparation room," which I couldn't help noticing, was appropriately decorated in various shades of brown. I looked for poop stains on the chairs and walls but couldn't find any. I was given a locker and kimono to change into. I could not figure out how to tie the pants so I held the string tight and put on the slippers and went back into the lobby clinging to my pants. My worst fear was losing my pants in front of a lobby full of Thai people.

A tall technician with long sideburns and a big smile came out to greet me in his pink scrubs (he was not in high heels, alas). He spoke nearly perfect English and greeted me as "Mister David." I asked him how to tie the pants that kept inching down — he showed me how to make a knot out of a loop in the front. I was still baffled, but at least I got to be close to him for a moment and at one point, he actually had to reach into my pants to tie them up. I was beginning to swoon — great, I needed a little distraction from an otherwise unpleasant procedure. He handed me a gallon of warm liquid in a bottle that looked like urine but smelled like orange Tang. He told me to drink it and let him know when I was completely cleaned out. He came to check on me a couple times and chatted briefly. I offered some of the laxative beverage to a couple of the women sitting in the lobby accompanying their spouses. They smiled and laughed — crazy Westerners.

Finally, after 2 hours of drinking the bitter orange liquid and 6 visits to the bathroom, I was at last ready! I found the smiling technician with the sideburns and he walked me into a room with a gurney, computers, flat screen monitors, and a big black hose that I figured was bound for my insides. Everything looked brand-new and sterile, in fact there really was no difference between this and any first-rate American hospital, except that the nurses wore high heels instead of comfortable gum-soled shoes. A nurse came in and put an IV line in my right arm and taped it up. Everyone left the room as they waited for the doctor to arrive.

This is when the waterworks started. Uh oh. I knew it was going to happen at some point but up until now I had gone into the role of blog reporter diligently scribbling notes every step of the way. I had to take off my glasses and put my notes under the pillow and so I just lay there for the 10 minutes of anticipation. No longer the reporter, suddenly I was just myself, very alone in a hospital for the first time at age 42, and a foreign hospital no less. It seemed like I was a really long way from home. What if there was a complication, who would I call on? I came to the realization that this is what I can afford as an aging man without health insurance in America: visits to foreign hospitals which would require braving these things on my own. I wanted to be a "big boy" but I couldn't stop crying.

The technician came in and noticed that my face was all wet. He stood next to me and rubbed my furry arm and gave me a soft smile of compassion, blinked slowly, and nodded his head. It must have felt odd for him rubbing my gorilla arms. He told me there was nothing to worry about. His softness, my feelings of being alone and nervous, and my crush on him all contributed to my being a blubbery mess. I'm not sure he understood why I was crying — for him this was routine, but he stayed with me anyway. I wondered if he was gay — a question that is asked a lot by tourists in Thailand — a country of fluid sexuality without much use for these western labels.

All of a sudden, the doctor rushed in with his entourage. Everyone assembled quickly and I was rolled onto my side away from the doctor. The technician untied my pants — a lovely last memory before the room went out of focus and I melted away as the drugs coursed through my open vein.

I awoke and looked at my watch. An hour had transpired without me. I felt no pain or soreness. I looked around — I was the only one in a long bay of gurneys with a view of the nurse's station. I watched the technician with the sideburns going about his duties. I blinked a few times and sat up. A nurse noticed that I was ready to move on. She had ordered a wheelchair for me which was waiting nearby. I waived off the wheelchair thinking I didn't really want to be an invalid just because I was a little groggy and bloated like I'd just had a beer and eaten a plate of refried beans. I waddled to the changing room and put on my clothes and went for lunch.

The hospital cafeteria was characteristic of the Bangkok

food courts — headless ducks hanging on strings, large woks full of vegetables and seafood, fragrant pots of curry. The smells were incredible and far exceeded any hospital cafeteria I have ever seen in the US. I ordered some vegetarian food, paid my $1.50, ate my lunch and crop-dusted all the way back to the GI and liver desk releasing several cubic feet of colonoscopy air.

The nurse directed me to the payment desk where I did something I've never done at the cashier: I laughed! The bill for the colonoscopy was $375. I could have spent that much at a day spa in America and I wouldn't be going home with a DVD of my intestines to show my friends.

The concierge at the front lobby arranged for a taxi to take me back to the hotel. Wending our way slowly through the gray and polluted streets, I thought about that news story of the woman giving birth in a taxi as we got stuck in traffic. I thought about the traffic cops of Bangkok who are trained in midwifery and about the technician with the sideburns. I now felt some odd sense of privilege to be able to travel half-way around the world for a procedure I could not afford at home. And then we pulled into the hotel and I promised myself a fun afternoon at the best gay sauna in the world with the cleanest colon on earth.

CHAPTER 2
SLOW BOAT TO LAOS
AND THE FLYING NUNS

*B*ack in the US, saving for my next foray to the
other side of the world, I came across an article in
the *New York Times* travel section about a French
colonial city called Luang Prabang in Laos. It looked a bit like
an Asian New Orleans. Being that I find the aesthetics of most
of urban Southeast Asia drab and cluttered, this place seemed
visually intriguing. There was also the promise of turquoise
waterfalls, night markets, and the famous dawn procession
of the monks in saffron robes. I was sold on the idea though
I only had to convince myself as this trip would be a solo
adventure. I worried about being lonely and slipping into a
melancholic state.

Getting to Luang Prabang is not the easiest proposition
unless you fly from Bangkok or Chiang Mai but then you miss
out on all the fun of overland travel. Because I was still new
to Asia, I felt the need to season myself with the adventure
of a slow boat ride down the Mekong River from Chiang

Khong, Thailand. It was purported to be a once-in-a-lifetime experience. I imagined sipping drinks on deck and waving to the mahouts leading their elephants along the riverbanks. Indeed, it *was* a once in a lifetime experience — more precisely — something you'd only want to subject yourself to once in your life.

The journey to Laos began in the northern Thailand city of Chiang Mai, where I stopped in at a local travel agency and inquired about the slow boat trip. The red-faced Australian man who was the front man at this travel agency signed me up for the trip while smoking and drinking his whiskey and soda at 11 am. His nose and cheeks were covered with rosacea. He promised me a nice hotel and a group dinner in Chiang Khong where we would spend the night and have a sumptuous breakfast buffet then board the boat to Laos first thing in the morning. I couldn't wait! I paid cash and he wrote out my ticket by hand telling me they would pick me up at my guest house the next morning at 9:00.

A Thai minibus is a rolling sardine can with tinted windows whose express purpose is to torture tourists. Getting on a minibus in Thailand means you will wait in front of your hotel for an hour…that is if they don't arrive a half hour *early* and catch you still in bed. Mine pulled up late with me sitting on my suitcase thinking they had forgotten me and I'd been ripped off. The minibus experience starts with the driver rushing you into a tiny seat in the "way back" while they rip and tug suitcases out to jam yours in under all the backpacks of other travelers. I found myself with my face jammed against the glass, angled slightly so that 4 large Westerners could fit on the bench seat. Forget about seat belts, and remember this: "TiT" — This is Thailand and you're not going to get what you paid for, you're going to get what they give you. My bladder was already beginning to whimper with control issues. I put on my iPod to calm my nerves as we then drove to 6 other guest houses to pick up more passengers.

About an hour after my hotel pickup we visit the last guesthouse and fill every cubic inch of the van. Finally, we are off on our journey...to the petrol station for a break. Why it didn't occur to the driver to gas up *before* picking everyone up, I don't know, but in Thailand you don't ask such questions. You *can't* ask such questions. I keep reminding myself this is not a vacation, this is *travel*.

After a few hours of the bus careening around corners, running through stop signs and nearly hitting water buffaloes on country roads, we pull into a rundown town full of banners, tuk tuks, and stray dogs: Chiang Khong — gateway to the muddy Mekong. I'm feeling psyched for the chance to see old Asia!

The van pulls to a screeching halt in front of an assemblage of corrugated tin and moldy concrete. Let me guess — this must be the package deal hotel. The driver ushers us off the minibus like pigs on the way to the slaughter house with his hand held out for tips. We are greeted by a tour guide who makes an announcement in something remotely resembling English. It is an earnest attempt but I get about 20% of it — something about this being the hotel where we would stay and that dinner would be served at 6 and to see him for a room key.

I got my key and grabbed my luggage from the pile of bags thrown on the ground and then went to find my room. The key opened a padlock on a pink plastic door that didn't quite fit the frame. I immediately went over to the bed to check the mattress as I thought I saw coils sticking out of a mattress that must have been from the 1950s. Yes, those were in fact coils — rusty metal coils — poking through the surface of the mattress. I had not yet learned to travel with an inflatable camping mattress and the sight of coils meant a sleepless night tossing and turning worrying about contracting tetanus. The pillow was a beige vinyl seat cushion from an old car with a greasy 100% polyester pillowcase loosely pulled over it. "No way, really? A car seat cushion for a pillow?"

In Thailand, one often sees tourist meltdowns. It's the

moment when the hapless tourist simply cannot abide the wholesale massacre of their expectations. They didn't say anything when the crosswalk was full of motorbikes. They didn't say anything when the roosters started crowing at 1am or the cats clawed each other to death outside their hotel room at 4 am. They didn't say anything when the hotel staff came into the room in the middle of sex. But *this?* That's where they draw the line. My "this" was the seat cushion-as-pillow. I stomped on the floor, "Son of bitch Australian who sold me this package deal. What next, a goat and some chickens on the boat?" Little Thai spirits hover unseen in the room scribbling down notes. "Mm hmm, he wants goats and chickens on the boat, does he?"

I went for a shower to clean up a bit before the sumptuous dinner. The shower area was outside in the courtyard in full view of all the "Scandafarian" backpackers sitting around drinking beer and twirling their fingers through their blond dreadlocks. I closed the corrugated metal door to have my shower, turned on the hot water tap and waited. And waited. It became clear that this would be a cold shower — not an entirely bad proposition in hot Thailand.

Returning to my room, I lay down on the bed. When I finally stopped bouncing off the top of the mattress coils, I heard the voices, the clearly audible and distinct voices of backpackers in the room next door. I touched the wall and the wall moved. It was not a wall, unless you call a piece of metal with some rivets a wall. I made the decision that no amount of Xanax was going to get me through this night.

I set out to find a new hotel when I ran into another woman who seemed to have that same sour look on her face that I surely was exhibiting. She was angrily hoofing it up the alley and appeared to be in search of a hotel.

"Not enjoying the 5-star resort, eh?" I ventured.

"Can you believe what they call a hotel room?" She rolled her eyes and shook her head.

We introduced ourselves. Yay, I found another cranky

American to commiserate with. I *needed* her. I couldn't bear to sit and talk about how great this trip was with doe-eyed, stoned backpackers. So far, this trip sucked and we both knew we had been hoodwinked.

She was Dianna from upstate New York getting to know the country as she had a son who had recently moved here and had had a child with a Thai woman in a town called Pai, in the north. We each set off for a new hotel and found half-way decent rooms and then convened for the dinner of pork fried rice with sticky coconut rice for dessert. To some this might sound delicious but to both of us, she a vegetarian and me a non-Muslim on a halal diet, the idea of pork and more bowel-stopping white rice was a gastronomic buzz kill. We pushed aside the dinner and went out for a walk to find something better on the street. I ended up with gristly chicken bits on a stick and some pineapple for dessert.

The boat ride to Luang Prabang began with a herding of the "farang" (the Thai word for foreigners) onto a boat that shuttled us across the Mekong River to the Laos immigration office. There we all sat on the garbage-strewn curbs with stray dogs sniffing us, waiting for our guide to come forth with our stamped passports and take us to the boat. After a couple hours of waiting we were herded onto a bus for a 30-second ride to the site of the embarkation, about 500 feet away. I stood at the top of the high river banks looking at the layers of plastic waste embedded in the mud under my feet. It was an entire archaeological dig through snack and candy wrapper history right at my feet. I watched plastic bottles and plastic bags flowing rapidly down river.

Carrying our luggage in hand, we were prodded toward the boat as the deeply descending muddy bank would destroy anything with wheels. The boat itself was a narrow-hulled, long, wooden vessel that looked like it would capsize if all the passengers gathered on one side to see elephants. Fortunately, I was advised to buy a seat cushion as the boat turned out to be full of wooden benches with the back set at a cruel 90-degree angle to the seat. Because I dilly dallied at the bank, looking at layers of garbage embedded in the mud, I ended up being among the last to board and took the only available seat — at the rear, next to the greasy diesel engine.

Once we were all aboard, the captain and his sons pushed the boat back and we drifted aimlessly down the river, turning and turning while they struggled to start the engine. I enjoyed the 2 or 3 minutes of silence before it was obliterated with the crushingly loud engine belching out putrid blue smoke that drifted with us as we headed downwind. I put in my earplugs and doubled up with my noise canceling earphones so that I could just enjoy the scenery and the bone-rattling vibrations of the engine.

The scenery was *really* something — perhaps even worth the discomfort of this trip so far. So far, that is, until after 7 hours of rattling and belching past rural villages, we arrived at the midpoint of our trip — Pakbeng, truly the worst place on earth. We stepped onto the banks to find our own accommodations (not included in the package deal for the good reason that they don't have electricity or internet in Pakbeng). Naked children and chickens wandered about the one dirt road through the main part of the smoky little town. Ramshackle houses in various stages of decomposition leaned over villagers squatting on the roadside next to pit fires.

Walking up the street to find a room for the night I reviewed my criteria: 1. A bed that didn't have springs sticking through the mattress; 2. No rats; 3. No electric generator next to my bed. I ended up in a room with all three. I lay in my filthy bed after a cold shower and waited for the town to settle down for me to go to sleep. The sun had set which means one thing in rural Asia — time to start the generators. The thin metal wall by my bed heaved as the diesel generator sputtered to life.

Fortunately, after a couple of hours, the generator ran out of fuel and when my ears adjusted to the silence all I could hear was the ringing in my ears. To live in Asia is to learn to live with noise and diesel fumes. When the ringing finally stopped, just before I was about to drift off to sleep, I heard the rats. It was rat happy hour in the exposed rafters of the guesthouse. The one light bulb was now out so I couldn't see the rats in the dark which of course set my imagination free to have fun with me. I feared rats would chew off my toes while I lay passed out in a Xanax stupor. I would awake to find bloody nubs and my power cords all eaten. I curled into the fetal position trying to avoid getting a puncture wound in my bony hip from the coils.

Morning arrived early as the locals rise with the sun and start the burning — the burning of wood for cooking and the burning of plastic bottles and garbage for housekeeping. Pakbeng is cut off from road travel to anywhere, so there is no such thing as a recycling program. Frankly, in most of Asia, the recycling program is called burn it, throw it in the river, or let the cows eat it. Smoke began to fill the guesthouse and signaled that it was time for the tourists to rise and shine.

I headed back to the boat early to get a better seat. This time I managed to get a seat amidships. I set out my pink plaid pillow and chose the aisle seat which turned out to be a wise choice as several of the backpackers aboard became violently ill from something they ate in Pakbeng. Tourists blowing chunks over the gunwales into the river framed my view of the

Mekong. I wondered if they ate that poor bleating goat that was tied up at the dock last night awaiting slaughter. Maybe they brushed their teeth with the sludge that came out of the faucet at their guesthouse. I offered up my acidophilus to the German guy next to me who was visibly green from nausea. The pro-biotic pills were all I had, but what he really needed was antibiotics. We were another full day's ride to the nearest pharmacy which meant he was going to be stationed near the edge of the boat for the duration. I wondered if the boat's toilet emptied its diarrheic load directly into the river but some things you just don't want to know about.

As Pakbeng faded into the smoke behind us, my spirits lifted. Only 7 more hours of sitting with my knees crammed against a hard wood seat back before we would arrive in French colonial paradise.

The slow boat to Luang Prabang earned its namesake as we chugged along with the current, stopping at various jetties along the way to pick up passengers. The few empty spaces on the benches were now filled...and then the aisle and then the edges of the boat and the floor space at the bow. I imagined someone would bring their goat on board, and well, in fact someone did. A small black goat was tied to a post near the rear of the boat and some woman carried on 2 cages of chickens which sat motionless and defeated with their beaks pressed against the bamboo mesh.

I pushed my way forward to join Dianna on the floor. We sat on a mat taking in the drama of the floating bus, watching in amazement as elephants lifted felled trees and farmers with conical straw hats carried buckets of water on poles over their shoulders as they watered their riverside crops. Boats zoomed past us with tourists wearing helmets and seatbelts on the fast boats known for being death traps when they hit logs or rocks. We passed villagers' houseboats with laundry hanging from the stern. Kids bathed in the murky, brown river. Mountains of Thailand on one side and Laos on the other side disappeared in the smoke like antique landscape paintings on rice paper. This was the old Asia — the Asia before the motorbike and the airplane. I was thrilled to see it even with a vomiting backpacker in the foreground.

I noticed 3 Laotian guys had boarded the boat at one of the small whistle stops along the way. They sat toward the front with wind blowing their feathery black hair. On closer inspection, I could see they were grandfather, son, and grandson — all of them beautiful in the various stages of their lives. They had the same square jawbones, button noses, and almond-shaped eyes. I wondered if the grandfather or even the father, as a child, had witnessed the American bombing of Laos from 1964 to 1973. I was just a child myself living in the Inland Empire of Orange County, California, but I remember seeing President Richard Nixon speaking of the war in Laos and Cambodia on our black and white TV. The U.S. dropped more bombs on the tiny country of Laos than were used in all of World War II. Surely the grandfather had stories of death and destruction that we could never imagine from the sheltered vantage point of suburban America.

After 2 full days on the boat we arrived in Luang Prabang. Dianna and I shared a tuk tuk into town and I went to my guesthouse which had not received my reservation request. I set out on my own, wheeling my luggage down the street to find a place to stay. It was Christmas eve and the town was booked solid. Finally, I found a small basement room down a dark alley off the main street. I checked into the humble guesthouse and took a long hot shower. I was immensely happy to be off the noisy, rattletrap boat, far from Pakbeng and on a mattress that didn't bruise me. I enjoyed my subterranean view of people's feet shuffling by outside my window. I watched the women fan their cook stoves and lay out their silk for sale on the sidewalk. I felt safe and comfortable like a mole in my little underground hovel in the heart of Laos.

The hotel staff were receiving English lessons from an English tourist. They would all stand and say hello to me as I passed through. It was here that I began my love affair with the Lao people. Much less cheerful than Thai people, their faces bear the burden of war and strict communist rule. They are more modest and smaller in stature than the Thai.

Signs on the guest house door warned about taking anyone of the opposite sex into your room. OK, not a problem, I thought. I even read an advisory to Western tourists from the People's Republic of Laos that said, "Welcome to our country. Please not to get sick because we don't have medical care here." I had noticed how young everyone in Luang Prabang was. It finally occurred to me that at that time in history the life expectancy of Laotians was only 65 years. (When I was born, the Vietnam war was raging and thus the life expectancy in neighboring Laos was a mere 44 years.) The whole of Luang Prabang seemed to be staffed by children who couldn't quite manage the enormity of the task. Nothing seemed to work properly and the food wasn't ever prepared or served quite right. It was like being in a pretend city with frilly French architecture all in some state of disrepair. But the people were kind, humble, and eager to connect.

Dianna and I met up for dinner and were invited to a "Kissmouth" party. I couldn't quite figure out what some young guy was saying when he kept repeating that he wanted us to come to his Kissmouth party. "Kissmouth KISSMOUTH! Melly Kissmouth." Oh right. Silly me, I forgot it was Christmas Eve. The invitation to a party was all very tempting but I opted for an early night after being sleep deprived from my night of horrors in Pakbeng. Dianna was leaving the next day, so we said our wistful goodbyes after dinner and agreed to meet sometime in her new home town of Pai, Thailand.

I woke early Kissmouth morning to smoke pouring into my room. Women making breakfast on the street with their wood-fired stoves were the perfect alarm for me to get up to see the procession of monks. At dawn the monasteries open their gates and the Buddhist monks and novices flow out into the streets by the thousands in their bright orange robes and golden sashes. In the dim light, they look like flames flickering about the town. They take their alms from the townspeople who sit with bowls of rice and money to give them with the hopes for good luck and prosperity in their own lives.

Throughout Asia there is a monastic mystique that is perpetrated by the non-monastic people. One is not supposed to touch a monk or a novice (the junior monks). They are allowed certain privileges like priority seating on buses and special waiting areas in airports. Townspeople give heavily to the monastery sometimes even giving their children. What I came to realize is that monasteries are essentially like frat houses for Buddhists. They are full of boys, after all, and what do boys do when they are not meditating, praying, or in class? They work out and play baseball. They watch violent Western television shows and porn. Yes, porn.

After a few days in my subterranean hovel, I was able to move up to the Sene Souk Guesthouse right across the street from Wat Sene Souk monastery. During my comings and goings to the guesthouse, I would stop and peer into the monastery wondering what life as a monk was like. One day, I noticed a group of novices sitting with their books at a picnic table under a big tree. I walked in the gate past a few novices who were sweeping the grounds with broomcorn brushes. They swept dirt and leaves from one side of the monastery and then back to the other as if they were just passing the time and not really interested in cleaning, perhaps practicing Buddhist non-attachment to outcome.

I was on my way to the table to chat with the monks when a novice said, "Hello, where are you from?" in near-perfect English. He was skinny, as most of the novices are, and flashed a big buck-toothed smile. He was unusually friendly to me and I had some sort of suspicion about his sexuality immediately. Why was he chatting up a single male tourist and ignoring the other tourists?

"My name is Oun," he said introducing himself.

"Hello, I'm David. I'm from America," extending my hand and then quickly retracting it realizing one doesn't shake a novice's hand.

"Are you traveling alone? Have wife?" he asked.

"Yes, I am alone — no wife. I'm gay. Do you know what *gay* is?" I said, lowering my voice so that the whole monastery wouldn't be subjected to this private conversation.

"Oh yes. I know many gay," he told me. I was amazed at how informed he was.

Oun had a sad, longing quality about him — something I could relate to being a lone gay traveler in an oppressive country. He told me he was studying English and invited me over to the table with the other novices to meet them and help them with their English. I was thrilled to have broken through the barrier that keeps most tourists behind their cameras and the monks silent.

His fellow novices were reading aloud to each other in between bouts of chatter and wicked laughter. Secular eyes seem to think that monks and novices are serious — that's at least how we want them to be, shunning earthly pleasures for piety. I came to realize that asceticism was only an illusion.

Oun introduced me to Lai, an adorable and muscular novice who was playful, goofy, and animated like the Dopey character in *Snow White*. "You may teach us English today if you wish," Oun suggested.

"Oh, what are you reading?" I asked. Lai pulled a small paperback from under his robes. It was a trashy romance novel. I laughed out loud wondering where they had gotten *that*. Oun started laughing with me and then he opened a page and read a sentence: "...and then she took his hand and pressed it to her bb..." he stumbled.

"Bosom!" I nudged. "Do you guys know what a 'bosom' is?" I laughed and told them. Lai grabbed some of the silk I had purchased in the market and threw it over his shoulders and pretended to be women touching her breasts.

"Yes! That's 'bosom.' Very good." Their laughter and playfulness were addictive.

They invited me to their room to see where they lived. I was brought into a big, dark, wooden room with no glass in the window frames. They all slept on thin mats on the floor. There was a small television with a set of rabbit ears antennae on top and a laptop computer that they all shared. How and where did they get *that* I wondered? They explained it was a gift from a local business to help them communicate with their families who left them at the monastery when they were children. Wow, it was all coming clear — this monastery was essentially an orphanage for dirt poor families who couldn't afford to feed their kids. I felt terribly sorry for them in a way that they probably didn't feel themselves. They had each other. I was the one traveling alone.

Lai asked me if I had Wi-Fi at the guesthouse and if they could have the password for their laptop. I didn't want them to be cut off from the outside world, so I scribbled it down on a piece of paper for them.

The next time I passed by the monastery I noticed no one was in the courtyard. I let myself in the squeaky iron gate and tiptoed through the courtyard feeling like an intruder without an escort. I gently knocked on the door of the bunkhouse and pushed the door open. There I saw something that would change my opinion of organized religion forever: the novices were all crowded around the laptop watching porn on the internet. I didn't know if I should admonish them or just silently observe what seemed like some great violation of Buddhist precepts.

The monastic mystique in my mind was irretrievably shattered. They turned to look at me and began laughing while pale bodies rhythmically writhed on the screen. I imagined that the novices were blushing but the room was too dark to tell. Not being particularly rigid in my beliefs of anything, I resolved in my mind that they were just teenage boys. I sheepishly covered my big grin with my hand and gave a shrugged-shoulders laugh back at them. They seemed to appreciate that I wasn't shocked or dismayed and that I wouldn't report them to their superiors. But the spell was broken. They slammed the laptop shut, adjusted their robes, and quickly ushered me out into the courtyard.

I had become fond of these guys and began to sense that they might all actually be gay — it was just a hunch. They seemed to like my companionship more than the other novices who kept their distance from tourists.

Oun seemed the most soulful of all and invited me on an adventure to a silk weaving village to purchase a wall hanging. We walked and talked about his life and his wishes to become a monk one day as we walked across the Mekong on a rickety bamboo bridge that swayed with each step.

"Oun, may I ask you a personal question?"

"Yes, of course."

"You know that I am gay and you mentioned that you have met many gay tourists at the gate, but what about *you?*"

"Oh yes, I gay too. But I in monastery and cannot experience what is like to be gay," he told me in a longing sort of way.

"Do you ever want to leave the monastery and find a boyfriend?" I pried a bit more.

"I think yes, but no. I must stay in monastery. My family no money. Here I have education and opportunity."

The intractability of his situation was depressing. On the other hand, I envied the stability of his life and the camaraderie he had with his fellow novices. Oun revealed that Lai was also gay and had in fact developed a habit of clandestine visits with other gay tourists at their guesthouses.

Later in my visit, Oun and Lai both took me on a river adventure to the pottery village. We walked down a long, muddy road lined with sugar cane. Once out of view of the public, they cut loose with their gayness, goofing off and talking about the hot guys they met at the gate. I was astounded but kept my responses cool — I didn't want to end up in a Laos prison for fraternizing with a novice. Oun stuck to his vows of chastity anyway, and I was apparently too young for Lai. Yes, too young. So, I just called them "the flying nuns" and enjoyed their platonic friendship for a few days.

When it came time to say goodbye, I made a point of stopping by to see them. The flying nuns were taking an outdoor shower out back in their bikini underwear. They were tormenting the younger ones by snapping them with wet robes and prancing around with towels on their heads like they were in a drag show. I found Oun sitting in a chair reading by himself, opting out of the more sophomoric monastic shenanigans.

He and I took one last soulful walk during which he revealed his desires for love and his misgivings about being ugly and skinny.

"What kind of men do you find attractive, Oun?" I asked as we sat on the bank of the Mekong watching kids jumping off the bamboo bridge and swimming ashore.

"Oh, I like Caucasian man."

"Really, why? We are selfish and have hair on our backs," I laughed.

"Asian man not attractive. We very small people. Not pretty. White man big, handsome. I *like* hairy man," he insisted. I marveled at the irrepressible nature of human sexuality.

"But what about kindness? That is more important than looks, no?" I asked.

"Some white people very kind. Many Asian unkind and selfish too," he insisted.

Before we parted, I gave him some money to help him on his upcoming pilgrimage to Bangkok and I also left him a packet of handmade writing papers. I inscribed on the first page, "Oun — never forget how beautiful you are," and wrote down my email address for him to use. I hoped Oun would write to me from time to time. I promised that I would go back and visit them.

That afternoon I boarded the small turboprop airplane bound for Bangkok. The plane swooped up and banked a turn right over Wat Sene Souk. I could see the yard where I first met the flying nuns and saw briefly the featureless orange dots moving in slow motion across the dusty courtyard.

China is now building a high-speed railroad to Luang Prabang. The volume of Chinese tourists this will bring will change the town into a Buddhist Disney World with its Main Street parade of novices. I got what I was looking for on this trip to Luang Prabang — a deeper sense of the old Asia that is in great danger of disappearing forever.

CHAPTER 3
NOODLES IN CAMBODIA

I met a man named Noodles on my return to Bangkok. Well, his name wasn't really Noodles, it was Yothin. Yo was obsessed with noodles: noodles for breakfast, noodles for lunch, noodles for dinner. In his sleep, I'm sure he was transported to a lip-smacking dream world of pad khi mao and pad Thai. A couple days after our meeting, it became clear that he needed to have the nickname Noodles. His body went limp with delight and bawdy laughter when I used his new name for the first time.

I met Noodles in a dark hallway in the Babylon sauna, his teeth gleaming in the shadows. He's a little guy, about 5 feet 5 inches weighing about 120 pounds. This meets criterion number 1 of my dream man: someone smaller than me. Growing up the runt of the family — the 90-pound weakling whom people liked to pick on — I swore that no boyfriend of mine would ever kick sand in *my* face, stand towering over me, or carry me over the threshold. So, where in the world does a relatively small Westerner go to meet someone even smaller?

The answer of course is Asia. It's a veritable candy store beyond all imagination with 60% of the world's population and over 4 billion little people. And Babylon in Bangkok is the preeminent dispensary of diminutive dudes.

Noodles and I connected immediately because his English was remarkably good and he had a lot of free time to spend with me. He grew up in a poor fishing family in the north of Thailand, then as an adult he met a French boyfriend who provided him with a beachfront condo in Pattaya which he now called home. When his French boyfriend was back in France, Noodles would head to Bangkok taking up residence in the halls of Babylon hoping to find a diversion from his lonely life of leisure.

He was some sort of part-time dressmaker, full-time bon vivant who had cut his teeth in couture working aboard a cruise ship sewing clothes for onboard shows. Growing up poor he developed a fetish for noodles. He swore like Scarlett O'Hara with his fists raised in the air that as god was his witness he would never go hungry again and thus he was never far from a supply of the slurpy goodness. I found him a wonderfully charming and playful companion.

Noodles was my first romance in Asia — he walked me around his favorite spots in Bangkok, possessively holding my hand through the crowded streets and back alleys of the metropolis. I wasn't sure who was prouder to have the other in hand. He showed me how accepting Thai culture can be toward not just Asian-Caucasian relationships and age-divergent ones, but also gay ones as well. Thailand seems to have few judgments about who is bedding down with whom. I was curious how this came to be considering the repressive neighboring countries of Malaysia, Cambodia, Laos, and Myanmar. The answer lies partly in Buddhism and partly in economics. Gays and lesbians account for a huge part of the tourist income of Bangkok, so while Thai people may not agree with us putting our peepers in poopers, the discrimination stops at the cash register.

41

I suggested to Noodles that we take a trip together to Siem Reap, Cambodia, to see Angkor Wat, the famous 12th century Hindu-turned-Buddhist temples that are considered one of the great wonders of the world. Noodles suggested we hire a driver and private car to Aranyaprathet on the Cambodian border and then change to a Cambodian taxi that would drive us the remaining way to Siem Reap. He took care of the booking, and a couple days later we were in the back seat of a Mercedes zooming through the Thai countryside with Noodles sound asleep in the backseat, no doubt dreaming of pad see ew — stir-fried noodles in sweet soy sauce.

Upon arrival in Aranyaprathet, we jumped out of the cocoon of the luxury sedan to face the dusty reality of a border town in Southeast Asia. Cambodia is painfully impoverished and scarred by the American war there and the ensuing reign of the brutal despot Pol Pot. Cambodia makes even Thailand look like a well-developed nation. We passed through the chaos of customs, teeming with folks carrying big bags, pushing and shoving, long lines attended to by bureaucrats who seemed inured to the mess. Once in Cambodia, we arranged for a taxi and then waited for the driver to find another 2 passengers. We sat having fresh coconut milk while watching the progression of vehicles lining up to pass through the border check on their way into Thailand. A huge, wobbly pushcart of denim stacked 12-feet high was being guided through the line by several Cambodian men when a tire exploded. The sound caused me to drop my coconut and then I laughed at my own reaction. The guys pushing the cart heard me and thought I was laughing at their misfortune. I waved to them as if to say, "No, sorry, I'm not laughing at you." They were even more confused by my waving. A group of men surrounded the listing denim cart to fix the tire, and we were summoned for our taxi ride.

The overland passage to Siem Reap is 2½ hours of bone-rattling, dirt road, post-apocalyptic hell on wheels. The taxis are old Toyota Corollas that are driven to the point where bolts and hubcaps unscrew themselves and shock absorbers are shattered. All that remains on the barebones car is what is essential to keep it rolling (and bouncing uncontrollably). It's the sort of ride through no-man's land that any sensible Western driver would take slowly, negotiating each pothole and bump. In Cambodia, however, the lead-footed drivers cross as fast as possible, skimming across the crests of the washboard corrugation of what appears to be some sort of road. The net result for a passenger is that you must keep your mouth slack jawed and your tongue toward the back of your throat so you don't bite it off on a surprise hard landing. I sat with my hands lifting me off the seat a few inches to cushion the impact on my spine and kept my head tucked slightly so that I wouldn't compress a disc should I hit the ceiling. I tied my trusty handkerchief around my face to absorb some of the dust.

Out the window I could see a light brown dust storm being kicked up by the car. Another rushing taxi or motorbike would briefly appear next to us before disappearing into the clouds of dirt. These dusty vignettes reminded me of Dorothy's tornado dream sequence in the *Wizard of Oz*. I expected to see Auntie Em go flying by, knitting in her rocking chair. Instead, I saw a motorbike with 5 Cambodians on it. Then a man on a motorbike chugged by with a pair of live hogs strapped to the seat with their bound legs sticking up in happy baby yoga pose (without the happy part). Rickety old trucks jam packed with live humans appeared outside my window. Women with babies sit atop the cab and in the open bed in the back, the carriage weighed down and teetering on the uneven road.

We finally arrive in the town of Siem Reap. I step out of the *Mad Max* mobile, blowing the dirt out of my nostrils, coughing and sputtering a few times when I realize I have wet my pants. This is not vacation. This is not travel. This is *hard* travel. Those people on the motorbikes and trucks who made brief eye contact with me had the astonishing ability to give a smile and friendly wave. They saw me as living a life of luxury they would never enjoy and they smiled in spite of their circumstance. The road has since been paved and so my once in a lifetime experience of that road shall thankfully remain just that.

Noodles and I checked into our guesthouse on the edge of town. The place had what I would call "rustic charm," which meant that the rats come out only at night. We opened the creaky old door to our room to find it full of mosquitoes and bloody splats all over the once white walls. I spoke to the front desk about the mosquito problem and while we went to the pool to wash off the day's dust, they sprayed the room with insecticide. I had to speak to them again to say the room was now full of toxic spray and that we couldn't breathe inside. The windows had no screens, so we couldn't open them and allow another fresh crop of winged vampires in. I'm not sure they understood the entirety of my complaint because the staff returned to the room and in true Southeast Asian style did what Southeast Asian hospitality does. If you've been to this part of the world, you know that the hotel industry is eager to please while being a little lean on practical solutions. When in doubt about any matter of cleanliness and smell, or really anything to do with the air, someone will unload a bottle of fragrant spray on the problem. Cloyingly, florally, sickeningly fragrant. So now we had both the pyrethroids and whatever else was in the air freshener to inhale.

This is a classic example of my own bumbling naïveté. Southeast Asians really don't fix much of anything. They will change your room, kick the fridge, jiggle the toilet handle, or make a phone call and a promise. But in the end, nothing is done. This is Buddhism in practice teaching us about non-attachment to material things like a functioning fridge or a flushing toilet. It's also Lao Tzu's famous quote, "When nothing is done, nothing is left undone," in practical application. In the end, we asked for mosquito netting which solved the problem with some finality.

Venturing into the town of Siem Reap, I encountered some

things that 'a girl ain't supposed to see' as Charlene sang about in the worst song ever written: *I've Never Been to Me*. Restaurant sandwich boards offered items like cow's intestine, cow's brain, and bull's sex. The center of town had a band of blind and limbless war survivors who were lying around on a mat playing whatever instruments they could manage with just a tongue or a stump. Noodles found it funny. I found this legless legacy of war and genocide horrifying. I pulled Noodles aside to tell him with pursed lips how laughing at desperate people was just not right.

Thus, I came face to face with another of the fundamental differences between American and Thai culture: they laugh at tragedy. I have seen Thai people crash their motorcycles into each other and step out of the wreckage laughing. It seems perverse to Americans who want to call 9-1-1 to report this incident and DO SOMETHING for god's sake! Not the Thai. Thai people will feel sorry for you if you get upset about anything. Outrage, in their eyes, is a sign of poor upbringing and must be ignored. As a result, they will not address charged issues with what we would call situationally appropriate emotion. In fact, should you have a hissy fit, your meltdown will be met with the famous Thai disappearing act. You will have suddenly rendered yourself completely invisible, banging your fists on the counter in a complete vacuum. You, dear righteous traveler, have been given what I call the "Thai timeout." Your tantrum will fall on deaf ears, and the Thai people who witness it will never forget the poor, pathetic person who soiled their serenity.

"But there's nothing we can do for them," Noodles explained. "If we are sad, then there is even more sadness in the world. But if we laugh, then we lift their spirits up, and everyone is better off."

"So, we are supposed to laugh at the poor people writhing on the ground like fly larvae with tambourines? What about feeling guilty?" I asked, incredulous about his justification and wondering if he knew what larvae were. I sighed and took a long moment to ponder his perspective. Given that he is Thai, his point was worth considering but I wasn't yet ready to join him laughing at other people's misfortune. We dropped the discussion and continued on past sandwich boards touting chicken person's nose, pig's feet, and other inscrutable and unmentionable animal parts being served for dinner.

The next day we got up before daybreak to visit Angkor Wat. Our tour guide picked us up at the guesthouse and drove us into the park down a dirt road alongside elephants being marched slowly to work. We situated ourselves beside a reflecting pond full of pink lotus flowers, floating water bottles, and snack wrappers. We waited for the sun to rise over the peaks of the ancient Hindu temple. Suddenly, a fight broke out between an Englishman and an American as they were jockeying for the best position to photograph the sunrise. I sat in the grass swatting mosquitoes and smirking at the lunacy of this moment. The sun poked over the peak of the stone stupas amid shouts of, "Hey asshole, you're in my spot! Fuck you! This ain't your goddamn spot. What are you gonna do about it mother fucker?" In moments like this I thought, it might just be more pleasant to stay home and watch the National Geographic documentary.

Unable to pronounce the letter "X," our adorable little Cambodian tour guide kept saying to me, "Mr. David, kiss me..." instead of excuse me. I tried to explain to him that what he was in fact asking for, he might not actually want. He laughed and would of course reply, "Oh solly. Kiss me, Mr. David." I found it endlessly amusing as I certainly did wish to kiss him but at age 24, he was already the father of 3 kids, so I assumed this meant he was not batting for my team. Of course, in Southeast Asia one never knows for sure.

Back at the guesthouse that afternoon Noodles and I noticed 3 tuk tuk drivers gathered in the shade of a tree watching something on a phone. With my curiosity piqued, I quietly eased myself into the group and saw that they were watching a porn video. Either I seem to have a sixth sense for discovering people watching porn in public, or Southeast Asian men simply don't have a private place in which to do it. The guys seemed delighted that I wished to join them. One of them even gave up his seat in the back of the tuk tuk for me. Ooh baby — a chance to be with the local guys. Suddenly, like the Grinch, I had an idea. An awful idea. A wonderful awful idea! I excused myself to my room for a moment and came out with my giant 17" laptop, and with the connection to the guesthouse's Wi-Fi, I dialed up some porn for them to watch. I had heard that Buddhists with their absence of homophobia and machismo, would switch unhesitatingly between men and women based on what's currently available to them, sexually. I wanted to test this theory and see for myself if they were not bound by the labels and divisions that we in the West cling to.

I started their flight of porn with heterosexual videos. They sat in fascination scrutinizing the screen intently, leaning in with wide eyes. Then, without warning, I switched to some bisexual porn before finishing them off with some gay male videos. At the end of my video tour across the Kinsey scale they leaned back and chuckled.

"Oh, cannot watch because might like too much," one driver said to me, but no one said anything unkind. No one ran screaming. No gunshots, no bashings. After a half-hour of watching gay porn, the novelty was wearing off and the guys seemed to be getting restless. I closed up the laptop and headed back to my room. The drivers went home to their wives and families with perhaps a story of what they'd seen that day. Perhaps not.

Noodles and I returned to Bangkok by minivan this time. He slept on the bus holding my hand tightly. I was so much enjoying the closeness with him and wishing I didn't have to leave so soon. In a couple days, I would be on a plane back to the States.

Conversation on our last day together was spare with lots of silently staring into each other's eyes through the steam rising off hot bowls of noodles on the sidewalks of Bangkok. This international affair was sadly at its end to either be continued one day a long time from now, or never.

The morning I left, I woke Noodles up in the hotel room to say goodbye. He stood naked and silent before the big picture window looking out over the hazy Bangkok morning. A new high-rise condo was under construction across the street. Cranes were swinging around lifting beams to the top floors. My mind was flashing back to the good times we had enjoyed over the past weeks. I had never really connected with anyone deeper than a one night stand in Thailand. Meeting Noodles gave me an insider's look at his culture and opened me up to the possibility of one day having a relationship here in a place where the men had always been available for an hour but not a lifetime.

"Yothin, I had a wonderful time with you. I will miss you back in America." I held him from behind. I felt his heart beating rapidly and heard him sniffle his little button nose.

"Yes, me too. It was very special," he choked out, prying

himself from my arms. He lay back down and covered his head with a pillow. If I had had more time, this could have turned into a very messy goodbye.

I wondered how many times he had been in this same situation, perhaps in this same room. I pulled the pillow off his head, licking the tears off his cheeks. I kissed him goodbye and promised to stay in touch by email. I lugged my suitcase down the hallway toward the elevator. I never saw Noodles again.

I returned to the States via Dallas and then on to Tucson. Back in Arizona, I took my place as a white suburban nobody in the risers of the University Community Chorus when something completely unexpected and miraculous happened.

CHAPTER 4
YOU NEVER FORGET YOUR FIRST

One ordinary Tuesday evening in Tucson while knocking out the sonorities and melodic intricacies of Mendelssohn's 42nd psalm, fate joined the destinies of 2 people burning up with longing. A petite German guy in ill-fitting clothes from Walmart sang with the tenors in front of me in chorus. He was the complete opposite of all things Asian: blue-eyed, blond, and white as a milk bottle. His name was Sebastian, a young man from Thüringen with manners as delicate as his constitution.

Our conductor asked the native German speakers in the chorus to raise their hands to help the rest of us figure out the pronunciation of "Wie der Hirsch schreit" and other German language tongue twisters in the psalm we were working on. Sebastian's hand went up. I now had an excuse to meet him and cornered him at the break asking him if he could help me with a few phrases. I melted as he explained that "schreit" sounded like I needed to hock some phlegm from deep in my throat and that "nach" sounded something like a cat hissing at a dog.

"Sebastian, how am I supposed to sing *that* and make it

sound pretty?" I asked with a bit of humorous sarcasm. His robust laughter thrilled me. "Hey, I'm having a sing-along piano party at my house on Saturday. Would you like to come?" I asked, putting the German lesson aside for a moment.

"Umm. Maybe. Hmm. OK. Yes, I would like to come. Thank you." I could tell the idea of coming to a potentially gay party was growing on him.

He showed up at my house for the party with an armful of German beer and a lifetime of questions. He asked none of them to anyone at the party. But in subsequent weeks, he came out to me by email and admitted that he'd never been with another man...or anyone for that matter. So, I invited him for dinner figuring he needed a big brother figure to explain everything. I was going to hand him my copies of *The Joy of Gay Sex* and *The Gay Kama Sutra*, but I had no intention of seducing him. In fact, I had arranged a date of my own to join us. My date fortuitously never showed up.

Sebastian and I dined alone that cold winter's night. I made a roasted chicken with root vegetables and a berry pie. This home cooked meal was manna from heaven for a guy living in a college dorm eating Subway sandwiches for dinner. I listened to his little moans of pleasure as he gobbled the meal down. My cooking had unintentionally seduced him.

He asked if he could kiss me after we watched my favorite movie, *Shortbus*. That was the beginning of an affair that would change both of our lives. We began a storybook romance that took us to Europe and Asia and back. Asia would eventually come between us.

This affair had come as a total surprise in a dull period of my life when I had sworn that I would never find a boyfriend in America, that my love life would be confined to Asia. My own country and people bored me and ignored me. Foreigners excited me with possibilities and differences — and a chance to see my world through their enchanted eyes.

Having grown up behind the wall in East Germany where holidays were spent in Bulgaria, Sebastian was fascinated by the vastness of America. I took him on an epic train ride from Arizona to Oregon. We camped out in the desert wilds of Arizona, surrounded by giant anthropomorphic cacti and coyotes yapping under the moonlight. We bicycled under canopies of trees in Portland's verdant streets. We sang Taizé songs under bridges in Leipzig, Paris, and Prague. We laughed at everything, everywhere. No one had ever loved me before like Sebastian did and I never had so much fun in a relationship. Finally, I got what I had always wanted and much to my surprise, the object of my affection wasn't Asian.

A year into our relationship, Sebastian and I planned a trip to Asia as I needed to make my annual medical pilgrimage. This trip would be a particularly fascinating one — his first through the portal to the East and my first visit with a boyfriend. We made our plans to start in Bangkok, then work our way to Chiang Mai in the north, and finish up in Luang Prabang in Laos. I wanted to visit Oun and Lai at the monastery so I wrote ahead to the flying nuns that I was coming with my new German boyfriend. We booked our trip.

On our flight from Thailand to Laos we boarded the Air Lao jet. We noticed that the seat buckles said Alitalia and the doors to the fuselage didn't match the rest of the plane. It seemed that this plane was built from the airplane pick-n-pull. Sebastian is more religious than I, and he said a few prayers before take-off. We bounced our way down the runway and landed in Luang Prabang feeling particularly lucky to be alive. Years later, that same airline crashed that same flight into the Mekong River killing all 49 on board.

Sebastian and I were celebrating our one-year anniversary and wanted to do something special. I had neglected to visit the famous Kuang Si waterfalls of Luang Prabang on my first visit, so we went together. The falls are a stunning, movie set-like collection of turquoise pools and gentle cascades set in a hilltop tropical forest. The place is so shockingly beautiful that it seems fake, like a pastoral scene you'd see in a mural at a dentist's office to calm your nerves before getting your teeth drilled.

Sebastian loved to climb, so he insisted we hike up the falls and see the view from the top. We slogged up the muddy steps to find a forest of fruit trees at the top. At the base of the trees were hundreds of butterflies feeding on the rotten fruit that had fallen — iridescent blue ones, alarmingly bright yellow and black ones, green bat-wing ones. We paused to behold the magic of the colors silently flitting around us, moving slowly through with our cameras in awe of the spectacle that no one else seemed to notice.

The next day, I took Sebastian to meet the flying nuns. Oun was sitting cross-legged under a tree with a book, looking like the Buddha under the Bodhi tree. I called out to him. He saw me with Sebastian but didn't get up to come and greet us, so we let ourselves in the old iron gate.

"Hello Oun! I would like to introduce you to Sebastian, my boyfriend," I said walking up to him in his chair. He stood up slowly and gave Sebastian a half smile of buck teeth.

"Se...bati...," he struggled to repeat his name.

"You can call me Basti," Sebastian rescued him from the multisyllabic name that ties the tongues of Asians. Oun stood silently not knowing what to say to us, perhaps harboring some jealousy. Lai appeared from the bunkhouse in a flash of orange robes, breaking the awkwardness of the moment. He wanted to plan an adventure with us.

Lai was as playful and silly as usual, running around with his robe falling off his shoulder revealing his nipple. They took us and an older gay American tourist friend of ours, Randy, on a trip to see the Pak Ou caves down the river. Oun led the way toward the boat through high grasses and down to the muddy banks. Lai and Randy lagged behind. Later on, I found out that Lai was busy hitting on Randy. The two met up late that night at a guesthouse to conjugate their burgeoning affair. Lai was careful to not be seen going in and out of our friend's room. Unfortunately, a party gathered outside their door during the evening and Lai got stuck inside 'til the wee hours waiting to sneak out. None of this really came as a shock to us. Lai broadcast sex on all channels. Our friend, in his 60s, was the right age, and in Lai's eyes, ripe for the picking.

Sebastian, however, was careful not to touch the monks. I watched him sharing a video game on his iPod Touch with the novices, leaning about 10 degrees away from them so as not to even bump shoulders.

That day on a walk along the Mekong, we had seen Laotians washing their freshly picked lettuce in a basket in the river — the filthy river with water buffalos pooping in it. "Wash it, peel it, cook it, or forget it," wizened travelers say. I say, "Even if it's washed, still forget it — considering what it's washed *in.*" That night, Randy and I both got a heinous case of food poisoning. We made the mistake of eating the lettuce garnish on a noodle dish at a nice restaurant — probably the very lettuce we saw them washing in the river earlier.

I paid the price for my disregard of travel wisdom, Randy, no doubt for his illicit transgressions with a novice. He vomited in his shoes on the way back to his room and I stayed in bed sick for 2 days listening to roosters crowing and temple bells ringing at all hours, wishing I were dead.

Oun and I found some time alone to talk. He told me that he was happy that I found Sebastian and that his pilgrimage to Bangkok was fantastic. He spoke of what a wonderful city Bangkok was. I wondered if there could be more than one place in the world named Bangkok — how could anyone think Bangkok was great? He told me he was going to remain in Luang Prabang and pursue being a monk but that Lai was planning to leave the monastery and pursue his gay life in Vientiane. I felt him crushing out any embers of his romantic fantasies with me that day. We said another round of poignant goodbyes at the gate of the monastery without a hug or a handshake. And that was the last I saw of him.

Sebastian and I returned to the States and spent the spring in Tucson and the summer in Leipzig, Germany, with him finishing up his degree. With his US student visa now expired and no way for him to immigrate (gay marriage with rights of immigration was not yet an option), our relationship had a soon-arriving expiration date on it. At the end of summer, we returned to the US from Europe to plot our next move when he sprung the news, "Daffy, I have applied to teach German in Guangzhou, China."

My romantic fantasy bubble was so severely exploded that I sat in stunned silence with my face flush and my ears ringing with the news. I was devastated. I helped mold him into the gay man he is today, and for the first time in my life, someone loved me back. Heretofore, no man had ever loved or cared for me. Sebastian was the game changer of a lifetime who showed me that a relationship was possible, that maybe I was worthy of being loved after all.

However, I refused to live in China. Asia, is after all,

a continent, not just one culture. Thailand and China may be nearby but the Thai and Chinese are vastly different people. The thought of 1.3 billion people living in a hybrid of communism and capitalism in the middle of an industrial revolution was off-putting, to say the least. Besides, I've spent enough time around unrefined Chinese tourists in Thailand to be horrified by the fashion, the spitting, the pushing, shoving, and shopping locusts. I was already soured on the same American boorishness, greed, and excess, and now China was well on its way to overtaking America as the most annoying country on earth. The Chinese had become the new ugly Americans. Sebastian planned his move, and I opted to stay in Tucson.

After he moved to China, I felt both the supreme loss of my first real relationship and the feeling of being spoiled — if I were to ever find another boyfriend, Sebby would be a tough act to follow. Our relationship was peaceful and playful. He had been my best friend and lover for nearly 2 years, and I plunged to the bottom of a terrible pool of grief that I simply couldn't get out of for over 2 years. I could see the world up at the surface but I couldn't rejoin life.

My grief recovery wasn't at all aided by taking a month in the middle of it to spend with Sebastian on the adventure of a lifetime through Myanmar. But sometimes kicking the can of grief down the road is just what one needs to do.

CHAPTER 5
A HAIR OF THE DOG

If you're going through hell, keep going.
— Winston Churchill

*O*n January, a year and a half after our breakup, Sebastian flew from his new home in China to meet me in Bangkok on our way to Myanmar for a 28-day country-wide expedition that would take us from Yangon to Bagan, then Mandalay, Pyin Oo Lwin, and Hsipaw. From there we would go on to Kalaw, Inle Lake, Ngapali Beach on the Bay of Bengal and end up back in Yangon. Sebastian and I made an extraordinary traveling duo — I booked the flights and rooms and chose an itinerary, while he did his research on the history, culture, and language. Whenever we arrived in a place, he would pull out a book or a program on his iPod Touch and begin reading, "Shwedagon Pagoda was built by the Mon people in the 6th century and stands today as the most holy Buddhist site in Myanmar." I would wander barefoot with my camera while he recited history. It was the sweet symbiosis of this partnership that brought us back together for this adventure of a lifetime.

Traveling on your own, it's always good to learn to say a few things — the usual things like hello, thank you, yes, no, etc. But saying no can be tricky in Buddhist countries like Thailand and Myanmar. There's something ingrained in the people such that they don't like to say no. In fact, in Thai there is no real word for no. It just doesn't exist. What they say instead is, "not yes." Let's practice speaking Thai:

"Would you like Donald Trump to slip his tongue into your mouth?" you might ask a Thai person.

"Not yes, thank you," they might reply.

"Would you like to watch *The Human Centipede* trilogy all in one sitting with the kids?"

"Not so much yes," is a good response and everyone is happy because no one was rudely rejected. Therefore, no feelings were hurt and most importantly, no one had to watch the worst concept for a movie ever.

As a result of traveling in Thailand, one starts to become acculturated to not saying no directly. But then there's Myanmar with the begging, insisting, and open hands wanting something — this is a culture where one really *must* learn to say no. When Sebby and I arrived by taxi at the Yangon train station on our way to Bagan, our car pulled up and was immediately surrounded by a group of men wanting to carry our luggage for us. They didn't really even ask, they just opened the trunk and walked away with our bags before I was even finished paying the taxi driver. We took off after our bags which were riding off on the shoulders of several Burmese guys. The men knew where we were going since there was only one train that day. They took our bags to the track and dropped them onto the platform and then demanded a tip. "Teep, teep. Teep, teep! Teep teep!!" It got progressively louder.

The men moved in to surround us tapping their open palms "One thousand. One thousand! One thousand!!" I thumbed through a 6-inch pile of bills we had gotten from a black-market money changer and handed them a 1,000 kyat note —

about 75 cents. We really didn't have a chance to say no, not that I even knew how. I left this job to Sebastian who was so freaked out to see our luggage disappear in a crowd that he forgot the word, leaving me to just pay what our friend later told us was highway robbery for carrying our bags.

It wasn't until wandering around an 11th century stone temple that we got to put the word "no" to good use. Sebastian had downloaded a Burmese language program for his iPod Touch and so if we needed to say no, we would tap the screen and out would come the "no." It had both a polite no and the no of no return — the no to end all no's...the nuclear no. We were at a temple in Bagan where a kid was following us around with postcards. He would fold them up like an accordion and then drop them out into a long strip of cards and announce the price. "Two thousand. Buy buy. Two thousand. Buy buy!" It was starting to work my last nerve as I was trying to photograph the ancient ruins. I asked Sebastian how to say no. What I had previously uttered to the kid didn't seem to have enough confidence or I had the tones wrong. I was probably in reality saying, "Please follow us around all afternoon and annoy us until we pay you for your dumb postcards. Please, ruin our day."

Sebastian put on his headphones and plugged them into his iPod Touch as he tested out the language program. He jammed the no button a few times before he beckoned the kid over to have a listen. He pushed the ear buds into the kid's ears, cranked up the volume and wailed repeatedly on the button. What came through the ear buds was loud enough that even I heard it while I was taking pictures. "Ma ho bu! Ma ho bu! Ma ho bu!" There was something perverse about watching that kid's face turn to stone as he walked away. He thought maybe we were about to play the latest Lady Gaga song or show him an amazing video game when really what happened was Sebastian threw the magic switch that gave us some peace. Sometimes even *my* guilty conscience is overtaken by annoying people. Sebastian and I burst into unrepentant laughter that we had unleashed the secret weapon of "ma ho bu" to be used only in extreme circumstances. We were able to finish our temple tour unaccompanied. On the way out, we saw the kid again who seemed to be sulking by himself. I went up to him and handed him 2,000 kyat for the postcards. He was of course befuddled by our purchase.

There are a few other pieces of travel wisdom I picked up on this epic journey through Myanmar. One was: do *not* under any circumstances drink the "purified temple water." Sebby and I met up with our veteran traveler of Asia friend, Larry, in Yangon. On our second day, we set off from the Mother Land Inn 2 guesthouse to visit some temples. Our first stop was the Sule Pagoda right in the center of Yangon. We walked around the temple in the blistering sun for an hour. I had finished all my water and was starting to feel a little dehydrated when I noticed a tall metal urn that had a sign clearly written in English: "Purified Temple Water." What it didn't say was *what* it was purified with or *how*. It didn't say, "Please help yourself to some delicious and *clean* water that has been boiled and filtered." Nonetheless, I filled up my water bottle with it and took a nice long drink. Ah, how, refreshing. I think I'll get ahead in my hydration. So I guzzled my bottle and refilled it. That's when I noticed the green moss growing in the glass tube that is used to gauge the water level of the tank. Maybe that was part of the purifying process? Why yes, the moss is used to leech out any bacteria that might be growing in the tank. This is how my mind worked to justify something that may have just put a nail in my coffin.

We returned to the guesthouse that evening, and that's when the intestinal theater began. Curtain time! Act one: the twisting. Second act: the gurgling, bloating, and nausea. I quickly downed some antacids at intermission but clearly this was a bigger production than that. The grand finale was coming soon to a toilet near me. In a matter of minutes, I was in the bathroom alternately hovering the parts over the toilet that were evacuating at the moment and flushing furiously.

How did this happen? I replayed the day's events in my head. No one *else* was sick. We all ate the same food, but we didn't all drink the purified temple water. Only I did. Therefore, only I have been purified. I lay on the filthy bathroom floor tiles with vomit streaming out of my nostrils confident that drinking purified temple water is the equivalent of walking into a Catholic church in Mexico and drinking the water at the baptismal font. It may very well have been blessed but it hadn't been purified in any sense of what we in the West think of as "purified water."

The next afternoon, Sebastian and I were to leave on the overnight train for Bagan, the city of over 2,000 temples. I was still sick when we arrived at the station and waited for the train to arrive. We booked first class passage on the 20-hour train ride north through the Burmese countryside. "First class" basically means that you have 2 bunk beds and share a large cabin with 2 other travelers. The train came lumbering in on the trash-lined tracks a couple hours late. We settled into the greasy and dilapidated cabin. I was still nauseous but the Imodium put a stop to the evacuations at about the same time the train started to roll. And rock. And bounce and shimmy. Burmese trains are known for being among the world's worst. Just Google "worst trains Myanmar" and see what comes up. This isn't something one does when researching a trip, especially if you're a rail fan like me. Bad trains are like bad pizza — even when they're bad, they're still kinda good. But this was bad. I mean *really* bad.

Sebby took the lower bunk and I took the upper one. Our cabin mates were two guys from Singapore who never spoke a word to us. (I made a mental note to skip Singapore for any future travels in Asia.) As the train left the slums of Yangon it began to pick up speed. However, speeding on *this* train was not a good idea as the tracks were laid by the British colonials over 100 years ago and probably have not been maintained since. We were shaken violently for 20 hours. In the middle of the night while I was trying to sleep, the carriage began to bounce so violently that I actually became airborne several times and was afraid I would hit the ceiling. I tried to get off the bunk to use the toilet and was thrown off the ladder onto the floor. I couldn't help but lie there laughing at my misfortune like a Thai person would.

The toilet was basically a large can with a hole in the bottom that opened to the tracks with a toilet seat placed atop it. I reminded myself that this was 1st class — 2nd class probably didn't have a seat. There was a strange water leak in the ceiling of the bathroom so I had to put on my raincoat or use an umbrella to sit on the toilet while bracing myself on the walls to stay on the seat. Returning to my bunk, I couldn't make it up the ladder without being slammed against the wall, so I just crawled into bed with Sebastian. A double dose of Xanax, and earplugs to dampen the squeaking and clatter still didn't deliver a wink of sleep.

We sat up at dawn, giving up on the notion of sleep entirely and took in the scenery. We raised the shades and opened the windows to let the breeze flow through the cabin. The daily train that clacks its way through the country villages draws the attention of the locals who come to greet us. Children wave and hope that you'll throw money. I watched as some tourists threw coins and candy. Children scrambled dangerously close to the moving train while their mothers stood by watching. I knew about this custom from watching it on YouTube, so before we left, Sebby and I had purchased packets of pencils to throw as an alternative to money or candy. When I threw pencils, the kids seemed terribly disappointed that it was something so practical. They picked them up and looked up at us like, "Jeez, really?" Sometimes they dropped them limply from their disappointed little fingers or threw them back down in the dirt. I fantasized that one kid would find that pencil, learn how to draw, and would be the next Robert Crumb. It's more likely that it would be used to stab some small animal to death that could then be placed on the fire and eaten. The pencil could be used to test the roasting meat for doneness or perhaps as a skewer. Me and my lofty ideas.

We passed water buffaloes cooling off in rivers, ox drawn carts, thatched-roof villages, and rice paddies. This was indeed a precious and dwindling view of the old Asia I had so wanted to see. As we slowly limped along the tracks, boys in tattered clothes jumped aboard the train to ride on the roof. I stood at the door of the carriage exhilarated to experience what would never happen in the US. Feet dangled over my head and I tickled the dirty bottoms of a couple of them.

"Hey, where from, where from?" a young voice yelled from atop the train.

"America!" I shouted looking up toward the roof.

"Obama number 1!" the boy yelled with a big, toothy grin. I wondered how in this poor and remote part of the world, so cut off from the free flow of news, they should know who the US President is.

We finally arrived in Bagan, a dusty desert town on the edge of the vast arid plains chock full of ancient temples. We checked into our guesthouse and took a long nap after that sleepless night on the train. In the evening after a sunset horse-drawn cart ride into the desert, Sebby went to bed not feeling well and I went to the internet room at the guesthouse to check in with the rest of the world. I noticed a young Burmese guy sitting in the room in a chair shivering. His name was Koko. I inquired as to why he seemed so sad there in the computer chair late at night.

"They rent my room to guest. No place to sleep," he told me with sad eyes trying to smile for the foreigner. He wasn't allowed to express his real discontent that after working 16 hours he had no place to lay his head.

"Oh no. That's terrible." I felt sorry for him and went to my room and got him a pillow, blanket, and the inflatable mattress out of my luggage. I set up a bed for him in the internet room. Koko was astounded and embarrassed by the attention I was giving him. He was, after all, the houseboy and should be attending to *my* comfort.

He lay down on the makeshift bed and as I was about to cover him with the blanket, I noticed something sticking up out under his longyi (the traditional sarong worn by men). Whoa, what is *that?* It was clear that the simple kindness I was extending to him was turning him on. I was flattered. I stroked his hair and we kissed a bit, which made him shiver even more. This was clearly a new experience for him. Koko's breath was stale and his lips were cracked and dry. He sat up and led me quietly by the hand down the hall and up 2 flights of stairs to the roof. He opened the short door, we ducked our heads and stepped onto the rooftop. The moon was shining brightly in the desert sky. The hotel's laundry was gently blowing in the wind (he had probably hung it there himself). He led me to an area behind the laundry line and grabbed onto me for a big hug like a child holding its favorite teddy bear. I was amazed that this was happening. We hugged and kissed for a long time but nothing much more happened. Koko told me he had never been with anyone before — man or woman (or teddy bear).

"First time?" I asked him again with incredulity.

"Yes, yes. First time," and his face nearly ripped at the seams he was smiling so widely. He laughed a little and nipped at my neck with his nose like a puppy might do. After a while of making out on the roof, he was starting to shiver again in the cool air. We called it a night and I tucked Koko into his bed and I went back to my room to sleep next to Sebastian noting the progression we had made from boyfriends to friends.

In the morning, Koko made me banana pancakes and a pot of tea and served them to me at a table in the guesthouse restaurant. He couldn't stop smiling and looking at me as he brought me extra pancakes and fruit. As soon as I finished eating, more food would be placed in front of me.

Later in the day, Sebastian and I walked to a fancy riverside restaurant owned by a gay German man and managed by his

Burmese boyfriend. The proprietor sat at our table noticing how sick Sebastian was and ordered a cup of Earl Grey tea for him. Sebastian took one sip of it and ran for the toilet. I chased after him and listened to him purging his guts.

"Oh Sebby, I'm so sorry. We'll get you some medicine later," I called out to him from outside the door.

I returned to the table to quiz the owner a bit more about gay relationships in Myanmar. I told him about my rooftop experience with the guesthouse staff member, keeping Koko's identity a secret.

"They're all tender, the boys here," he said puffing on his cigarette and speaking perfect English with a vague German accent that made his S's whistle. He spoke with a knowing confidence about such things. I trusted what he was saying — his words would ring true throughout all my years in Asia. I watched as his Burmese boyfriend was busy in the kitchen bossing the staff around.

"What exactly do you mean by 'tender?'" I was curious.

"Look, these boys have nothing. They work 16 hours a day, 7 days a week. They sleep on the floor in shacks with no furniture. Look how skinny they are! They are very oppressed and isolated with this corrupt government. When someone exotic and wealthy like you shows up and treats them well, they can't help but be turned on. But it doesn't mean they're gay. They don't know such distinctions — those labels are constructs of Europe and America. Here those labels are useless and serve no purpose to them. These boys will all grow up and have a wife and children. And they may have a little something else on the side," he told me looking toward his boyfriend.

Sebastian returned from his ride on the porcelain bus looking weaker and paler than his normal milk bottle white — more of a bluish white. I escorted him back to the guesthouse and put him to bed, kissing him on the forehead.

I went out for a walk with Larry and his friend Carole who had arrived from Portland to join us on the trip. We set out in search of some meds for our sick friend. Sebastian, in his infinite travel wisdom, purchased a little placard containing illustrations of people in various forms of purging and hurling. On one page was a little stick figure of someone on a toilet with a spray of brown coming from its backside. There was also one of a figure bent over blowing chunks. And then there was one perched on the toilet with nothing at all happening. We stepped into the open-air pharmacy bearing this card and pointed to the illustration showing diarrhea in action. The pharmacists all gathered around to have a look. After much laughter and thigh slapping, out came some traveler's diarrhea medicine. Success!

In the morning, I moved Sebastian to the lobby to wait for our bus to Mandalay. I stuck a thermometer into his mouth, and he blinked tenderly at me as we waited for the mercury to rise. He still had a fever. I held his overly warm hand for a few minutes of sitting in silence, looking into each other's eyes. Our eyes spoke what our mouths couldn't. Thank you for taking care of me. I still love you. Me too. And what in God's name did I eat?

I went back to get our luggage and Koko was sweeping the room. I closed the door behind us and locked it. We passionately kissed — his lips were a little moister, his breath a little fresher. His longyi lifted up again. This time we took care of that and then we hugged a long goodbye. We exchanged email addresses and once again I was leaving someone I had made a nice connection with, promising to stay in touch. The odds were against us ever connecting again.

Koko carried our luggage to the bus and stood on the street watching us climb aboard. I sat down and looked out the dirty window as he stood there on the curb with his big mound of Leonid Brezhnev hair holding firm in the breeze. He couldn't muster a smile or even a wave as the bus pulled away leaving him in a cloud of dust and greasy blue diesel fumes. And then we were off...on the worst bus ride of our entire lives.

CHAPTER 6
VASS DID YOU EXPIKT?

$\mathcal{N}$o one knows how to ruin a bus ride like the Burmese. But here's their secret in case you want to try: First, break all the chairs so that you're leaning back at a 45-degree angle and then slightly tilt each one to the side. This means that the seat in front of you will be basically in your lap. Make sure the windows are grimy and covered with food smears and handprints so that you can't see out. Next, crank up the sound system that long ago blew out the woofers so that it's not just bad music, it's loud music, *and* it's distorted. Then make sure that the onboard toilet (if there is one) is out of order. Next, turn the air-conditioning so high that even though you put on everything you're carrying in your backpack, you're still freezing. Then, fill the aisles with people sitting on their backpacks so that you can't get up and foment a rebellion. And that's just the inside. Make sure that the shock absorbers are removed and the exhaust system is re-routed inside the bus. The diesel fumes and noise will comfort the locals, making them feel at home wherever they are traveling. Finally, be sure that a gear or two is missing in the transmission so that the bus will lurch and chug as it cycles from gears 1 to 3 to 5.

Such was the 9-hour bus ride from Bagan to Mandalay. Travel books warned us about the road conditions, and as the bus set out of town on a nice smooth road I thought, "What are they talking about? This is fine." Then the paved portion of the journey ended with a thud as we belched our way down rutted dirt roads. The bus rattled and shook nervously. Bags fell out of the overhead compartment. Burmese passengers were hit on the head and not even awakened.

I've always been astounded how Southeast Asians can sleep through anything. I've seen road construction crews on their lunch breaks sleeping in the median of a major highway with motorcycles and dump trucks passing by. I've seen security guards sleeping sitting up in a chair in a busy parking garage. No one ever complained that they couldn't sleep through the fireworks of the daily occurring holidays that require something to be blown up or set on fire.

This ability to effectively tune out such clamorous noise is a lifetime achievement for Asians and evidenced by the white noise app I have on my phone. Among the comforting sound modes to choose from are: clothes dryer with shoes inside, a screaming hair dryer, cars driving, city streets, crowded rooms, and a vacuum cleaner. What about waterfalls and the sound of wind in the trees to lull one to sleep?

Naturally, being the only 2 foreigners onboard the shit bus from hell, we were the only 2 people awake with a mixture of indignation (how could they sell tickets to this?), self-blame (we did this to ourselves), and at some point, humor (can you believe how bad this is?). I cycled through that range of reactions and landed on humor for a change. Perhaps I was getting used to Myanmar — at least I wasn't sick. Sebastian, however *was* still sick. I loaded him up with Imodium before we left, and that pretty much sealed off his back door. In a few days, we would be back at the pharmacy pointing to the picture of the constipated stick figure, but for now he wasn't going to shit himself on the bus. I wonder if Asians could sleep through *that?* A smelly event of that type and magnitude might be where they would draw the line and ask for us to be thrown off.

Sebby was nauseous and my laughter at the hideousness of this bus ride was not amusing him at all. I watched him shake his little fists in frustration at the bus, "Oh come on, really? What the fudge!" He is a good Christian boy and reluctant to use the full three and four-letter expletives that I bandy about freely in such circumstances. Fortunately for him, I had packed a bottle of cheap whiskey in my backpack. That and half a Xanax and we were both out for most of the rest of the ride. Tune-it-out in bottle and pill form work just fine since we didn't grow up with the kind of assault on our senses that would have organically prepared us for this.

We checked into our large and strangely empty government run hotel in Mandalay. The room was the most luxurious we'd found in Myanmar thus far. It had a proper bathroom though the hot water didn't work. Luxurious means that the bathroom door actually fit and closed, we couldn't feel the springs on the bed, and our toes didn't poke through holes in the sheets. We were seriously road weary and skipped dinner just to get a shower and get into bed for a peaceful night's sleep.

Then at 5:13 am, in the middle of a blissful sleep, the call to prayer screamed into our hotel window, "Aaaaaa-aaaaa-llllllaaaaaaah!" The cry damn near gave me a heart attack. We threw open the curtains to see that the giant loudspeaker of a mosque was mounted outside our window — not just next to our window — pointed right *at* our window.

Mandalay turned out to be in the running with Pakbeng, Laos, for the worst place on earth. Let's just call it the worst big city on earth, though I've never been to Jakarta which I hear could leave Mandalay in the dust. Mandalay is such a nice name — it makes me think of the Mandalay Bay in Las Vegas with its palm trees, swimming pools, water slides, and the lobster buffet. Mandalay in Myanmar by contrast has no trees, no traffic lights, no streetlights, millions of motorcycles honking their horns, and almost no restaurants. Walking at night through the streets is a post-nuclear holocaust game of survival. Motorbike headlights scan the dusty air as their drivers dodge cars driving blindly through intersections beeping and tooting our ears into oblivion. Pedestrians cling to the curb shared with rats as there's no sidewalk or if there is one, it is used as motorcycle parking and completely impassable.

We spent a few days touring around the city and suburbs by car. Our drivers kept one nervous finger tapping on the horn at all times. They honked for every car, pedestrian, and cow they saw. But it finally dawned on me what made driving in Myanmar sheer madness. Myanmar was once a British colony and so everyone used to drive on the left side of the road while the cars' steering columns were on the right — as they should be. This alone is confusing enough for Europeans and Americans as we often look the wrong way and get run over crossing a street, or heaven forbid we should take the wheel ourselves, we end up driving on the wrong side and making menaces of ourselves.

However, Myanmar takes the driving madness one step further by moving traffic to the *right* side like America but the cars' steering columns remain on the right. As a result, the driver is hanging out on the edge of the road and can't see oncoming traffic should they want to overtake another car. In fact, all the driver can see is the cows and garbage on the roadside. The front passenger has to tell the driver when it's safe to pass or they just lay on the horn and blindly move over into the oncoming traffic. When I finally figured out what was so completely wrong about this driving configuration, the horn-honking made perfect sense.

After a couple of days of nail-biting car trips around the city to see the gold leaf pounders, the marble sculptors, and the teak monastery, we shared a taxi with Larry and Carole and traveled upland to the small cities of Pyin Oo Lwin and Hsipaw. In Pyin Oo Lwin we all gathered for a meal at a fancy restaurant. Another big mistake in super poor countries: don't try to treat yourself to a nice meal out. They don't have the know-how to run a nice restaurant and as a result, you're better off eating simple local food. Larry and I both got food poisoning just as Sebastian was finally feeling better.

Bowel management had become the overarching theme of our month in Myanmar. It is what we talked about over our fiber-less white rice and white toast breakfast. "Mine was like a rock that got stuck half way out. I couldn't shake it loose." "Oh my gosh, mine was like lava. Remember that scene in *Bridesmaids* where the women shit all over the bridal store? That was totally me in the guesthouse last night."

Each meal we wondered if this was going to be the meal that would kill us all. Dining was like playing Russian roulette, and this evening Larry and I took the bullets. I lay in bed at the guesthouse the next day counting the minutes until my next gastric explosion while Sebastian toured the botanical gardens complete with loudspeakers broadcasting annoying music. "What about this trip is pleasant?" I called out to Sebastian as I ran to the toilet. I got no answer. "I guess I'm going to get a good blog story out of it but frankly, it's just not much fun."

"What did you expect?" he asked me, laughing and echoing some German tourists we ran into on the streets of Yangon when we were searching for a restaurant, any restaurant. We saw the only other Caucasians on the street and asked them if they knew where we could find something, anything to eat. Their answer was not directions to an eating establishment. Instead, they gave us a cross look and, "Vass did you expikt?" and they walked away from us in disgust. They were answering our facial expressions of disenchantment rather than the question at hand. Perhaps they were hungry and cranky themselves. "Vass did you expikt?" became the catch phrase of the trip applied at every mishap and crappy moment, of which there were many.

On the last night of our visit to Pyin Oo Lwin, our taxi hit a stray dog that limped off squealing into the bushes to die. "Stop! I want to go help the dog," I yelled to the driver. He did nothing of the kind. He was smart enough to know that a tourist wandering into the dark woods to help a wild dog was not a wise idea. Dogs in Southeast Asia are not the pampered pets of the West. They are street scavengers that skulk around the cities at night turning over trashcans and picking open garbage bags for scraps. They are ragtag packs with their ears chewed off from fights, legs broken from cars, teeth marks, and patches of mangy fur missing. Our smushed dog experience wouldn't be our last.

Hsipaw was our next destination — "an idyllic gateway to the Shan State" if you read the *Lonely Planet* guide. In fact, this scrappy little city is gateway to the muddy Duthawadi River which flows from China through Myanmar serving as the central garbage conveyor belt. It delivers its payload of bottles and bags to the Andaman Sea so people can enjoy tripping on them on the beaches of Thailand. Hsipaw turned out to be essentially a stopping point for fuel trucks on the way to China. Our guesthouse sat just feet away from the main highway. The thin walls rattled as the trucks shook the ground, their mighty horns sounding like elephants in the jungle.

More importantly though, Hsipaw is the home of Mrs. Popcorn's Garden. We stumble into her magical garden restaurant while looking for what *Lonely Planet* called "Little Bagan" which turns out to be just a couple of crumbling stupas overgrown with weeds and surrounded by packs of wild dogs. Mrs. Popcorn's Garden offers serene refuge from the dusty chaos of trucks and ox carts on the dirt road just outside her walls. As we pass through her gate, Mrs. Popcorn herself gets up from her wicker chair where she sits reading beneath large shade trees waiting for customers. Some days she receives none.

A quiet and contemplative Shan woman in her 60s, Mrs. Popcorn has a warm, soft face and kind eyes behind her dirty and outdated wire rim glasses. She lives in a small ramshackle ranch house with her family who helps her harvest and prepare delicious local specialties. We sit reclining in big wooden chairs in the shade and ordered some fresh fruit shakes served with ice. The shakes are so good and the atmosphere of sitting in a garden so pleasant that we don't ever want to leave.

We order her set lunch, and her daughters spring into action. The wok is thrown on top of a wood-fired flame and then the dishes begin coming out — stir fried okra, beans soaking in chili oil and garlic, bok choy, noodle dishes and rice. The food is all vegetarian and remarkably good considering how difficult finding a decent restaurant in Myanmar is, and especially one that won't lay you out for a few days popping Imodium and Cipro.

Mrs. Popcorn's name derives from, you guessed it, Mr. Popcorn — her now deceased husband who was the town's corn popper and proprietor of a factory nearby. She sat with us and talked wistfully about her husband and his business and in hushed tones about the changing winds of politics in Myanmar. Then she excused herself to attend to the next course of the meal — the tropical fruit platter of red dragon fruit, mangosteen, and pineapple.

Leaving the Eden-like sanctuary of Mrs. Popcorn's Garden was hard, but we handed over our $1 for the meal and went back out into the filthy fray. Sebastian and I continued down the dirt road and crossed over a small tributary to witness a group of women washing their laundry while their kids swam and bathed. This open-air toileting was all being done about 30 feet downriver from a farmer herding his horned water buffaloes across the river. One of the beasts stopped mid-river to take a huge dump which kerplunked in the water and drifted slowly toward the bathing family. They seemed oblivious and smiled and waved to us as we walked past. The gleeful kids jumped and played and dipped their heads in the river, filling their mouths with the brown water and spitting it out like elephants. What kind of stomach flora do *they* have? Whatever it is, I want some.

Back at our truck stop slash guest house (which I noted was situated next to the unfortunately named "KKK" guesthouse) we settled in for an afternoon of trucks gearing down and cigarette smoke coming through the loose rivets of the metal walls dividing us from some European tourists who liked to smoke in bed. Our guesthouse attendant Tun Tun was a muscular guy in his 20s who took delight in showing us his washboard stomach and biceps. I opened the shutters of the room to find him in the courtyard working out. We cheered him on, "Yeah, curl that iron, lift those dumbbells!" He laughed not understanding what we were saying. I encouraged him to take his shirt off which he did without hesitation, revealing a model-pretty, smooth, brown body. He came to the window to let us rub his six-pack through the bars and take pictures of him as if we were in jail reaching out to him as our jailor.

"Yeah, that's right, work it for the camera," I told him as I snapped a few shots. He was flattered that we found his body worthy of admiration. I don't think he suspected for one minute that any man would or could harbor desire for him. That concept simply didn't enter his mind, never having had any encounters with gay culture. To Tun Tun, we were just a couple guys admiring his hard ab work — that's what guys do.

The following morning Sebastian, Carole, Larry, and I all took a boat tour up the Duthawadi River. The first stop was a temple and farm on the banks of the river. We jumped out of the noisy long-tail boat to be greeted by a tiny old woman. I mean tiny. I mean old. She was about 4½ feet tall with very dark skin and wrinkles so deep you could drive a Matchbox car in them. Hers was not the face of a woman who wore PABA-free, non-comedogenic, dry touch, broad spectrum sunscreen, with a minimum of SPF 55 for the tropical sun. No, she stood there, unprotected and content in the blistering sun to greet us and welcome us to her land, burnt skin and all.

"She is the oldest woman in the village, and she is here to greet you as her distinguished guests," our tour guide Mr. Bean told us.

"How old do you think she is?" I queried.

"Really old. Yes. Very, *very* old." He repeated with furrowed brows as if we would never meet anyone as old again and that she might die at any moment.

"Mr. Bean, how old do you think she is?" I insisted.

"She's 60 years old."

"Yes, OK, I see." I nodded slowly pursing my lips and turning to Sebastian to note that both Carole and Larry were 60+ themselves. For an hour, the little lady was not the oldest living person in the village.

After our tour of the temple to witness the novice monks sitting around watching a violent wild western movie, we set out again on the horrifically loud long tail boat. We beached the boat at an old railroad trestle built over the turbulent river by the British in the early 1900s. Sebby and I took off up the hillside to walk the trestle while the others remained on the sandy beach. Sebastian wanted to walk across the trestle and so he set off alone.

"But Sebby, what if a train comes?" I cautioned him and I stopped to turn back. I noticed there was no landing onto which he could jump should a train come by.

"Oh, I don't think there will be a train. We're in the middle of nowhere," he assured me.

"Yeah probably true. Well, if you hear a horn, you better run!" I warned him like his mother.

I returned to the beach to join the others. We waved to Sebastian, as he was half way across the bridge 40 feet above the raging river. As I sat on the beach eating my lunch, I heard the train approaching the trestle. I felt weak in the head as I imagined Sebastian being run over by a speeding train. I wasn't sure Sebastian heard the horn as he was directly over the rapids which probably drowned out the roar of the train.

"Sebastian, get off the bridge! The train is coming!"

I yelled at the top of my lungs.

He didn't hear us. All the local villagers on the beach jumped up and started running around, pointing, and screaming. They were panicked that he had not heard the horn and wasn't listening to us — he thought we were just waving hello and he waved back. Finally, he heard the horn. He stopped for a painfully long moment and then began to run back and then he stopped again. We thought he wouldn't make it to land and should step off onto the concrete pier holding the trestle up.

"Get down, no, GO!" We yelled to him with mixed panicky messages.

The train was getting closer and louder. We could hear the wheels clacking. Sebastian didn't quite know what to do — stand and try to let it pass, or run. In the end, he made the smart choice to run for his life to the bank where he started. I managed to film the whole thing with him running like a chicken on the wooden railroad ties. He made it to safety without becoming the village's first German pancake and I thankfully didn't get the best fail video of all time.

CHAPTER 7
SEE YOU IN THE NEXT LIFE

*M*yanmar was proving to be a fascinating glimpse of old Asia in the middle of its own disappearing act. Much of the old grace and beauty is being mowed over by motorcycles and plowed under by shopping malls. The country's military dictatorship, while oppressing the people and keeping them sheltered from progress, had the unintended result of making Myanmar one of the last places you can still find cows being herded on the streets, or grandma taking the ox cart to the market. Traveling in Myanmar was rough — we were all sick at various times from the ambient filth. At the same time, wherever we went we found astonishingly lovely people — people humbled by the bamboo curtain that has kept them isolated and stuck generations behind. Myanmar is the Cuba of Southeast Asia. Like Cuba, things are changing rapidly in Myanmar and the country is opening its doors to commerce with China. That change, however, has provided a whole other set of challenges for the country — the stamp of industrialization — as now you can find villages and monasteries with massive gas pipelines running through them. Characterless Chinese hotels and concrete apartment buildings are being erected in places where previously there were only bamboo shacks with tin roofs. Freight trucks belching diesel smoke dominate the roads as they export Myanmar's natural resources to China. Fake Chinese silk products made of polyester have infiltrated the silk market. The country seems poised to be completely depleted and manipulated by their economic giant to the north.

From Hsipaw, we took the train (the very train that would have had a small white German guy plastered to the front) back to Pyin Oo Lwin across the famous Gokteik viaduct made in America and assembled by the British in 1900. Crossing over the Gohtwin stream at a height of 820 feet, the bridge is mentioned in Paul Theroux's acclaimed travelogue *The Great Railway Bazaar*. In this book, he describes the viaduct as, "a monster of silver geometry in all the ragged rock and jungle, its presence was bizarre." There's something dubious about a 111-year-old metal structure holding the weight of a train, especially in a country that can't fix a toilet. However, this adventure was *my* idea and if this mass of silver geometry were to eat us and we plunge to our deaths because someone forgot to tighten a bolts or check for rust, only I would be to blame.

Approaching this gorge on this broken, old train was a religious experience, if not for the spectacle of it, for the prayers even non-religious people like me say before crossing.

First you go through a massive fern-lined tunnel carved out of the mountain. Then the abyss and the bridge over it are revealed to you as the train comes to a full stop. Once the engineer has confirmed that the trestle is still standing by giving it the eyeball test and we've taken on a few more stowaways, the train begins to creep at a deathly slow pace. We head across the 2,260-foot-long structure as if taking baby steps to test its stability. I think the engineer should just gun it and if the old bridge collapses, at least some passengers would make it across and survive.

As we crossed we could hear the structure taking the massive weight. It began groaning loudly and then it pinged, popped, and creaked. I stood at the open door to our carriage with my camera in hand while the locals all avoided looking out the window.

In the US, if we had such a train ride, we certainly wouldn't have been allowed to stick our heads out of a window or stand at an open door and look straight down. Sebastian and I filmed each other hanging out the window in sheer awe of the century-old ingenuity. In America, a volunteer docent wearing lots of pins would be blathering on a microphone about the history of this marvelous structure, recounting 111 years of whad'ya knows. On this train though, there was an eerie silence save for Sebastian's gasps and the sound of straining metal.

The ride was truly exhilarating for a train that went no faster than a tortoise emerging from hibernation. I could have actually gotten off and walked along the viaduct faster.

The next day we set off for Inle Lake by plane. Our arrival at the airport in a country without computers or cell phones means we hand the gate agent a handwritten ticket that has carbon paper slips in it. They check to see if we are on the clipboard. Yes, the *clipboard*. After several minutes of flipping through pages while I get very, very anxious, we are remarkably confirmed on the flight. Then of course the next question is, when is the flight actually going to leave? For that they have to check another clipboard. Then with shrugged shoulders, they invite us to please have a seat in the lobby in any available broken chair.

But what about security — don't we have to go through security? Oh yes, we already did that without our even knowing. We are foreigners — we passed the stringent security test of some guy with red stained teeth seated on a plastic stool by the entrance spitting his betel nut juice into a can. Let's call him The Eyeball. He is in every airport in Myanmar. The Eyeball will give you the once-over. And if he is in a good mood, you go. If he's not, he will stop you, inspect your bags and seize your plastic utensils as he did mine in Yangon. Not, mind you, the plastic knife, fork, and chopsticks that I was also in possession of, just the spoon. It was a nice extra thick spoon that I had carried through many countries and eaten many a bowl of yogurt on train platforms with. And I left my prize spoon with The Eyeball. He may never know how much I resent him *to this day* when I reach into my backpack and pull out a crappy plastic spoon that has broken into 2 pieces and I have to eat my yogurt instead with a fork.

When it came time to board the flight, we walked out onto the tarmac through a sliding glass door that might open out onto someone's backyard pool at home. There we see our plane — the one with the flat tire. The one with the flat tire THAT THEY ARE NOT FIXING!

"Sebastian, look at that — the left rear wheel of the plane is flat, isn't it?" I say to him choosing to share my anxiety with him because anxiety needs company.

He screws up his face and looks worried. "Oh my gosh, it is. Should we say something?"

"Oh, like they're going to do anything about it. They could spray some air freshener on it maybe," I tell him, remembering my afternoon in Cambodia.

Onboard, our fears are amplified when we open the Air Bagan in-flight magazine and the first page is a letter from the president of the airline with a fleet of 5…now 4 planes. The letter apologizes for "the unfortunate and tragic incident last Christmas." What incident? Get me off this plane. I can't do this anymore. We don't know what that incident was, but I assure you it's not that someone threw up on the plane.

Sebastian calms me down, "How likely is it that they'll crash 2 planes in 2 months?" This was brilliant thinking on his part and it did actually allay my fears for the 45-minute flight, which went just fine except that we seemed to be listing a little to the left upon landing.

One of the greatest sites to behold in all of Myanmar is that of the Inle Lake fishermen in straw hats casting their conical nets at dawn. They move out in groups in the morning mist in long, wooden skiffs, propelling themselves silently, and in perfect unison with just one oar each. The men stand balanced with one leg on the stern of the boat and one leg hooked around the oar and with a characteristic j-stroke the boat inches toward the middle of the lake.

We were out at dawn on a long-tail boat tearing up the quiet of the morning when we spied the fishermen in the golden light. I waved and shouted to our driver to slow down and let me take some photos. He obliged. The rest of Asia uses deafening motorboats, but Myanmar is delightfully about 60 years behind. We were thrilled to have seen this water ballet — a vestigial sight from old Asia.

At the end of our month in Myanmar, Sebastian and I returned to our point of entry and the beginning of our journey, Yangon, once known as Rangoon. Over 5 million people live in its bleak urban canyons strewn with rocks, garbage, and low-slung power lines. Concrete apartment buildings with faded colors dominate the landscape with lines of laundry strung up outside their windows like prayer flags.

We had one free night in Yangon before returning to Bangkok. We each had several thousand Burmese kyat left over to spend or give away. Since there aren't really any nice restaurants, we decided to eat cheaply at a Shan buffet and then just walk down the street and give the rest of the money away, keeping enough for the taxi ride to the airport.

On our way back to the guesthouse with money burning holes in our pockets, we passed a couple digging through trash piles lining the streets that looked like Dresden after the blitzkrieg. We walked up to them and handed them 2,000 kyat (abut $1.50). The haggard couple looked at us perplexed, as if to say, "No, that's not mine, why are you giving this to me?" We insisted they take the money. They looked at us and then at the bills and then at each other and just started laughing. We walked away slowly, looking back as they just kept laughing with incredulity.

We continued on our philanthropic parade down another bombed-out looking street past an old monastery with moss growing on the drab concrete walls. We heard chanting coming from inside the gate. All the novices were in one big room with bare fluorescent bulbs doing their evening prayers. We stood outside the main gate listening to the masculine drone, when a couple of novices approached us. "Hellooo. Where from? Come to English class. Special guest you."

We went in and sat down on the floor of a large, austere room with 6 novices who had their books open and were reciting English with very heavy Burmese accents. Sebastian and I offered a few pronunciation tips and read from their books for them. They sat smiling, eager to learn from native speakers (if you can call a German a native speaker).

Afterward, they wanted to take us on a tour of the monastery and show us their living quarters. They led us up some decrepit stairs to a room full of mats and tarps strung through the bare rafters of the building. Wires ran all over the place to power various devices and a small TV from the 80s.

Small statues of the Buddha were adorned with dusty plastic flowers. The place had the feel of a grimy, spiritual barracks. The windows were open, allowing the noise of the city and the humid night air in. The novices all seemed eager to show us which mat, tarp, and bookcase was theirs. We visited each novice's space, looking at the pictures of their families they had pinned up on bookshelves.

We sat on the mats talking with several of the boys. One slightly older novice in saffron robes with the characteristic red betel nut stained teeth was the spokesperson for those whose English wasn't as good. They all were so attentive and thrilled to have guests visit them. No one was face down in any device. They appeared slightly malnourished.

The novice with the red teeth told us what their lives were like and where they came from. The story was similar to what we had heard before — the boys arrived at the monastery when they were 9 or 10 years old, sent by their poor families in rural Myanmar. Host families in the city "adopt" them and welcome them for a meal or to give them money and gifts, racking up Buddhist brownie points for themselves.

"We get up before dawn and pray and chant together. Then we cook breakfast and clean the monastery. We have a cold bath and then we have 2 hours of class and more prayer. Then we have lunch and study more. After that we do not eat for the rest of the day."

The novices were curious to know about our lives, made us some tea and asked about our trip through their country. Many of the places we visited, they had never been to. We told them stories of the trains and the temples and how much we loved the Burmese people and how kind and welcoming people had been everywhere we visited.

Their bedtime was approaching and we stood up to leave. They all insisted on a photo. We lined up in 2 rows and posed for the camera. Sebastian and I were the only ones smiling as we stood shoulder to shoulder. Snap — the moment was immortalized — our parting shot of a magnificent and trying month in Myanmar. We gave them the last of our money, a few thousand kyat.

The novice with the red teeth spoke for the group when he said in a very profound and decorous way, "We will never forget you. See you in the next life." He looked around and the novices all laughed and repeated together, "See you in the next life!"

Red Teeth walked us to the gate and said goodbye, pointing us in the direction of our guesthouse. We hired a bicycle pedi-cab back to Mother Land Inn 2. Sebastian and I sat facing backward as the driver with muscular legs in shorts pedaled us slowly and silently through the city's canyons glowing with small curbside fires of burning plastics. I reflected on our month in this noisy, polluted place with rats and rickety trains, and the days spent sick in bed. I also remembered the majestic temples of Bagan and the fishermen on Inle Lake, Koko and Mrs. Popcorn. Though I wasn't yet grateful for this trip, I thought about the novices at the monastery as spokesmen for our unforgettable time there. I could never forget them either. Myanmar in all its raw glory was a rare glimpse behind the bamboo curtain.

Immediately upon our arrival back in Bangkok we turned on the TV — something we had not done since we left. The horror unfolded on all channels. The most devastating event that a gay man could endure his entire life had just occurred. We sat on the bed awestruck and in abject grief by the breaking news. Yes, Whitney Houston had died of an overdose.

Oh dear god, no! I was going to have to say goodbye to Sebastian and Whitney in the same week. This compound farewell was going to blow my emo circuitry. There were not enough hankies in Bangkok to accommodate this big crybaby. As Sebby and I walked the streets counting the hours to our departure, *I Will Always Love You* was blasting from every store, bar, and pirate CD vendor. Sebastian and I had had an incredible month together, but still I wasn't ready to let go. We had shed the romantic love attachments, but he was still my best friend, my travel buddy, my partner in adventure, and someone I could always laugh with. But that was all coming to a close, as he would return to China and I to the States. We had no future plans to see each other, and I doubted I would ever see the little guy again.

Hearing Whitney belting out that song over and over was all I needed — I began to lose my composure as I walked Sebastian and his luggage to the Bangkok subway station near the guesthouse. I found myself having to take deep breaths and exhale slowly, focusing on getting him to the station on time. We got to the subway turnstiles when I collapsed. I had spent a year and a half grieving the loss of him as my lover and partner and then I just spent an extraordinary month traveling side by side with him. Saying goodbye to Sebastian was one of the most painful things I've ever done.

"Daffy, don't worry, we'll see each other again. *I promise,*" he comforted me with a tight hug at the turnstiles.

"I know that. But I don't know when that will be and that's the hardest part. I just want you to know that I will always love you," I choked, quoting Whitney in an admittedly cloying and lugubrious way. I've always hated people who quote songs in profound moments and now I found myself doing it, but sometimes you're just grabbing for a line and pop music is there to deliver the it.

I held onto Sebastian's small, sweaty body and soaked his shoulders even more. He was wearing the same threadbare shirt he wore when we traveled Europe together. Sometimes you just have to lose your shit and your dignity and this was one of those moments. I didn't care if everyone in the subway station was looking at us and wondering what kind of drama was unfolding. My crying turned into gasping for air in a not-so-silent way.

I could tell Sebastian was getting slightly uncomfortable with this spectacle. He eased himself to the other side of the turnstile putting necessary distance between us. He dragged his luggage through. I reached out for him one more time putting an over-emotionalized finishing touch on our goodbye. He tentatively stepped onto the escalator.

I tortured myself by taking in every second of his descent into the underground. Then I lost eye contact with him and it was over. I had to go back to the guesthouse. Alone. I could barely breath the whole way back. Money boys called out to me from the street corners. I ducked into a quiet restaurant and ordered a beer to calm my nerves. The perfectly attired lady boy server could see I was crying. She sat down at the table with me looking at me with compassion.

"You very sad," she noted. I appreciated that she didn't laugh at me.

"Oh yes. I just say goodbye to my friend."

"Special friend you," she tried to console me. "Don't cry. You friend, see again." She handed me some tissues and I blew my nose.

"I hope so," and I finished my beer, trying to muster a smile, and went to Babylon, which turned out to be a terrible mistake. There's nothing worse than someone with a broken heart going to a sex club. All that enchanted me in previous trips to Babylon now disgusted me. Hands reaching out in the dark seemed like tentacles that would strangle me. I couldn't get out fast enough.

"Vass did you expikt?" I asked myself aloud limping back to the guesthouse. Uttering those words made me laugh and cry at the same time. The 4 words were a poignant and humorous summation of my month with Sebastian in Myanmar. Truly, what *did* I expect? It was over with Sebastian, and that meant letting go and getting on with my life.

I packed my things for a midnight flight back to America, and back to the bottom of the pool of grief looking up at happy people on the surface, knowing I wouldn't be able to be one of them. It would be another year and a half before I returned to Thailand on a surprise visit — an emergency exit from a bad situation in the South Pacific.

CHAPTER 8
SURFACING

You can find me lying here
Just whispering your name
'Til your memory goes away
Or I get used to the pain
— Country singer John Anderson

t was late winter and I had to restart my getting over Sebastian from the beginning. Never one to shy away from emotional self-torture, I watched Whitney sing that damn song on YouTube over and over and over. I bought Eliza Gilkyson's Requiem and put it on repeat in my phone. I cried until my tear ducts ached — I guess I got used to the pain. Then, after a few months of self-pity I just couldn't grieve anymore. I fell back into my routine as a downwardly mobile gay male — melancholy and marooned in midlife. I threw myself into the things that gave me some small pleasure — cycling, singing, photography. But the spark of my life had really gotten lost somewhere in Asia. I reminded myself how lucky I was to have had the love and companionship of Sebastian for the time that I did. I tried to remember that he gave me a view into what was possible with love — being cared for in a way I had never known before. Still, I failed to find anyone to replace him, so I walked around like a zombie with a black hole in the center of my chest devouring light. Friends distanced themselves from me because of my darkness. Jim Beam spent the weekends with me, lording over my gloom from a shelf by the bed.

Then I got a wild idea, but not a new one. I would run away — this time to New Zealand! My friends Tom and Steve had moved to Wellington and were texting me photos and stories to try to entice me to move there. The trip seemed like a journey of redemption. Simply booking my flight put the spring back in my step. I found myself excited and enthusiastic about life again. And then there was the *reality* of New Zealand.

In the summer of 2013, I landed in Wellington right in the middle of an extra-tropical winter cyclone and my friends' bitter divorce. Between the time they extended the invitation for me to join them in New Zealand and the time I arrived, Tom and Steve's relationship had gone sour. Screaming and door slammingly sour. Everything was wrong about New Zealand. It was expensive, freezing cold, windy, rainy, and my friends' drafty apartment had become center stage for their shouting matches. I spent my days trying to stay out of their way. I sought shelter in museums or hid in the guest room with the heat on full blast, chatting with a couple local guys on line. This is when Asia once again came to my rescue and gave me the biggest, warmest hug that I needed. My life raft came in the form of a Chinese guy named Yee, living in Wellington with his mother.

Yee and I agreed to meet in person one afternoon in front of the Te Papa Museum in downtown Wellington. I saw him walking through the crowds of tourists and knew immediately he was the man I was looking for to escape the matrimonial madness at my friends' house. Yee kind of looked like a Chinese Robby Benson — tall and slender, unkempt black hair, and a broad Cupid's bow smile.

"Hellooo! You are David?" he said to me boldly over-compensating for his shyness.

"Yep that's me." I leaned close for a hug to introduce myself. He pushed back and shook my hand instead.

"No, no, no. Not here." He explained that he was not out to anyone. In fact, he had used a former partner's photo in his online profile. I wondered why he looked more than a little bit different in person.

"But this is *New Zealand!* How can you be in the closet? This is the most gay-friendly country on earth. If you can't be out here, where can you be?"

One thing I've learned is that Chinese mainlanders are nothing if not stubborn. There's no talking them into or out of anything, especially a closet. Yee grew up in an oppressive culture and brought it with him to New Zealand. Our affair began with me — as it ended with me — telling him to lighten up a little, have some fun, kiss me in public. We carried on the bulk of our affair in cafés, museums, and the dark cubicles of a downtown Wellington sauna as he was not welcomed at the house-o-door-slamming. We lay in each other's arms in the bathhouse cuddling and giggling while businessmen on nooners jiggled our door handles. The sounds of people having ruckus sex banged and bowed the thin walls of the cubicle next to us.

In the weeks that followed, Yee would sneak away from his mother, pick me up at the museum, and take me on adventures. We went to sheep-covered hills and windswept beaches and cliffs. We snuck into the woods to make love and sat on cliffs holding hands and dreaming about being together somewhere else. But we couldn't quite figure that part out. Yee was intractably beholden to his single mother, as are most Chinese boys. He could never leave her alone nor could he ever disappoint her by telling her he was gay. He lacked the backbone to get himself free.

We played in the windy afternoons when his mother was at work, before Yee went to his evening job at a Chinese restaurant. I wasn't sure if I was in love but I certainly was feeling something for this man, and I knew he was for me. Yet the connection felt as doomed as it was with Sebastian. I was eventually going to have to flee the domestic mess that my friends had gotten into with their divorce. Thus, I found myself in another date-stamped relationship.

I met Yee to talk one afternoon at the museum. We circled around the grotesque giant squid exhibit — the world's largest invertebrate. I couldn't ignore the irony that I was with the 2 largest animals on earth without backbones.

"Yee, I could fall in love with you," I told him getting misty-eyed and trying to hold his hand. He shrugged off my hand and turned away nervously. There was no question that he felt similarly but he simply couldn't handle any forthright discussions on matters of love.

"Shhh, not here!" The conversation made him uncomfortable — not just the nature of it, but having to have it in public, in front of a creepy 18-foot squid soaked in formaldehyde.

"Where else are we going to talk about it? We can't go to my place and we can't go to your place, and frankly, I can't afford another afternoon at the sauna." The conversation got tabled.

Things were becoming intolerable at home with Steve and Tom, so when I wasn't with Yee, I was scouring the web looking for my escape flight. I considered islands in the South Pacific, Australia, or maybe going back to the States. I also thought it might be a good time to go check on Koko in Myanmar. He and I had been corresponding by email ever since I left him on the street in Bagan. He told me he couldn't swim as he'd never been to the sea. I came up with a plan.

First, I would fly to Bangkok and get caught up on medical stuff, then go to see Dianna (the woman from the slow boat to Laos) in Pai, and then on to meet Koko in Yangon to take him to the Indian Ocean for swimming lessons. The excitement of the trip began to warm me from the inside. Finally, I would be able to thaw out, eat some food I could afford, then regroup and figure out where to go with my life from there. But this escape plan meant I had to say goodbye to Yee. My heart sank but what could I do? If he came out to his mother and welcomed me at their home, I'd stay, but that would never happen. I clicked to purchase the flight and broke the news to Yee who seemed strangely OK with it. We had 2 weeks left to cement whatever we might continue elsewhere, or we would just let go forever.

We spent our last chilly night together in downtown Wellington. Yee met me in a bar during their jazz festival. Unwilling to take time off from his job and mother, this was the first evening date we were able to have. Unfortunately, this was also our last date, but something surprising and beautiful happened: he held my hand in public while lounging on a sofa listening to a band playing jazz standards. This sweet gesture gave me some small shred of hope that this relationship might continue somewhere else in the world. We talked of plans for him to meet me in the States after my trip to Thailand. He would work on getting his US tourist visa the next time he was in Shanghai.

The jazz band finished and packed up and I walked Yee to his car up the block. We stood shivering in the freezing wind. I leaned into him for a final hug, and for the first time, he didn't pull away. I kissed him goodbye right there on the street by the parking meter. His lips were warm and his body trembling but he let me hold him for a what seemed like a long time. Finally, he broke away shaking and choking back some tears in silence. Then he turned, came back and kissed me some more, boldly in full view of drunk passersby — a long and passionate kiss. He kissed me like he meant business. I was excited for his own liberation and thrilled that something had shifted for me. There's nothing like the power of Eros to lay to rest a broken heart. That evening I finally stopped grieving about Sebastian.

Yee texted me in the morning as I was at the airport

waiting for my flight to Bangkok. He said that he was not feeling well. He felt sick to his stomach. I had to translate: this "illness" is a Chinese boy his having feelings. It's was easier for Yee to say he was sick than to say his heart was aching, but I knew what he meant. He thanked me for the best 6 weeks of his life. I thanked him for giving me hope and helping me to the surface where I could breathe again.

I imagined Yee wearing his little white cook's hat with his hair sticking out the back, manning the wok at the Chinese restaurant near his home, unable to tell anyone about his secret. I felt terribly sorry for him. My plane took off for Thailand over the beautiful city of Wellington with its pastel houses dotting the windswept green hills and then I was gone. Yee never followed up on his promise to meet me in the US. Our conversations became less frequent and more distant. The line eventually went dead.

CHAPTER 9
THAW

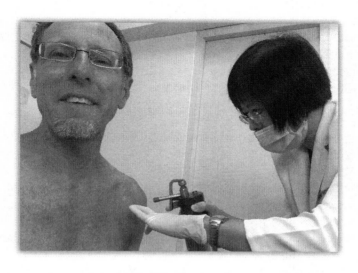

A year and a half had passed since the Sebastian / Whitney doubleheader meltdown in Bangkok. I felt so relieved to be back in the warm climate of Thailand, enjoying the easiness of the people, the creamy-tangy-spicy food, and the affordability. Thailand was everything that New Zealand wasn't. However, Bangkok had become a place of romantic ghosts — Noodles and Sebastian — so I set a course for the north of Thailand.

First, though, a visit to see Dr. Kittiporn at the hospital to get a year's worth of dermatology work done. Going to the hospital in Thailand isn't a sullen affair. For me it's a chance to jump on the back of a motorcycle taxi, close my eyes and go for the ride of a lifetime. We zoom up on sidewalks, down alleys, through parks, in between cars stuck in traffic. The vibration of the engine and the chance to hug a little Thai guy the whole way is a cheap thrill. I arrive at the hospital flush from the experience and in need of a change of underwear. Oh, it's good to back!

95

"Hello Dr. Kittiporn. How are the children?" I ask the doctor at Bangkok Christian Hospital. I wonder if she has any clue what her name means in the West? She draws the curtain, snaps on her gloves, and comes at me with the liquid nitrogen gun. The procedure of burning off my pre-cancerous spots is excruciating, but the whole bill ends up being about $30. I waited no more than 7 minutes for my walk-in appointment. After a quick chicken curry lunch in the hospital cafeteria for $3, I head over to urology. Another doctor snaps on *his* gloves and gives me a manual digital prostate exam. "What, only 1 finger this time, doc?" I mutter under my breath as he goes in. He doesn't hear me.

Then I'm on my way back to the hotel. I peruse the line of men and their motorbike taxis waiting outside the hospital. I choose the most petite driver with the tuft of chin hair and show him the card from my hotel. He nods. We agree on a price, he mounts his steed, and within seconds I'm out on the super slab inhaling a metric ton of carbon emissions.

Twenty-four hours in Bangkok and bang zoom I'm back at the airport on the way to Chiang Mai, ghosts in the rearview mirror. Founded in the 13th century, Chiang Mai was once the capital city of the Lanna Kingdom until it was, little by little, dissolved and annexed as part of the Kingdom of Siam. Remnants of the old city's brick wall still stand with a moat surrounding it, but that's about all that is left of the city's past. Chiang Mai is now a sprawling city of nearly a million people. The appeal for Westerners is that the city is a bit cooler than Bangkok and the air quality is arguably better.

At the airport, I hop into a taxi to my guesthouse and immediately rent a junky old Chinese bicycle with wobbly wheels. This will be my only mode of transportation for my time here. I cycle around the quiet alleys of the old town ringing my bike bell as I pass the various shops I have come to know. First, a ding to Tu the tailor. She looks up from her vintage black Singer sewing machine to give me a big smile and hello, "Aww. Sawatdee ka!" Tu has sewn almost all the clothes in my closet. I tell her I will visit her after the fabric market tomorrow.

I ding past the Denar tailors. Their 2 boys are getting bigger. They wave and smile. They've made beautiful suits and vests for Sebastian and me over the years.

I pass by Wee's Italian restaurant. He's outside arranging flowers. "Oooh Sawatdee! You back. Looking good. Ravioli tonight. We have good time." He winks at me and wags his tongue in a lascivious way. I laugh and tell him I'll see him later. Across the street, Adam, the proprietor of the Tri Gong house is out watering the planters. I wave but he ignores me — he has disappeared me. I used to stay at his place until he acquired 3 little dogs — Whipped Cream, Money, and iPad. After their arrival, there was no sleeping, so I stopped staying there. Who names their dog iPad, anyway?

A ding of the bell goes to Gavalee, the tailor on Sri Poom Soi Nung. She looks up from her glasses and glares at me. She never liked me.

A double ding for Ponapa the lesbian chef at Ponapa's Kitchen where she cooks wonderfully spiced curries out of her garage and sets up a few tables. I'll sit with her for a meal later. "Aww! Bai nai, David?" She asks me where I'm going.

"Bai tee ow. Le ow pop khan mai!" I'm going out. See you later, and I wave to her.

Thailand's cities are giant quilts of little villages sewn together, and mostly populated by people who grew up in the countryside and migrated to the city for commerce. Each alley is a new village. Everyone knows everyone, and they never forget you as a good customer. (They never forget you if you're a bad customer, too.)

The last ding of the bike bell is for Lek, the shake lady. She lights up revealing a mouthful of crooked teeth when she sees me and I stop in for an avocado and green apple shake. Her business is doing well. She's moving down the street by Wee. She seems to flirt with me even though I know she has a husband.

My first couple of days in Chiang Mai are spent on a mission to find the best fabric for some new clothes and to get the cloth to the tailors before I take off on some other expedition. I cycle over to the Warorot Market just outside the city's walls, plunging into the wonderful world of fabrics. I start my day at the Muslim fabric store on a side alley near the main market. The sidewalks are lined with bolts of fabrics of all kinds spilling out into the streets — plaids, checks, dots. The Thai Muslim families usually have the best selection of linens and cottons. Today I'm looking for Japanese linen for some tropical shirts. This trip to Thailand was a surprise, having come from the New Zealand winter with nothing but warm clothes.

The first Muslim store doesn't have what I am looking for so I cross over the street to the one opposite. Massive piles of fabric bolts covered with dust bunnies are strewn as far you can see. Minna, the owner comes out and says hello in perfect British English. "I hear you are looking for Japanese linen today." I give her a quizzical look and she says that her brother across the street has alerted her that the guy in the blue hat is looking for linen.

"I have some fabrics upstairs that you might be interested in. Follow me." We climb over bolts and up the stairs to find some buttery soft white Japanese linen with green stripes and some orange Chinese linen in a Burberry plaid pattern. I am convinced and buy enough for a couple shirts. She sells me some contrasting fabric for lining the collars. Then I scoot off down the street to the button store. I squeeze down the aisle meant only for tiny Thai women and pick out packets of shell buttons and a few little decorative add-ons. By the afternoon, I am at Tu and Dinar tailors with my drawings and instructions for the shirts which will be ready for me to pick up in a few days.

In the evenings, I cycle around the old city looking for a new or interesting restaurant, any festivals or night markets, a cheap cocktail, or just someone to talk to. As a lone traveler, small chats with strangers keep me from slipping so far inside my head that I become completely unsociable.

One beautiful, cool evening I packed a bottle of Sang Som rum in my backpack and went to enjoy the sunset at the ruins of the 14th century temple Wat Chedi Luang. As the skies darkened I secretly dipped into my bag for a few sips from the little bottle. I felt the stresses of the day lift from my shoulders. Ah, now all I need is a little massage. Well, the Buddha must have read my mind. A passing monk stopped to talk to me.

"Hello. Where from?" the standard question from anyone in Thailand.

"Hi. I'm from America."

"You here with wife?" he inquired.

"Oh no. Not married." I responded kind of wondering where this was going. I was sure he was going to tell me that I should have a wife and kids.

"Not married?" he asked again just to confirm and then he got to the point, "You like massage?" I sensed this was starting to go off in a direction I had not anticipated.

"Yes, I like massage," I told him.

"Come to my loom. I give you Thai massage." He walked ahead of me showing me the way as it would raise suspicion for him to be seen walking next to me. I had heard about people being seduced by monks at monasteries, but I had written it off as urban legend or locker-room talk. I had a sense that either I was being seduced or that I was going to get talked into making a large donation to the monastery.

The monk took me to the dormitory, a long, nondescript building a bit like army barracks. Little novices scampered around talking to him and pulling on his robe. I'm sure they were asking about me. Perhaps they were saying something like, "Well, that's the 5th one this week!" He shooed them all away and they rushed off into their rooms. He led me into his room, closed and locked the door, and stuffed a towel into the gap at the bottom. He was serious about this, whatever *this* was. His room was more decorated than the monastic digs I had previously seen — it had curtains which he closed abruptly, little twinkly lights, and some nice statuary.

Immediately he told me to lie down on a mat. He said it in a very bossy way like one would talk to a dog. Take off shoes. Come here. Lie down. Roll over. Good doggie. I complied with his demands not really knowing where this encounter was headed but considering I was in a monastery, I figured it probably wouldn't involve me being hacked up.

He squatted next to me, his robes parting in the process revealing his unfettered devotion. Holy cow, this monk had been going commando while on his tours of duty at the monastery. He began the massage which went something like this: press on my calves, press on my inner thighs, grab my crotch. He wasted no time going right for my junk within about 6 seconds of the commencement of the "massage."

I figured that considering his openness to such nefarious activities and the openness of his robes, I would reciprocate in kind. I slowly reached into the folds of golden fabric and just as I was about to gain purchase, my hand was swatted away.

"No cannot," he scolded me.

"Why cannot?" I asked.

"Cannot."

"Why cannot? You touch me. I touch you?" I asked, pressing the issue.

"No cannot. I am monk. Cannot touch monk."

"Ah, OK, I see. You monk. You touch me. I not touch you." I restated to him what he just said attempting to get clarity on his intentions while at the same time illuminating the sheer lunacy of his reasoning. I guess in his mind, molesting me wasn't considered a violation of Buddhist precepts, but if *I* were to initiate contact and touch *him,* that would be a violation. The logic mystified me, but hey, I went with it since I was already lying on the floor with my pants around my ankles *in a monastery.*

He nodded and squeezed out a dollop of lotion into his hand and then went to town. In my moment of passion, I reached under his robes again just to test his will and was swatted away once again. All I could do was lie back and enjoy, and he wasn't bad, actually — I suspected he'd had a lot of practice. I could hear novices scurrying about outside his door and my nervousness brought about a quick conclusion to this scene.

As soon as I was finished — in fact, *before* I was finished — he was mopping up and ushering me out the door while I was still buttoning up my pants. He peered into the hallway motioning away any potential witnesses, then he flung open the door and pointed to the exit telling me to hurry up. I started down the empty hallway and I looked back. Poof, he was gone, the door was closed and that was the last I saw of him. No cuddle, no hug, no sharing of his dreams for the future. I stepped outside into the slightly cool air, still flush with incredulity about what had just happened. I took a swig of Sang Som, slipped on my shoes and hopped on my bike back to the guesthouse. I kept replaying the scene in my head, still in disbelief. Did I *really* just get seduced by a monk in a monastery?

CHAPTER 10
PAI TIME

*M*y first view of the little Thai mountain village of Pai was from the clouds. Most people arrive by bus or minivan. I couldn't bear the thought of the notorious 762 curves on the mountainous road from Chiang Mai. I get motion sickness just turning my head, so I opted out of the vomitous route and took the small, single engine plane that seemed to literally jump over the mountains. Aboard the Kan Air flight, I could see the winding road below. I imagined the vomit chunks rolling around people's feet as they took each hairpin turn for their 3-hour journey.

On the day of departure, I received a phone call at the guesthouse that my flight was leaving an hour early and to come to the airport immediately. It sounded something like this: "Meetuh Davit, fright reave erry. Must to come light now." I do the accent translation and then I panic, rushing to pack my bags.

I got to the airport an hour ahead of time so we can wait. We were to leave early because of the inclement weather, but then we were delayed back to our previously scheduled time because someone from the Thai royal family was in the airport gumming up the flight schedules. In my haste, I managed to slip my boxer shorts on backwards, which wasn't really a problem until I needed to pee. Thanks to the Thai royal family, I now had some unexpected time to discover at the airport urinal that there was no fly in the front. I stood at the urinal digging around and around, trying to find the fly. My fishing around inside my pants and my confused and frustrated look surely gave the impression to the gentlemen standing beside me that I simply couldn't locate my penis.

Finally aboard, the tiny plane bounces down the runway and darts into the clouds as if it weighs nothing at all. When we finally loop around Pai, I can see the airstrip. We drop down out of the sky like a hawk after a mouse, missing the runway entirely. I'm in the seat directly behind the pilot and can tickle his neck if I want to. Maybe I'll try that and just give a little wave to remind him that he has passengers to drop off and that landing the plane on the airstrip might actually be a purposeful thing to do today. But I don't because in Asia I am just a tourist and a witness rather than a backseat pilot. I watch with wide-eyed curiosity as we get a second pass over Pai. Circling the whole city, I see temples, rivers, and a giant concrete Buddha under construction in the hills. This time we swoop down and land on target, puttering over to the tiny terminal. Outlandishly dressed Chinese tourists with big floppy hats step off the plane, grabbing hold of the wings and what appears to be sensitive navigation antennae. They hold up 2 fingers for selfies with the plane. I roll my eyes and head off to see Dianna waiting for me with her Thai-American grandson, Pansa.

Dianna lives at Ing Doi guesthouse aka Yawning Fields aka Center for Pork Healing, a nutty conglomeration of huts off a muddy road in the middle of several acres of rice paddies. Her American son Jake and his Thai wife Mink run this funky but fun haven for backpackers and ducks. The pork healing name has something to do with the fact that Mink loves pork and Jake is vegetarian. It's a loose play on words that in the end sounds like a veterinarian center for barnyard animals, but in fact is just a great place to lay your head and eat some delicious Thai food served up by Mink. The place is crawling with ducks, the occasional snake, and alternative travelers from the US, Australia, England, and Russia.

I was put in a small bamboo cabin with thatched roof overlooking a preternaturally green rice paddy. I opened the French doors, parted the sheer curtains and breathed in the humid, peaty smell of the rice fields. I sat in a hammock with my book, watching the farmers wearing their conical straw hats tending to the baby rice plants. They moved like chess pieces in slow motion on a rice paddy chess board. Beyond them were layers of green mountains with that giant Buddha construction barely visible in the haze. This was the closest I'd come to paradise in Thailand. At $15 a night, with stunning views of old Asia, I thought I could stay here forever. That's when I heard the scream. It was a man's voice and it wasn't a scream of delight.

I went to the door and witnessed him backing away from his cabin quickly — not something you hope to see in paradise. He saw me and called out in his British accent, "There's a giant snake in my cabin. I heard it poke its head through the thatch and then it dropped down onto my bed. We must do something!" Oh, dear. Like what — call 9-1-1? Release the attack ducks?

He went to the main lodge and got the help of the Thai gardener who seemed unfazed by the news of the snake. The gardener picked up a hoe and shovel and headed into the cabin with amazing poise. I grabbed my camera. Within minutes he emerged with a big grin holding up a 6-foot long snake with its head now flattened. I wondered where he was headed with the serpent but I was sure that it was not going to be wasted flesh.

I borrowed one of Jake's bicycles and took myself on a cycling tour of the town. I was thrilled to be on a bike, out of the cold, wind, and rain of the New Zealand winter. The sunset was nearing, so I circled around a rice paddy and parked my bike. I grabbed my camera and walked along the little ridges of mud that divide one farmer's rice from another's. I was clicking away capturing a green and gold sunset when I noticed some farmers in a hut in the middle of the field. They were drinking Thai whiskey, smoking cigarettes, and laughing. They invited me into the hut, motioning me to sit on a log and join them for whatever was in the pot simmering over a small pit fire. I was curious what was in the pot and they motioned me to have a look. I took the lid off and to my horror, it was full of boiling eels. They laughed at my shock and then to further the tourist torture, pulled the lid off of a basket of live ones writhing and wiggling inside and shoved it at me. I nearly screamed as they gestured their hands to their mouths, inviting me to stay for dinner. I thanked them and graciously backed out of the hut and resumed my photography. My nerves were fried by slithery things — maybe tourists just aren't supposed to duck their heads under the thatched roofs of little huts in the middle of rice paddies in Asia. My bad.

It was in Pai that I first began to notice the growing discomfort between the Thai people and the mainland Chinese tourists. If you haven't been out traveling the world, you probably haven't noticed that China's rising middle class has yielded a large crop of first-time tourists taking to the air. They flock to Thailand by the millions in their oversized hats and garishly colored clothes paired with ill-matching accessories. They seem to always travel in large tour groups

— ensuring there will be no chance of connecting with people from a different culture. Or is it to shield themselves from the ridicule they invite? I've come to refer to these big groups of Chinese tourists spitting, clearing throats loudly, and yelling across airport terminals as "Mainlandia." Pai is no stranger to invasions of the Mainlandia.

One day I was sitting in a restaurant having lunch in downtown Pai when I spied a Mainlandia family traveling with their one government regulation baby. During the course of their lunch, they lifted the toddler onto the table with his shoes on, pulled down his pants and lifted a water bottle up and encouraged the boy to pee into the bottle. He filled it up, they capped it, flicked the boy's little wiener, pulled his pants up and placed the bottle on the table. My attention was diverted from my lunch companion as I stared in silent disbelief at this spectacle. The family paid for their lunch and left the urine filled bottle on the table.

The Thai wait staff stood by watching in horror at the unfolding table urination scene. They joked about who had to dispose of the pee bottle. Though I couldn't understand the language, I was sure that it was something like, "You do it." "No, *you* do it! I did it last time." I decided to join in the conversation and went over to the pee bottle and held it up to the giggling staff and motioned that someone should drink it — that it might be quite tasty. They doubled over laughing.

Evenings in Pai means it's time for the fashion show of Chinese evening wear. Mainlanders see the crowded, smoke-filled street market as their Oscars red carpet runway as they hop out of their tuk tuk as limousine into the crowd to get their chicken on a stick. They imagine flash bulbs and interviews with the press.

The more matronly women dress in flowing pink and white polka dot terry cloth mumus, light blue, ruffle bodice chiffon gowns paired with tangerine clogs. The more petite come out in black micro-mini cocktail dresses, lace stockings, and 6-inch stiletto heels. They often accessorize with big sun hats and scarf ties — very useful for evening affairs. These women take being out of touch with the local culture to a very high art. The net result is that in this funky, hippie town, they look like hookers working the parking lot of the Barnum and Bailey Circus. The men dress in oversized t-shirts and saggy pants, carrying the giant COACH knockoff purses for their wives and girlfriends.

I became acquainted with a tender yet tough lady boy named May who worked at the Relax Massage parlor in Pai. Thailand is chock full of transgendered women such that if you're a straight guy on the prowl, you best be prepared for a surprise, or just don't go below the waist if you're not absolutely sure. Because Thai guys are not particularly big and muscly like lots of us from the West, their petite bodies can make a convincing transition to female, should they choose to do so, and lots do. In Pai, there is only one lady boy (that I'm aware of) and she's not super convincing as a woman. As a dude, she was a mesomorph — short, stocky, and strong as an ox, but as a woman, she's still short, stocky, and strong as an ox…only now in a bra and lipstick. She is a kick-ass massage therapist who will knot you up like a pretzel and then deftly unknot you. Thai massage is painful for delicate creatures such as myself and no matter how you tell May to take it easy, she can't — she seems not to know her own brute strength.

After a few massages with May, I couldn't take the pain anymore, so I switched to another gentler massage therapist who wouldn't leave me with bruises and in need of a full body cast. His name was Noom. Noom is Burmese and one of the most beautiful straight men I've ever laid eyes on, all in a miniature package standing about 5'2" and weighing about 120 pounds. He looks like an Olympic swimmer scaled down by about 40%.

In his spare time, he practices Thai kick boxing. Noom would take me into the steam room at the massage parlor, rub salt all over my body and then oil me up for a full body massage. It was like being in a non-sexual, interactive porn video. But I couldn't tell May because she might very well be overcome with jealousy, tie me up and send me to the Bangkok penis reattachment center with my junk in a Ziploc bag.

My visits to see Noom had to be arranged by the boss when May was off duty. One day she came in and caught me being massaged by Noom. She sat down next to me on the mat and a tear came to her eye. "I pretty too," she said to me in the most tender way.

"Yes, you pretty too," I reassured her. Just the words seemed to make her feel better. We held hands while Noom massaged me. Over the weeks in Pai, May and I developed a sort of girlfriends relationship.

Late one evening May and I made a date to hang out. I went by the massage parlor at 10pm and waited for her to finish with a client. After she cleaned up and let her hair down, we jumped on her motorcycle and drove up the dirt road to the guest house. I know what she wanted (or I thought I did) and was a bit wary of inviting her into my cabin knowing that with her strength, she could date rape the hell out of me. But estradiol therapy has the amazing ability to defeat all the ugly behavior traits of testosterone. We cuddled like kittens in my cabin — fully clothed. Instead of throwing herself on me with indignity, she pulled out her phone and logged onto Chatroulette.com. She held up the phone as people from all over the world started clicking in on us. Faces appeared for only 2 seconds, had a laugh, a look of surprise or disgust, and then clicked off to the next person. Some bland looking white guy appeared from Iowa. It was early morning out there on the farm and we had a brief chat in English. I told him I was in bed with a lady boy in the middle of a rice paddy in Thailand. "Hum. You don't see that every day, do ya?" And then he was gone. After a few dozen clicks of this self-esteem bashing, May got bored with Chatroulette and me, and she was gone. I heard her motorcycle zoom off into the dark of the rice paddies.

CHAPTER 11
VASS DID YOU EXPIKT? *REDUX*

A couple years had gone by since I last saw Koko, the gentle houseboy from Bagan, Myanmar. After our little rooftop tryst, I had left him standing on the street in front of his guesthouse. We Skyped a few times without speakers or camera which meant I typed, and he read and responded to me by voice. I could hear him but couldn't see his face. And he could only read my typing, characteristic of Burmese dysfunction.

Still, we managed to keep current on each other's lives. I sent some money to him via an American friend who stayed at his guesthouse while on a tour. I asked him to save the money to take a bus and meet me in Yangon. I would fly up from Thailand and we would go to the Bay of Bengal so I could teach him to swim as he had never been to the ocean or even a pool. I was excited to see him and envisioned the romance of him holding on to me as he floated in the sea for the first time.

As soon as I boarded the flight from Chiang Mai to Myanmar, I knew something was not right about this trip. The plane was painfully hot inside — the air conditioning was not working properly. Then there was the traffic choked taxi ride to the guesthouse in downtown Yangon. I had to pay extra for the air conditioning. Most people would agree that Yangon is not charming by any measure but oddly the vehicular noise is minimal since they outlawed the pervasive horn honking that destroys serenity in the rest of the nation.

Low-strung power lines crisscross the narrow streets that are brimming with cars, rubble, garbage, and pedestrians avoiding giant holes in the sidewalks. Corded telephones are set on TV tables in front of shops to serve as phone booths in a country with little or no cell phone coverage. Trees and vines rooted in the cracks of once beautiful British colonial buildings threaten to splinter them. Women hang out laundry on tiny balconies with decorative wrought iron that is now rusting to the point of failure. Old wooden shutters sag and rot in the humid air. More than 5 million Burmese call this city home.

When I check in at the shabby but friendly guesthouse, the women at the front desk inform me that Koko is already in the room. His arrival is a miracle since he doesn't have a phone and I've had no way to be in touch with him other than occasional emails and Skype. I open the door to the room and there he is, skinnier than ever, his giant wad of hair taking up more space than the entire rest of him. He's all smiles and no talk. I greet him with a big hug. His body is like a plucked bird, I can feel his heart beating wildly through his ribcage. He pokes at me with his nose as if he were sniffing me without the inhaling part. I wonder about this — is he inspecting me or showing a sign of affection?

"It's good to see you! How are you, Koko?" I get no answer, just the nod of a head, seeming not that dissimilar to the Skype chats we've had. Hmm, life imitating technology. I speak, he nods, shakes, and occasionally chirps something, but no full sentences. I wonder if I should type my questions to him.

"Right, OK, let's go get some food. Are you hungry?" He shakes his head in that diagonal way that Indians often do. To

110

a Westerner, it's not clear. It's both a shake of no and a nod of yes with a little wiggle like the doggie with the spring neck you put on the dashboard of your car. I guess we'll go eat — he certainly *looks* hungry and I'm going to fatten him up on this trip, I tell myself.

The front desk gives me a map of Yangon and points out only a few restaurants. Walking down the streets, you'd think that restaurants were banned in this city. No one seems to eat out or there are not abundant and reliable suppliers of food for restaurateurs. So, we walk and walk and walk and cannot find a restaurant. I check the map because GPS doesn't work here. I show Koko the map and ask him to help me find the dots that indicate a restaurant. He can't seem to figure out the map or how it corresponds to the streets. We fail to find a street sign and it's getting dark and there are no street lights. I started feeling a little concerned that we might get lost. We double back to where we started and count the streets to the nearest restaurant. It's seeming like we're in a dark forest leaving a popcorn trail and some little bunny is eating the popcorn behind us.

It turns out that either Koko cannot see well or he cannot read Burmese, or both. Silly me, I imagined that he would be my tour guide and would interpret the language, make connections, read maps and guide me on a magnificent journey behind the scenes of Myanmar. Nope. He is both shy and possibly illiterate which, in a tour guide, is a bad combo. Koko in fact, is more freaked out about being in this big confounding city than I am — I've been here before so I already have one up on *him*. Navigating and stumbling through the language barrier is going to remain my responsibility. What Koko does is hold my arm and the umbrella as it begins to rain and I'm on a street corner flipping and turning the map around, terribly disoriented.

Somehow, I forgot to check about the weather before coming to Yangon in July — it turns out that July is peak monsoon season. While I fiddle with the map, it begins

111

pouring, not just buckets but waterfalls. The streets turn into ankle-deep rivers. Buses tear by drenching pedestrians.

In a way, it delights me when nature overpowers man in cities. And then a turd floats by my ankles. I don't dare pick one up to confirm it is indeed a turd, but I'm old enough to know what a turd looks like. And *that* is a turd. We're walking in a giant toilet looking for a restaurant. Maybe we will float away in a chocolate river like Augustus Gloop in *Willy Wonka & the Chocolate Factory*.

At last we find a restaurant! I don't even check to see what kind of food it is. I don't care that it is lit with one bare fluorescent tube on the ceiling as long as I can dine on something edible without feces tickling my ankles. The server comes around and says something I don't understand. I ask Koko what she said. He flashes me a look of befuddlement. Right.

"Koko, tell the server that we would like some vegetables and chicken, OK?" He looks down at the table. I can see that he is very sorry that he can't help.

"Why can't you help me? Can you *please* order some food for us?" I'm begging at this point. Still nothing from him. He gets more and more withdrawn, and I don't know what to do. I start flipping through my Burmese translation guide to find "chicken." I point to what looks like bubbles, squiggles, and doors. Even the prices are inscrutable as they don't use Arabic numerals. In the back of the book I find "vegetables" and I cluck like a chicken and the server nods and disappears. She eventually returns with some food that resembles exactly what I had hoped for — stir fried veggies with chicken. I'm thrilled and start to dig in when I realize that Koko hasn't stopped staring at the table in embarrassment for not helping.

"Koko, please eat some food." He looks at me and cannot smile. Suddenly I'm having an aha moment: Koko has never been to a city, he cannot read, and he has probably never even been in a restaurant seated at a table with a white person. He may need glasses and maybe has a stomach bug because he has no appetite and I have no way to communicate any of this or any way to remedy the situation. He's like the Burmese Helen Keller. Jesus, Buddha, and Muhammad, this is a very sad multi-point stalemate and I don't know what to do. What have I done to this poor young man? I've brought him to this big city where he is clearly disoriented to the point where he can't even eat.

He took a couple bites of the food and then put down his chopsticks. I suddenly feel flush with embarrassment that my whimsical notions of Koko were tremendously far afield from any practical reality, and who do I think I am anyway? Some sort of rich and powerful benefactor come to wave a magic wand and grant some poor Burmese guy his wishes? This is where the fantasy trip ends and now we get to walk back to the crappy guesthouse in the sewage. I think I became a shade less idealistic about international relationships that night.

Back at the guest house Koko and I lay in our boxer shorts under the accusatory light of the bare fluorescent tube buzzing overhead. A ceiling fan clicks at every wobbly revolution. Cigarette smoke makes its way into the room from the hallway. A TV in the lobby blares some silly game show with lots of sophomoric sound effects. None of this makes me feel particularly amorous toward Koko or hopeful about this trip. What I feel is pathos and that's not sexy. I don't even know if a sexual encounter is what Koko wants... or needs. After my dinner revelation, I became more of a parent than a playmate for Koko. We tried kissing a little bit, but his breath was so bad and his lips so chapped that I just couldn't do it. I suggested he brush his teeth but he waved me off with the diagonal head bob. He took a long shower that included a couple little moans at the end so I could only imagine what he was doing in there so long.

The next morning, I went down to the community breakfast at the guesthouse and shared a table with a young gay American who was on assignment for Outright

Action International to work toward advancing gay rights in Myanmar. I listened with envy to his stories of trying to get press coverage for gay causes in Yangon. Why is it that he was here doing so much good and I'm here as a playboy just tinkering with this young man of undetermined sexuality? What good was *my* being here doing anyone? I thought about the swimming lessons in the Indian Ocean. I mentioned this to the American activist. He laughed, "It's monsoon season, the beaches are closed. Good luck!" And then he was off to do work that I would love doing. Instead I had to go back to the room, rouse the sleeping Koko and try to imbue us with the enthusiasm to do something, *anything*.

I remembered how to get to Alan, the travel agent who helped Sebastian and me with the previous trip. He was somewhere near the train station. If I could find the train station, I could find Alan, who spoke English. He would make everything better and come up with a travel plan for us.

A person standing bewildered on a street corner holding a map, turning it and then turning it again, usually draws attention, but especially a white person in this country. An older Burmese gentleman in glasses came up to us and in perfect British English said, "May I offer some assistance?" I nearly cried and grabbed onto his longyi.

"Oh, thank god! Yes, I'm trying to find the train station."

"Well, you're in luck. It's just behind those buildings there," and he pointed in the direction we should head.

"Thank you so much! Tell me, how is it that you speak perfect English?" I queried.

He explained, "All the older people in Myanmar speak English. The country won its independence from the British in 1948. After that, they stopped teaching English. But we old folks still speak it. Now everyone wants to speak English because it is the language of commerce and the country is opening up."

The gentleman looked around to see if anyone was spying

on us and leaned in close enough that I felt his breath on my face. "We must be careful. The government might follow you and question me for talking to you. Whatever you do, don't take pictures of the police or soldiers. They may be opening up now but it's not like your country here."

I thanked him for the advice and digging into my money belt, I offered him a tip, but he turned it down. "Oh heavens, I am happy to help and am delighted to finally see tourists in our country. We've waited half a century for you to come back. I hope you have a good time here. Good day to you!" And we were off on our separate ways. I wish I could have invited him to join us.

Koko and I found the train station where Sebastian and I had set off for Bagan a couple years before. Then we found the travel agent. We went in and asked to speak to Alan.

"You're back! Couldn't get enough of Yangon, huh?" he laughed so hard he started coughing. I didn't laugh so hard.

"Well, honestly, I've had enough and I need your help to get out of here."

"Where do you want to go," he asked as he sat down at his computer terminal. I marveled at the first modern computer I'd seen in Yangon.

"I want to take my friend Koko to the Bay of Bengal to teach him to swim." I was starting to sound like Dorothy trying to get to Emerald City.

He began to laugh at me, then covered his mouth and coughed a little to regain his composure. "Well, look, it's monsoon season. You can't get there by bus because the roads are washed out. You could fly but there's only one flight a week. But even so, there's some 'political unrest' (he winked) on the coast. The Buddhists and Muslims are fighting and there's a curfew. You would be stuck in a hotel room in the rain and might not be able to get back."

"Oh dear." I said crestfallen and dejected. "OK, when can you get me out of here? I want to be on the next flight to Thailand."

"It's Monday. The next flight to Chiang Mai is on Thursday afternoon," he told me with a grim face.

"I'll take it. Book it, please."

He attempted to book the flight but my credit card was denied. Shit! I forgot to tell my bank that I would be in Myanmar. To them this looks like credit card fraud — what tourist in his right mind would be in Yangon? I emailed my bank from his computer but of course it's the middle of the night in America. I would have to wait until evening for a resolution.

"Look, take your friend to see some temples, go on a day trip to Bago."

"Ooh baby, more Buddhas," I said in a terribly disrespectful and irreverent way. "If there weren't temples in Asia, there would be nothing to do."

He pursed his lips and shrugged his shoulders and said, "What did you expect?" That made me finally laugh out loud for reasons he would never know.

Koko and I made the best of the 3 days in Yangon. We took a lackluster taxi trip to Bago. I got used to him being of no help as a tour guide. However I enjoyed how he held my arm everywhere we went. It somehow made us both feel special. I've never had anyone hold my umbrella for me, rain or shine, but Koko insisted on holding it for me in the monsoons and shading me from the sun. Maybe it gave him a sense of purpose so I let him do it. We sat in restaurant after restaurant with him pushing the food around his plate. I clearly wasn't going to fatten him up if he refused to eat. I asked if he would like to see a doctor and he shook his head diagonally again. I took that to mean no.

Back in Yangon, it continued to pour down rain. We stood under awnings watching the streets turn into rivers. One rainy night we went up to the fabulous Shwedigon Pagoda where I had been with Sebby. It's a place that strikes me dumb with amazement that such a poor country would lavish itself with such an extraordinary temple strewn with gold and jewels. And of course, ancient Buddha statues must all have blinking LED halos placed behind their heads. I couldn't believe the marriage of elegant antiquity and tacky modernity. I cornered one tour guide about it.

"The blinking LED lights depict the Buddha's enlightenment," he explained as if I didn't know what they were.

"Yes, I know. But why do you need cheap blinky lights? You can buy those lights at Walmart! Why not leave the ancient sculptures the way they were?" I pleaded with indignation.

"We think it makes them more beautiful," and he walked away satisfied for having fully answered my question. With that rationale, I could see the Burmese putting a pair of cherry red 2(X)IST boxer briefs on the statue of David. And they would too, if they could figure out a way to get his legs through the holes.

I kept slipping on the wet marble floors that surround the main stupa at the center of the temple. My bare feet were sore from the hard surface without my beloved orthotics and then I noticed a red carpet had been laid out to circle the whole stupa. Fabulous, I thought to myself, I'll go walk on the red carpet while Koko sits staring at the stupas in some sort of disoriented wonderment. The carpet felt soft and welcoming beneath my feet. This is when I noticed an army of men with linked arms moving toward me to chase me off the red carpet.

As the men got closer, I stepped back onto the wet marble and let them pass. I realized they were in a circle and protecting someone at the center. An umbrella was held above someone's head and the entourage surrounding her held their heads below hers. Wait, I recognize that face! She smiled at me as they passed quickly by. It was her royal highness, Princess Sirindhorn of Thailand, on a tour of this great Buddhist shrine. I remembered her from an exhibit of her photography that I had seen in Bangkok. After they passed I stepped back on the royal red carpet until they came to roll it up, and I was back again to my bare feet on wet marble.

On Thursday morning, I got up early and packed my suitcase. Koko was already awake and standing on the rickety wrought iron balcony off the 4th floor of the guesthouse. He was staring out at the patchwork quilt of faded colors on the building opposite us. Two women stood on balconies, arms resting on railings, watching the street come to life below. Vending carts with bells, stray dogs barking, and pigeons flapping in flight all made more noise than Koko who stood in perfect silence. I stared at him for a long time trying to know what was on his mind. I made an attempt to ask him and in his usual manner he gave me a tight smile and looked at me with his peaceful almond eyes. What he was thinking was entirely inscrutable.

I put Koko on a bus back to his life in Bagan giving him all the spare cash I had on me. He didn't jump for joy, nor did he seem sad. I set off to the airport for my flight back to Thailand with a hug and a wave, and our lives unceremoniously diverged. The whole trip we hardly said 5 words to each other. There was no anger, just silence and the poignant realization that without a common language, we are deprived of any enduring connection.

In the end, I felt I had no business poking around in

Myanmar. What positive effect does my presence have on the locals? I'm not leaving them better off showing up with my irrepressible Western ways and expectations. Besides, am *I* better off for having been there poverty gazing? I comfort myself knowing that I can put on my ear buds and play soothing music for myself, sleep in my air-conditioned room, and ultimately be back on the plane to my own land of luxury and order.

My 2 trips to Myanmar have been the most uncomfortable travel of my life. At the same time, the visits have been more meaningful than any other trips I've had. Developing nations either wear you out or inure you — neither are desirable states if you are to be of any use to anyone on the ground. I conceded after Yangon that I am done traveling in poverty-stricken nations (other than my own where I can make a difference). Witnessing this seething mess of humanity and environmental degradation is just too painful. The realization that I didn't have the skills or money to make any significant difference in Koko's life left me feeling that I was simply an interloper. I wasn't willing to invest the time to go to his village and get to know him on his terms. So, I had to question what my intentions were and whether it made any sense for me to continue pursuing relationships in countries where we don't have a common language or a shred of cultural commonality.

Leaving Myanmar this second time, with my ass thoroughly and completely kicked *again*, I swore I would never return. However, the plight of the Burmese people was indelibly imprinted on my heart. I would just have to let them come to me next time.

CHAPTER 12
NEAR MISS

*B*ack in Chiang Mai, reeling from my failed swimming lessons with Koko, I decided to bicycle over to House of Male, the gay sauna outside the gates of the old city. There they have an open-air gym, swimming pool, and bar. Lying around a pool with gay men drinking cocktails seemed like the perfect way to recover from the gravitas of 4 days in Yangon.

At the gym there, I met a handsome Thai guy in his 40s who kept staring at me. Finally, between sets of lifting weights, I volunteered a hello. He could barely muster a smile — uncharacteristic of the Thai. But, he insisted on getting my phone number which I was happy to provide. I always appreciate connecting with locals and especially someone closer to my own age. After his workout, I watched him ride off on his giant, sleek Honda motorcycle covered with chrome. This was not the cheap, ubiquitous motorbike of Southeast Asia — something was up with him. He texted me a few times and offered to come and pick me up at my guesthouse and take me to see his house outside the city. A sanitized suburban adventure was just what I needed after wading through sewage.

He picked me up the next morning and I jumped on the back of the motorbike throwing my arms around him to hold on. He immediately un-pried himself from me. We drove around and around outside Chiang Mai to the point where I lost my bearings. Then he took me on some highway and accelerated. I had the distinct feeling he was either trying to impress me or scare me.

Finally, we arrived at a really upmarket suburban neighborhood with a guard house. The streets were lined with mature tropical trees like one would find in suburban Miami. We pulled up to his 2-story white house with terra cotta tile roof. The gate slid open upon entering his code into a security box. Then the garage opened and we pulled inside and dismounted the bike. He wasn't friendly or welcoming but he did ask me if I wanted a coconut. Sure, I told him, not wanting to say no to his small gesture of hospitality. He got out a machete and sharpened it on a work bench. This made me slightly nervous. I was in a garage in the middle of nowhere and some unusually surly Thai guy was sharpening his knife. I made mental notes of the exits and all the doors and gates that closed behind us as we entered in case I needed to escape. Getting over the fence outside would be challenging — I might snag my fine Italian linen pants on the sharp finials. I would be seen running down the street in horror of the damage done to my hand-sewn shorts not to mention having escaped being murdered.

The guy went outside to the side yard, climbed a ladder with a knife in his back pocket. Clearly, he didn't grow up wealthy. Rich Thai people don't climb coconut trees, they sip coconuts from a straw when someone puts one in front of them. He stabbed at the tree with fury and some coconuts plunked to the ground like heads. I caught a picture of him at the top of the tree giving me the evil eye for pointing a camera at him. This is when I noticed a body-sized mound in the lawn near the tree where the coconuts landed.

"No photo, no photo!" he yelled at me. Hmm. One more mental note: seems like he has something to hide. He climbed back down, grabbed a coconut and led me inside.

The house was furnished like a vacation rental in Florida would be — overstuffed pastel sofas and chairs, glass tables, lots of mirrors and some fake flower arrangements. It was all so *not* Thai. While I was looking around the expansive living room he placed a glass of water on the coffee table.

"You sit down. Sit down!" he ordered me, pointing to the sofa. "You drink!"

"Oh no, that's OK, I have my water bottle, thank you."

"Why you don't drink?" he asked seeming upset that I wouldn't drink his water.

"No, not thirsty. Mai au kap," I told him in Thai that I didn't want it.

"You must drink!"

The more he insisted the more I resisted. I began replaying scenarios in my head of tourists being poisoned, robbed, and buried in the yard — in that mound outside by the coconut tree? That possibly poisoned water was not going down my throat unless he forced it.

"You live here alone?" I asked trying to figure out the probability of his homicidal tendencies.

"Yes."

"How long you live here?"

"My boyfriend he dead 2 years," he told me. *Interesting*.

"Oh, so sorry," I said, "Where your boyfriend from?"

"Australia."

"What he die of?" I figured I'd go for broke and ask.

"He fall down stairs."

I'm thinking that he didn't fall at all, he was *pushed* down the stairs the minute he got his Thai boyfriend a joint bank account and that mound in the side yard is his final resting place. I started feeling a little hot in the head like maybe I need to leave before I get snuffed out.

Just then he took the coconut and hacked it hard on the counter with the machete. I jumped off the sofa in a panic. Shards of coconut hull flew all over the kitchen and living room. This is the first time I saw him smile. It was an evil, rotten smile. He smashed that coconut with delight — like it was my skull. I was now 100% convinced of this guy's nefarious nature and I really needed to be out of there.

I texted a few friends to let them know that I might be in danger and to be aware that if they didn't hear from me soon, I have been abducted. I typed quickly and precisely, "I don't know where I am but I'm in the house of some crazy Thai guy and he's hacking up coconuts and I may be next. All I know is that we are near the airport and jets are flying close overhead. I don't even know his name but we met at the House of Male and he drives a fancy motorcycle."

I realized to get out of there, I needed to stay calm and beat this guy at his own game. If I panicked, he might sense my fear and then I would be doomed. I puffed myself up, went to the kitchen and plucked some coconut shards off the counter and ate one of them seductively, "Say, how about you let me give you a little massage?"

"You give *me* massage?"

"Yes, I give you famous American massage!" not really knowing what I was about to do but it sounded like something a Thai person would want.

"We go upstairs." He led me to the dreaded stairs but I pushed myself ahead. If I were in front of him, he couldn't push me down them. It's amazing what your mind can do to survive when your blood is coursing with adrenaline.

We got to his room and got undressed. I did indeed give him a nice massage figuring that my chances of being in that mound outside might be reduced if I soothed his savage beast. Amazingly, he seemed lighter. He relaxed and even fell asleep snoring on the bed.

I grabbed my iPhone and got the GPS location and snapped a screen shot and sent it to my friends just in case. After a while, the guy woke up and insisted on taking me home right away.

"Oh no, so soon?" I feigned my disappointment figuring reverse psychology would accelerate the process.

"Yes, we go *now!*" And within seconds he was dressed and heading to the garage.

I felt enormous relief to be back on the motorcycle heading to my guesthouse alive. I wondered if he had any other plans to dispose of me but I guess the ol' American massage trick worked and I was safe in my room that evening. Maybe that mound was just a mound and my imagination had gone a little wild? Or maybe my distaste for being alone had become a fatal flaw if it was putting me in situations like that? I would never know the answer to the former. The latter was clear to anyone more willing to look than myself. Off the hook this time, I would return to my predictable life in the States and be safe from dangers like that. I couldn't have been more wrong.

CHAPTER 13
ENGRISH LESSONS

*O*n my way back to the States I had to change flights
in Bangkok. On the way to my gate I passed a
bookstore featuring a cookbook called *Cooking
with Poo* by the community organizer and chef Khun
Saiyuud Diwong aka "Poo." I considered how her full name
just doesn't roll off the Western tongue and how if she wants
to sell a cookbook, using the name Poo could actually work
if for no other reason than as a gag gift. The book certainly
caught *my* eye. I snapped a picture of the cover and sent
the glowing face of Poo around the world to my guffawing
friends in America — her marketing strategy proving itself
to be brilliant.

Thailand is notorious for its "Engrish" (the misuse

of English by Asians) and even its decorative use of the language. Throughout Asia, English has become not just the language of commerce but also the language of coolness and chic with little or no regard for actual meaning. So, you'll find restaurants in Bangkok with wallpaper that says things like HUNGER SUGAR EAT CAFFEINE CHEWING in giant words, or banners that say "Aroma goes farther." These are not words or phrases that we would normally use in connection with food in any delectable sense, they are simply words used because English makes something look legitimate and worth spending money on.

In Thailand, I found bed linens with a cute little maggots and hearts pattern with the saying "Maggots in Love" as well as t-shirts that said "Racist" and featured rainbows and hearts. You'll see kids wearing shirts that say, "Crap Your Hands Make Noise" or a bottle of hand cream that says, "An Oily Substance." But that is just the beginning.

Now I'm no expert on foreign language myself. I can barely attempt Thai with its 44 consonants, 32 vowels, and 4 tones. I find it completely impossible to learn more than a few phrases. Thai people are amazingly unforgiving and will laugh at you if you get the tone wrong or seem perplexed by what seems like the slightest variation in tone you just uttered. If you get the tone wrong, you'll end up with a to-go box when what you really wanted was brown rice. In this specific instance, getting the tone correct is crucial — and I have never managed to get that one right. Many a meal has been brought to me with a box which I assure you is not going to add more fiber to my diet than white rice.

Ordering cocktails in Thailand is only for the truly adventurous. Once in Chiang Mai at a gay bar, I ordered a greyhound — a simple drink of grapefruit juice and vodka. I watched the flustered bar staff consulting their bartender's guidebook, flipping furiously through the pages. Rescuing them from the frustration, I approached the bar and told them the ingredients.

"Greyhound. Grapefruit juice. Little bit vodka. Finish."
They all shook their heads knowingly.

"Gay hound Ok, Ok."

"No, not *gay* hound. Greyhound." This confused them so I conceded. "Yes, OK, gay hound. Grapefruit juice and vodka," I reiterated, turning my back on them. Note to self: never turn your back on novice bartenders in any country.

What arrived at my table was unrecognizable and undrinkable. The drink was purple and smelled like Smucker's grape jelly. It was grape juice and vodka and tasted like cough syrup. I tried to explain to the drag queen cocktail waitress that grape fruit juice and grapefruit juice were two different things. Her eyes glazed with confusion. I put it aside, pretending to like it. Nom, nom, nom.

So, I ordered a martini. An extra dry martini. The waitress with Adam's apple and large hands took off with confidence, returning with a wine glass that smelled a bit like grandma's mothballed sweater chest. It was a big glass of Martini brand extra dry vermouth. An accomplished bartender might splash a martini glass with dry vermouth and shake it out before finishing the classic cocktail with gin and olives on a spear. A professional mixologist might use an atomizer to give a hint, a note, a *pentimento* of vermouth to a dry martini. How lucky I was that I got a full glass of it. I put my lifetime supply of vermouth aside and ordered a beer.

Admittedly, I am a goof with foreign languages. I'm the one, after all, who, in Costa Rica, confused pecho and pedo in Spanish telling my date that he had a very sexy fart as I was running my fingers through his chest hair. (Pecho is chest. Pedo is fart.) But it was an honest mistake and as such I have no right to criticize people for their mistakes in language translations.

However, I'm not in the business of extracting money from Thai-speaking people. For Thai people, a significant portion of their income is from tourism — English-speaking tourists —from the UK, Europe, Australia, and America.

The Thai have a well-earned and award-winning reputation for routinely butchering English beyond recognition.

Take for instance this sign I saw posted in a Chiang Mai apothecary: "For keep, the post-meal morning, the cold, before lie down (superior effective go up)." If I were running a business that catered to English speaking tourists, I might check in with a native speaker of that language before posting that sign. I would probably just ask some blond person, any of the numerous blond persons cavorting in Thailand, to read this before I print it on my giant beauty salon sign: "Pluck a leg below" and "Pluck Eyeblow."

Maybe it's just me being a picky language bitch, but I would probably ask someone to confirm that Gents for the men's room and the counterpart of "Lad" for the ladies' room were in fact the proper gender terms, because those actual signs I saw in a Chiang Mai mall would give me a little more gender confusion than I want at the bathroom door.

If I were running a restaurant for Western tourists, I would ask any of the English-speaking patrons to review my menu before I listed items like, "Chef's balls in cream and beer mustard sauce." I might also ask them how the cream, beer, and mustard sauce actually tastes. The answer to both of those inquiries might be surprising.

Perhaps after dining on the "chef's balls," one could treat oneself to a "hot herbal ball massage" at the local massage parlor — if one were so inclined and feeling ballsy. Me, I prefer to dine on "chilly chicken" or maybe some "sweet and sour porn" with "vegetable gourd soap." For dessert, how about some "ancient ice cream" or a "puppy seed muffin" and a cup of "coffree?" Yummy. And please "beware of your belongings" when you leave.

Leaving Thailand is always a bittersweet prospect. If you are returning to the States, you're returning to a place where you can drink the water, breathe the air, read the food labels, and call the police (and they'll come). Being in America means that the spice level on the green curry at your Main Street America Thai restaurant will be throttled back for your delicate gut.

But being back in the States also means the party is over. The hospital you go to won't know what the cost of seeing a doctor is, the massage you get will be free of hanky-panky, and there will be no more laughing at tragedy.

This trip to Asia was a good one — the warmth of Thailand saved me from New Zealand where I was freezing and starving to death, caught in the middle of my friends' ugly divorce. But at some point, one has to go home — wandering aimlessly without a plan can eventually wear thin. I don't happen to be one of those people who gets homesick the minute they zip up the suitcase, heading out the door. For me, that suitcase zipping sound is glorious. It is the sound of freedom — freedom from something I want to leave behind. After so many months of travel I began to forget what it was I was running from...or toward. So, I headed home, if Tucson could still be considered home.

Apparently, however, I was none too eager to be home because I nearly got stranded in Korea that winter. My flight home was on Korean Air's Airbus 380, the world's largest commercial passenger jet. When I arrived in Seoul to change planes from Bangkok, I forgot to set my watch 2 hours ahead. I arrived at the departure gate about 3 hours early watching people board the magnificent double-decker A-380. How wonderful to see this aviation marvel — light blue with a bulbous nose like a beluga whale. It began to snow, and I delighted in seeing the fluffy flakes dusting the plane and the tarmac. Peace came over me and I kicked off my shoes and did some reading, fiddled with my camera, texted various people, checked my email, and went for some noodles.

I came back and the terminal was deliciously, wonderfully empty. Lovely, now I can listen to some music in peace while I wait for my flight. I was listening to Fauré's Requiem mass, the In Paradisum movement. La la la. "Oh yeah, listen to the organ and the boys choir. [Mitter Gimmer!] This has to be the most beautiful choral music ever written. [Mitter Gimmer!] Musicologists say he wrote this requiem to comfort the living, not to scare them into contrition like other masses," I thought to myself while blissed out in my iTunes world.

"Mitter Gimmer. Passenger Gimmer!?" The flight attendants walking past me were insistently calling out into the empty terminal.

"What? Shut up. Go *away!* Who is this Mitter Gimmer?" I wondered with annoyance for bringing me out of my Fauré induced coma. Gimmer. *Gilmore?* Oh no! I pulled my ear buds out and addressed the frantic flight attendants. "Are you looking for *me?*"

"Are you Mitter David Gimmer?"

"Um yes, I am, I think."

"Hurry or you miss fright," they frantically pleaded with me.

"No, no. My fright doesn't reave until 3pm. It's only 1pm."

"It's 3pm, Mitter Gimmer. You must run make fright!"

"Why would the flight leave 2 hours early? Look at my watch. Oh crap!"

I looked at my watch which was displaying Bangkok time. How could I be so stupid? The answer of course was free cocktails on international flights (and my inability to say no to them). I grabbed my bags and ran to the boarding gate, flashed my boarding pass and rushed down the lower jet bridge. Two more flight attendants stood at the jet door looking at their watches and giving me Korean stink eye. In fact, all the passengers on the largest commercial jet known to man were seated, ready for takeoff and giving me stink eye. The Caucasian delayed the plane's push back by at least several minutes and they were pissed. I rushed down the aisle and plopped into my waiting seat, pretending that my connecting flight was late.

That's when I smelled vomit. Baby vomit. Someone's

infant just hurled on the floor and the flight attendants rushed to clean it up. All of this delayed our push back even further. Then the snow started coming down heavily. The soonest they could get a de-icing machine tall enough to reach a double-decker plane was 2 hours. Thus, we sat at the gate for 2 more hours while the baby threw up a couple more times, and I began to feel some relief that at least *I* wasn't entirely to blame for the delay.

The flight across the Pacific was 11 hours of being shaken to the point where I thought the wings would come off. The jumbo jet shook so much that I couldn't even read my book. When we finally got to Los Angeles, we had lost our place at the gate and so we had to wait another half hour while they found a gate big enough to take this monster jet. Then it took about a half hour to deplane that many passengers and another 45 minutes to offload all their baggage. After all that, I had long missed my connecting flight to Arizona. I caught the next flight to Phoenix, spent the night there and took a shuttle bus back to Tucson in the morning. Total travel time was 46 hours. I would not do this flight again anytime soon. Count me out of flying on the largest passenger jet in the world, and from now on I answer to *anything* remotely resembling Mitter Gimmer.

CHAPTER 14
EPIPHANY OF THE YELLOW BUS

*W*ith my mid-century mark fast approaching I planned my next visit to Southeast Asia to celebrate. Surely my 50th birthday in the US would end up with me eating in a cheap burrito joint in Tucson, singing *Happy Birthday* to myself. I opted instead for something a little more grandiose and exotic: a big birthday bash in Pai, Thailand. I began making plans to rent "the big house" at Ing Doi, inviting various friends from all over to join the celebration. My trip started out at my parents' home in Florida where I was visiting them for my annual dose of Italian family drama with a side of lasagna.

To get to Pai, I would fly from Ft. Myers, Florida, to Atlanta to Los Angeles to Seoul to Bangkok, then to Chiang Mai and finally Pai. This meant I was going to have to engage in my least favorite activity on earth: pooping on a plane. My morning "comfort" must occur in a serene environment. I prefer a nice fluffy rug beneath my feet, fresh air from a window, the sound of birds outside, an array of essential oils, and reading materials like the *New York Times Magazine*. However, pooping on a plane is something akin to being stuffed into a broom closet that is shaking like a 6.0 earthquake, sitting with my knees touching the door while little Korean women with cheap perms jiggle and pull on the door handle. "It's not stuck, it's *locked!*" I yell to them. Yelling of course freezes my peristaltic action, causing further delays and a long line of antsy persons waiting outside the door with their knees clamped together. I imagine these women are returning from their first trip to the US to visit Las Vegas. This might even be their first time on a plane and they haven't quite figured out in-flight toilet etiquette. I have to start over with my breathing and relaxation techniques.

Flushing, however is the worst part. I have a quite possibly warranted fear that if I flush the toilet while still seated, my thighs will form a perfect seal on the rim and that my guts will get sucked out and I will fall over dead with my entrails extending down into the plane's hold. That has yet to happen. Yet.

The other offense of having to poo on a plane is that toilet flushing is so deafening that I have to drop the seat to trigger the flush and then quickly cover my ears before the enormously loud roar and rush of wind. The roar of the flush excites the line of passengers waiting outside the toilet door. I try not to flush until the last minute or they might kick the door open and throw me out.

On this flight from Los Angeles to Seoul on Korean Air, I went to use the lavatory and threw open the door to find a woman perched atop the toilet in complete shock to be

133

exposed while in the middle of her business. She shook her head in hysteria, bad perm curls flopping wildly, and clasped her hands over her face. (I would have preferred she hide her exposed parts instead.)

What about Korean women on this flight cannot grasp the concept of a locked toilet door regardless of what side of it they're on?

I was in Chiang Mai for a month preparing for the birthday bash when it came time to leave the country to renew my visa. To do this, all you have to do is cross over the Thai border to any of the surrounding countries, come back in and be stamped for another 30 days. I reviewed the surrounding countries: Laos — check. Cambodia — check. Myanmar — check. I'd been to all those countries.

That leaves Malaysia. Hmm. What do I know about Malaysia? I know there's a city that sounds something like a lumpy koala. Oh yes, Kuala Lumpur. I looked up Malaysia on line and read that the country is mostly Muslim and not particularly gay-friendly. I read that Malaysia is an uneasy mixture of Malay, Chinese, and Indian. Its main draw for me was the Indian food, the Islamic Arts Museum, and the world's tallest twin towers — the famous Petronas Towers which I had read about in architecture books. Homophobia notwithstanding, I booked a quick flight on AirAsia to spend 4 days in Kuala Lumpur aka "KL." I was somewhere between excited to try something completely different and nervous to be negotiating as a gay person in a Muslim country, something I had never attempted before.

At this point in my life I don't make a lot of advance travel plans other than the flight and a place to sleep. For Malaysia, I booked myself into the Hotel Summer View in the Little India section of KL called Brickfields. I arrived at the old Kuala Lumpur International Airport and walked about a quarter mile in the rain from the plane to the terminal which was a teeming mess of construction noise and rather plump brown people scurrying in every direction. The airport has since been rebuilt and now you can walk a quarter mile *indoors* with teeming masses of plump brown people pushing and shoving their way through passport control in air conditioned comfort.

There were two white people in the whole terminal. Me and a hippie chick who was probably from America, wearing a rather sheer sarong without underwear. Her firm and decidedly white buttocks became exposed when she had pulled on her large backpack — which got caught on the bottom edge of her sarong. It was like the curtain went up and it was *show time!* I watched in amazement as she wandered through the terminal completely unaware that she was not only exposing her bare ass cheeks but that she had picked up a cadre of salivating Indian cab drivers moving in for a closer look. The Malay seemed bound by Islam not to stare at such fleshy delights. The Chinese were too disciplined and busy to take the time to stare. But the unabashed Indians went right up to her, pulling down their spectacles, giving her the once over, the up and down, and a little bit of lip licking behind her back. I thought about informing the woman about the growing entourage behind her, but it did cross my mind that she actually knew what was going on and enjoyed the attention.

I took a bus to the big transportation hub in Little India where I purchased my ticket for a taxi to the hotel. I was forewarned that the taxi drivers in KL are among the worst in the world. I steeled my defenses and paid my $4 at the kiosk. The taxi driver asked my destination, I handed him the ticket and then he gave a little snap of his tongue. We pulled out of the bus station and drove 1 block to the hotel where the car stopped abruptly. My 1 block, 1 minute taxi ride cost $4 US dollars. Couldn't someone have told me that the hotel was just across the street from the bus station? I had to laugh at myself. The grumpy attitude and the lasciviousness of my first hour in Malaysia set the tone for the trip — in a way I got all of Malaysia right up front.

I could sense the darkness of this city, unlike anyplace

in Southeast Asia I had been. In Myanmar, the people were beaten down by the military dictatorship but still very kind and eager to help. In Thailand, there's an air of excitement and foolishness and a desire to connect even if for monetary reasons. In Laos, there's a simplicity and kindness in the people. In Cambodia, there's a palpable sadness and humility from the war and the despotic rule. In Malaysia, I could tell there was a gravitas — a heavy feeling that maybe came from Islam and possibly the fact that this rapidly expanding city was changing too fast for the people to assimilate the growth. There was also an underlying insidious racism that I couldn't quite explain yet but was palpable. After Thailand, the sobriety of Malaysia was strangely enchanting. Being a not particularly cheerful person myself, I dove in feeling I was in a country of kindred curmudgeons.

First things first, I went on my iPhone and checked the geo-social apps to see who the gay guys were in the near vicinity. Upon landing, my phone had sent out a beacon revealing to all the gay men in KL that I, a white male from America had arrived. By the time I logged onto the hotel's Wi-Fi, I already had several dozen messages waiting. I sat on the bed and read each one carefully. Wow! I was astounded that these guys were middle class, educated, and wrote nearly perfect English — an artifact of being a former British colony. I got full sentences complete with prepositions and subject-verb agreement: "Hello and welcome to my country. Where are you visiting from? I would like to meet you and take you out to show you the city." I was blown away. Never had I experienced this level of sophistication in my travels anywhere in Asia. The only trouble was, in the time I was on line reading these greetings, more messages came pouring in. And more and more. My phone was lighting up and dinging like a slot machine on a lucky night in Reno. I couldn't keep up with 4 apps and dozens of messages in each one. I was forced to start cherry-picking: whoever had the most interesting profile and the best English would get a response.

One message that stood out above the others was from a Malaysian-Sri Lankan man named Ash. His face in the photo looked like a sub-continental prince — very dark skin, coal black hair, almond eyes, and the squared-off features of a Westerner. His profile seemed refined and educated. We made a date to go for a cocktail downtown. He picked me up in his Range Rover — a sign of Malaysia's prosperity. Ash drove me around the city with the windows open and my head hanging out looking up at the blazing Petronas Towers, their 88-story spires piercing the clouds.

Ash was attired beautifully in dress slacks and a long sleeve shirt. He possessed an elegance I'd never seen in Southeast Asia. I was immediately taken by him and wondered if maybe he would be dateable if I spent more time here. We sat in Claret, a cocktail lounge on the 23rd floor of a Norman Foster building near the Petronas Towers. I was impressed that he knew the architect.

"Oh, David, I hate KL. It's a terrible place and I can't wait to get out," he told me with his modified British colonial accent.

"Really? It seems so nice by comparison to Bangkok and Yangon. What don't you like about it?" I probed.

He leaned in and lowered his voice. "I don't like the homophobia. The government is terribly corrupt, and the traffic is awful."

I chewed on this for a bit while sipping my hugely overpriced cocktail taking in the sparkling view of the city. I could see his point about the homophobia for sure. However, that played right into my hands so I was reluctant to hate Malaysia for it. The Muslim government's disapproval of all things gay is off-putting to LGBT travelers and so most gay tourists in the region head instead to Thailand, Bali, or even now Taiwan. As a result, gay folks in Malaysia are desperate to meet other gays from the outside world which is why my dating apps were swamped when I arrived.

There is, however, a visible gay presence in KL — if

you know what to look for. It is conveyed covertly by attire, gestures, winks, nods, and occasional frottage in public places. Being in KL is like going back to the 70s in America when gays were in the closet and all identification and connection was underground. Strangely I felt right at home. The only problem I could see was how expensive my cocktail was. Alcohol has a "sin tax" placed on it by the Muslim government which forbids the Malay from alcohol consumption but permits it for the rest of the citizenry — albeit at a premium price.

Ash took me back to the hotel after another driving tour of the city. He parked the car at the hotel and came up for a night cap. We lay in bed beside each other cuddling and talking about our lives. This is when he revealed that he is actually a married man — married to a German man.

"Dammit! I mean, good for you. But *dammit!* Finally, I meet a smart, wonderful guy I have things in common with and you're taken."

"Oh, don't you worry," he reassured me, "you will have no problem meeting tons of great guys here. Trust me." His words replayed in my head for the rest of my time in Malaysia. I felt like a prospector of the heart mining for a boyfriend in Southeast Asia and I wondered if Ash could be right and I'd finally found the mother lode in Malaysia.

The next day, I met Roy, a Malay guy who worked for Petronas. He invited me downtown to come and tour the twin towers using his employee discount. I took the subway to the city center, and we went for a little lunchtime nooner in a seedy rent-by-the-hour motel nearby. He told me to hide behind the bushes while he got the room key at the check-in desk. Roy spoke perfect English, was extraordinarily beautiful, and charming. However, there was something about him that led me to believe he was carving notches in the bedposts of seedy motels — that this was not a *meaningful* nooner. Some indication of this is given by the time it takes for a man to jump out of bed post-coitus. With Roy, it was a matter of seconds. No, milliseconds.

After the tryst on the bed with dirty sheets, I took a shower behind the shower curtain with cigarette burns. How does one get a cigarette burn on a *shower curtain?* Roy waited impatiently for me to finish my shower before taking me back to the city center. I said my rushed goodbye to him and then it was off to the 2:00 Petronas Towers tour. From the top of this architectural masterpiece that looks like 2 steel cobs of corn, I could see the tropical green of parks below and the sprawl of the concrete jungle extending for miles into the haze of air pollution. I noticed a giant penis-like shadow of one of the towers poking the unsuspecting people on the street below. Was this a foreshadowing or just a coincidence?

After my tour of the towers, I took a walk through the park that spreads out beneath them. The sun was stiflingly hot and the 90% humidity made it downright miserable. I was enjoying the cool of a giant tree when a tall, young man walked past giving me a lingering, but not accusatory look. One corner of his mouth went up and his eyes went down, checking me out. Holy cow, it was the 70s and 80s in America all over again — gay men actually still go cruising in parks here. This man came closer and we struck up a conversation. He was from Morocco here to study English. He didn't identify as gay (does anyone in Morocco?) but he wanted to come to my hotel to prove that he sure wasn't strict about his religion. We took the subway back to the Summer View Hotel where the security guards at the elevator were starting to wonder about me. They silently glanced at me and the young Moroccan guy at my side. Then they looked at the hotel desk staff. Without a word the guard pressed the elevator button for us. This silent treatment was the classic Malaysian disapproval and tacit acceptance of what we were so obviously up to.

Their religion forbids gay sex and technically they could have called the police on us and had us arrested and caned for being in bed together. That almost never happens and would require by law 4 male witnesses to relay the intimate details of the encounter to a judge. Something about having 4 witnesses standing around taking notes could possibly be a buzz kill obviating the need to report any sexual activity. Further, the Malay may be Muslim, but they are mostly modern-ish Muslims and so they turn a blind eye to what they don't approve of. More importantly, they are *Asian* Muslims, which means they don't like to make a scene. The end result is nothing is ever done either for, or against gays, in the name of Allah.

In the middle of my little fleshy foray into North Africa, my phone chimes. Oh gosh, it's 5pm and I have to go! Sanjay is coming to take me out to dinner for curry puffs. Let's see now…on this trip so far, I've sampled the goods from Sri Lanka, native Malaysia, and Morocco. Now it's time for some Indian and then I simply have to have some Chinese before I go. This trip was surprising me by turning into an international tail trip. Why did I think I was going to be lonely in my room practicing my clarinet, waiting to go back to Thailand?

Unfortunately, Morocco was still in the room, and I was having a little international crisis about how to make a seamless transition from North Africa to India. How could I keep my composure and do the handoff in the lobby with dignity and grace? Sanjay texted that he was now in the lobby and to come down. Yikes. I told Morocco to finish it up in a hurry because I have a friend waiting for me downstairs. The minute the elevator doors opened in the lobby, Morocco would have to pretend he didn't know me. We exited the elevator as planned and Morocco walked right past India as I extended my hand to greet Sanjay. My heart was pounding as I worried it would all go wrong and a big scene would be made in front of the front desk and security.

Sanjay was an Indian student studying marketing at a nearby university. He had discovered my travel blog in advance of my trip and got in touch with me telling me he would like to meet me when I came to Malaysia. He never said he was gay or interested in anything more than friendship, but when I met him in the lobby of the hotel for the first time, he insisted on coming up to "see my room." The security once again pushed the elevator button. I heard someone's rush of air through their nose. Surely, they had never seen anything like this before. I looked at the guard and said, "English teacher," and smiled and waved as the door closed.

Sanjay got to the room and within seconds he was peeling off his clothes and asking me for sex advice and for me to give him a massage. Jeez, dude. Can we sit and chat for a bit first and what about those curry puffs you promised? I needed time to metabolize a heroic dose of Cialis capable of satisfying a nation of repressed men. It was really clear to me how eager and hungry Malaysian men were to connect with foreigners — Ash was right. There were indeed legions of gay men who don't regard themselves as "sticky rice" (Asians who prefer only Asians) and so they sit on the likes of Grindr, PlanetRomeo, and Scruff just waiting for the odd jetlagged tourist to stumble in on his way to Bali or Borneo.

After 3 days of all this attention I was delightfully worn out. I took a breather and visited the Islamic Arts Museum which featured a world class collection of textiles and decorative objects all in the beautiful geometry of Islamic design. Look, if this is what living in a Muslim country is all about — gorgeous design and the attention of so many amazing men — sign me up. I texted my expat Malaysian friend Dennis who was now living in Norway with his husband about my experience so far in KL. He wrote back, "Kuala Lumpur is the best kept secret for gay tourists."

"Clearly that's true, Dennis," I wrote, "and why on earth didn't you tell me this before? I wasted a lot of time in the surrounding countries."

"You didn't ask," was his response (a response that I got to know quite well in subsequent months). I guess he was right. I didn't ask. How was one to know that Malaysia was Asia's secret gold mine of gays? What would ever make me think a Muslim country would turn out to be such a hot spot?

There was, however, one piece missing in my knowledge gap — China. One Malaysian Chinese guy kept pestering me for a date. I told him I just didn't have time this trip. He seemed so sad even though he put an LOL at the end of every sentence. Sometimes LOL *was* the sentence.

"Please, can we meet just briefly? LOL"

"Daron, I'd love to but I'm out of time," I wrote. In actuality, I was out of sexual stamina. I needed a break.

"Oh, that's too bad. LOL I guess you don't like little Chinese guys, huh? LOL"

"Actually, 'little' is the magic word," I texted, revealing my love for petite men.

"LOL"

He told me about his life as an artist and an accountant. In the end, I couldn't resist Daron's super-nerdy look. He was 5'2" and weighed about 110 pounds (not unusual height-weight proportions for Malaysian born Chinese) and had thick, goofy glasses and buck teeth. He looked a bit like a miniature Asian Austin Powers. We met for vegetarian Indian food in Brickfields near the hotel. I was astounded by his good manners and how earnest he was — earnestness being the hallmark of the Chinese and good manners coming from his humble Malaysian upbringing. Mainland Chinese may be pushy and smack their lips while eating, but they tend to be industrious and sober. Add in some Malaysian born humility and British colonial refinement, and you've got a nice combination. He looked up at me and asked me questions about my life as we walked back to his car. When we got to the car, he seemed a little disappointed that that was where the evening would end.

"I brought my toothbrush just in case," he told me blinking at me through the giant magnifying glasses attached to his face. His pleading eyes seemed twice as big through the lenses.

"Do you snore?" I asked.

"No, but I like to cuddle," and he laughed out loud.

I invited him up, one last time ushering someone past the Nepalese security guards who at this point were certain it was a late-night English lesson. I winked at them as the doors closed, tempting fate.

Daron was a wonderful lover in spite of, or maybe because of, his size. At one point, he jumped on my back holding me as if I were wearing a warm, bony backpack with waist straps.

We shared this lusty last evening together, and then he was off to his day job as a staff accountant for an international insurance company. I sat in the lobby restaurant of the Summer View Hotel eating my breakfast, surrounded by a large mainland Chinese tour group. The sound of them eating with their mouths open was so loud it was echoing off the ceiling and I could barely reflect on the last few days. I texted Ash to tell him he had given me the hope of finding a boyfriend. He wrote me back to once again assure me that I would have no problem in Malaysia, if that's what I wanted to do. Was that what I wanted to do? Did I want to stop being the international playboy and move to Kuala Lumpur and settle down?

Then came the epiphany of the yellow bus. This time I walked the 1 block to the bus station and boarded the big yellow bus with the frilly curtains bound for the airport. I was heading back to Thailand for my 50th birthday. The bus was the usual mixture of Malaysian ethnicities. I was contentedly the only white person aboard. I sat down and put on my headphones to collect myself from a very intense few days. With all the distractions and immediate gratification of being man about town in KL, I had forgotten what I started fighting for, to quote the REO Speedwagon song, *I Can't Fight This Feeling Anymore*. That big question loomed in my mind: should I bring this ship in to shore and throw away the oars? The cheese-o-meter of pop music wisdom had just gone into the red.

My thoughts began to coalesce and clarify. I had been on a long journey of fun and fantasy here in Southeast Asia, but why did I come here in the first place? The first time was for a colonoscopy and a little fun in a new and exotic place. But I kept returning looking for something. What was it? What was I doing here, year after year? Clearly something was continuing to draw me to Asia. Was it just the easy, recreational sex? Perhaps the allure was what it *didn't* offer me. Asia didn't deliver what my own country gave me in spades: wholesale rejection. In Asia, I wouldn't be passed over for being the white, middle aged guy that I am. No, in Asia being white was precisely what made me special. And special was exactly what was missing in my life back home.

After enjoying being the center of attention on every visit to Asia, it became increasingly difficult to return home. With no one to join me for happy hour, a bike ride, or a movie, my life slipped almost irretrievably into melancholy in the States. Asia seemed to be making me an offer I couldn't refuse — redemption for my heart. For my life.

But, would living in a soberer country than say, Thailand, net me a boyfriend? I had spent a couple years grieving the loss of Sebastian. Maybe it was time to take the leap of faith and just leave America and finally stand in front of the warm fire. I needed some advice. So on the yellow bus bound for the airport, I asked:

"Dear goddess of little brown guys with perky butts, please grant me the wisdom and grace to know if I should move to this place." The answer came back immediately and was, "Adapter plugs."

"Dearest goddess, what kind of answer is *adapter plugs?*" I demanded telepathically, without opening my lips and frightening the other passengers with my obvious direct line to a deity.

"Helloooo, are you not listening to me? Turn off the 80s-pop music and listen up. If you move to KL, you will find true love and you will need adapter plugs for all your precious electronics. You've got a flight to catch. Signing off now. Go get 'em! LOL"

I can't say that auditory hallucinations happen to me very often. Usually this kind of wisdom arrives only after a double bourbon on the rocks, but *then,* I can't remember what the revelation was the next day. This, however, was in the morning and under no fog of intoxication, so I gave this celestial message a little more credence. Hmm, I thought, "true love?" That sounds about as cheesy as the REO Speedwagon song playing in my head, but I got the essence of the message. I was willing to give it a try — what did I have to lose? Just a dull and lonely existence in America and a life of meaningless folly in Thailand. I could give up both of those and maybe get what I've always really wanted — it was worth a shot.

I watched Kuala Lumpur disappear knowing that I would be back to find a special guy and sweep him off his feet. I couldn't wait to reveal the epiphany of the yellow bus to the friends assembling for my 50th birthday party in Pai. I was feeling mighty close to something big and the cheese was getting very loud...

And even as I wander I'm keeping you in sight. You're a candle in the window on a cold, dark winter's night. And I'm getting closer than I ever thought I might.

I accepted Asia's invitation. LOL

CHAPTER 15
A SHOT IN THE DARK

I returned to Thailand with a 30-day stamp in my passport and a new direction for my life. I couldn't wait to tell everyone that I was moving to Kuala Lumpur. First things first: I had a birthday to celebrate in Pai.

Jake and Mink rented me the "big house" to serve as party central. Mink and her assistant La began preparing food: lasagna, and an array of Thai dishes. Anon who is the chef and co-owner of Om Garden Café made a chocolate cake and carrot cake.

The guest list was short but esteemed. I was a bit nervous when at the last minute, Sebastian surprised me with the announcement that he was coming. He would be flying in from his new home in Hong Kong along with a few other friends from the US. I had not seen Sebastian since my Whitney Houston emo meltdown at the Bangkok subway station a couple years before. We were in the middle of a no-contact period but he had read the invitation I posted on my blog and decided to come. I had not spoken to him in 9 months, and I had not told him about the yellow bus epiphany nor of my impending move to Malaysia.

The day Sebby arrived I walked down the dirt road through the rice paddies to pick him up at the bus station. The town was bustling with tourists renting motorbikes and shopping. I saw him standing amid the crowd with his little backpack, wearing the same clothes he had worn the years we were together: the gray argyle sweater and the blue plaid shirt, and he was still carrying the vintage leather camera case I bought for him when we lived together in Germany.

I called to him, "Hey, Sebby! You made it to Pai — all 762 curves. And you're still wearing the same outfit that you wore in Tucson 6 years ago." He lifted his shoulder to his chin in a familiar shy gesture of acknowledgment.

"Hello Daffy," he said coyly using the nickname he gave me years ago. It felt like seeing an old family member, a brother maybe, without any of the romantic charge or pain.

"Good to see you, Sebastian," I said with a long pause as the town seemed to whirl around us. "Let's go get lunch." I led him to Om Garden Café which was teeming with the hippie glitterati of Pai sipping Anon and Mark's fabulous fruit concoctions and enjoying the spectacular fusion Thai food served up in an outdoor tropical garden setting.

"I have some amazing news to tell you, Sebastian," I said over a bright fuchsia dragon fruit drink, "I'm moving to Malaysia."

"Malaysia, OK. What is it about Malaysia that's calling you?" he asked, not seeming particularly surprised.

"I had a vision in the middle of an 80s pop song. Well, I had a vision. I am going to find my boyfriend in Kuala Lumpur. He's there. Seriously. I can feel it. We haven't met, but I know he's there."

I was beginning to embellish the vision to the point that the identity of a boyfriend had been preordained. I just didn't

147

know who he was…yet. I could see Sebastian's face glazing a bit (like so many would upon my telling them just that). His face said to me essentially, "Good for you, Daffy. I hope you don't get your heart broken again." He knew enough about my stubbornness to not attempt to disabuse me or caution me about such a reckless pursuit to the far ends of the world. For a gay man to move to a Muslim country because he had an epiphany on a yellow bus with frilly curtains was bordering on delusional, but he *knew* I would do it.

"And what about you, Sebby," changing the subject off of me for a bit.

"Well, I hope this doesn't hurt you but I, um…I have a boyfriend now," he confessed.

There was no pain for me in hearing this good news. I found some small place in my heart to love him and celebrate his new relationship. After all, I had my upcoming move to be excited about.

"Tell me all about him." I leaned forward with my chin on my hands, eager to know about Sebastian's life that had evolved in Hong Kong entirely without me. The old movie *Casblanca* was haunting me: of all the fruit shake joints, in all the towns, in all of Thailand, he walks into mine. In the words of Humphrey Bogart, this was the beginning of a beautiful friendship.

The birthday celebration was a ruckus affair. Sebastian played DJ for the evening, we sang Taizé songs in Latin and German for the crowd, and I played *Young at Heart* on my clarinet — drunk as a skunk — which sounded more like someone choking a goose. The crowd was stupefied to silence. "Damn. I worked so hard on that," I slurred. I had been toting my clarinet around for months working on that.

"OK, well. Thank you very much for that, Daffy!" Sebastian said with a certain amount of irony in his voice and his hands clasped together unable to muster some applause.

"Should I play another piece? Who wants an encore?" I asked the crowd. Radio silence. Sebastian cleared his throat giving me the hint to drop it. "OK, maybe not. Let's dance. Hit it, Sebby!" He took his place back at the stereo. We rocked the rice paddies until the wee hours.

In the days after the party, Sebby and I won quiz night at the Almost Famous bar and visited the spectacular white Buddha on the hill behind Wat Phra That Mae Yen. From there we could see all of Pai, and we continued our tradition of saying goodbye in high places.

"It was really good re-connecting with you. I'm sorry I made such a mess of myself in Bangkok that time saying goodbye. I promised myself no tears this time, but I'm not sure when I'll see you next, Monkey," I said, using an old pet name for him and keeping my promise.

"Daffy, you'll be living in Malaysia, so you'll be just around the corner. You can come visit me in Hong Kong. It's even in the same time zone," he reminded me, and we went off to Om Garden for one more piece of Anon's famous carrot cake.

The other birthday guests dispersed by bus, and Sebastian and I flew on the 12-seater plane back to Chiang Mai together. We said our farewells in the airport as he headed off to Hong Kong and I to Bangkok for my flight to the US. This time with dry eyes. I was excited to be heading home to pack my things for my big move to Malaysia. All was put in perfect perspective with Sebastian, and we flew off in different directions as we always had.

Sebby's birthday gift to me was a silver pen and little diary for me to record what makes me happy. I looked forward to writing in it when I got back to America. As expected, my return to the US didn't produce a lot of entries in the little book of happiness. The list went something like this:

- A clean sink and toilet
- Flannel sheets
- Watering and pruning
- Brussels sprouts in the oven
- The color pink
- Big naps
- Goat cheese and roasted beets
- The sight of water ripples on the bottom of the pool
- Dreaming of travels

"A clean sink and toilet?" "The color pink?" Really? That's what makes me happy? My American life had come to this: a short list of simple, slightly self-indulgent pleasures. What about seeing the Jean Paul Gaultier exhibit at the de Young in San Francisco? What about the discovery of dark matter or Noam Chomsky's latest book? What about learning a new Chopin nocturne on the piano or helping Syrian refugees? I was embarrassed by my own suburban American dullness. I needed to get out of there and fast before the tentacles of ennui and ordinariness grabbed hold of me never to let go.

And that's when someone tried to shoot me. Perhaps this was the kick I needed to get my ass in gear and get on with my life in Asia. I was riding home on my bicycle late one night listening to music, singing along as I pedaled through the darkness. My head-mounted lamp illuminated the bike path ahead of me but also provided an irresistible moving target for a sniper in the dry river bed alongside the bike path. I heard the loud pops over the music and saw the orange fire spitting out of the barrel of a gun pointed at me from the center of the riverbed — about 200 feet to my left. I doused my lights and pedaled as fast as I could, up a small bridge and back down the other side. When I was off the bike path and out of firing range, I called 911. My heart was racing so fast I could barely speak.

"911, what is the nature of your emergency?"

"I just got shot at on the Rillito bike path."

"The *what* path?"

"The *Rillito.*" I repeated impatiently.

"Have you been injured?"

"No but the shooter is still there and people are on that path!"

"What are the cross streets?" the woman asked.

"There are no cross streets! It's on the river path about 1,000 feet east of Campbell. Can't you tell from my cell phone where I am?"

"What is the address where you are?" she asked as if she had heard nothing I previously said.

"Jesus Christ, are you an idiot? I'm on the Rillito bike path!" Silence at her end.

"Do you need medical assistance?"

"No but if you don't get the choppers out there, there may very well be casualties. Hurry up! You're wasting time."

"Can you tell me the cross street of the Rillito?"

"I just told you, are you not listening?" I started yelling into the phone.

Ugh. The US is supposed to be the most sophisticated and wealthy nation on earth and this is what you get in a life and death situation? By the time I got to my house, a few neighbors were standing outside as they had heard the shots and asked me if *I* had heard them on the path.

"Yes of course I heard them! They were fired at *me.*"

The helicopter came about 20 minutes later and scanned the river with its searchlight to try to locate the gunman, but they were too late to apprehend a suspect. An officer came to my door about an hour later and told me that I was lucky I didn't get hit and that people have been shot on their bicycles before. He filled out a report and left.

Warning shots had been fired across my bow. If I stayed in America, I might not have the chance to grow old and miserable. I might just be lying in a pool of my own blood shot to death in a park. In the following days, I booked my one-way trip to Malaysia. I was not planning to come back.

In the aftermath of my near-death experience, I began earnestly reaching out to some of the guys I met on my exploratory visit to Kuala Lumpur, along with a few others I didn't have time to meet when I was there. By the time I arrived in KL in July, 2014, I was in daily contact with Dez, Fizz, Iz, Bibi, Bunny, and Buddhi.

Then on June 1, 2014, I began the 6-week journey toward expatia, the end of which I hoped would land me the boyfriend I had been searching for. To get to Malaysia, I took a train from Tucson to San Francisco, then flew to New York and then sailed across the Atlantic to England. From London, I took the Eurostar to Paris, then flew to Venice, drove to Slovenia and Croatia, then flew to Qatar and finally to Malaysia.

The ocean liner passage across the North Atlantic Ocean was the most memorable part of this emigration. My ancestors had sailed across the Atlantic from Italy to New York 3 generations ago. They came to America like most immigrants in search of a better life, some protection from religious intolerance, and a chance to start over. I was leaving America for some of the same reasons. America had become intolerable to me. In the US as a 50-year old gay man, I was by most measures undesirable and invisible. Add to that my inability to afford health care, and the final straw — being shot at on my bicycle. America seemed irretrievably in a state of decline and I wanted out.

I stood on the deck of Queen Mary 2 somewhere over the final resting place of the Titanic remembering my great grandparents pregnant with my forebears in 1905. I could see them passing by on the same well-traveled patch of blue with hopes of a brand-new life and yet so many unknowns ahead. I nodded to the empty space where their steamer once chugged by with the huddled masses in steerage yearning for that first sight of the Statue of Liberty. Here, a hundred something years later, alone on the deck of the world's last great ocean liner, I hoisted my drink to toast the ghosts and went back to my cabin to dress for dinner.

After a couple of weeks making my way across Europe, I flew from Italy to Malaysia, arriving in Kuala Lumpur in the middle of Ramadan. It was almost the same day as the 2nd Malaysia Airlines crash — this time the one from Holland.

When I got to Kuala Lumpur and put a local SIM card in my phone, my email app began filling up with notes from friends and family who were in a panic as they knew I was flying to Malaysia from Europe around the same time. They were concerned that I had been among the dead shot down over Ukraine. "Please let me know you're OK. I'm worried sick," some friends wrote. I took the time to write telling them I was lucky enough not to have been on that ill-fated flight from Amsterdam. I called my mother in Florida.

"No, mom, I'm fine. My plane didn't crash. No, I wasn't on that plane, mom. Yes, I'm sure I wasn't on that plane. No, I'm not dead. I'm sure. No, I don't think moving to Florida would be a good move for me, mom. No, they don't behead gay people here, they just cane them. Cane them. Cane. Like candy cane without the candy. Anyway, don't worry. I'll email you soon."

I wasn't dead at all. On the contrary, I was in Asia and was just coming to life. In fact, I had gotten bumped up to business class on Qatar and was enjoying champagne and my first taste of caviar, ever. It seemed like a good omen to welcome me to my new home. Everywhere, though, in KL, people were fixated on the TV screens crying and watching the breaking news of the smoldering wreckage of their national airliner. I wasn't sure how to interpret *that* omen.

On the train from the airport I sat across from a young Malay man and his much older Australian boyfriend. Their age spread was about 50 years and yet they seemed to be so happy together. I told them of the yellow bus epiphany and that I was here to find my boyfriend. They welcomed me to Malaysia and were very excited for me and my prospects of finding love here.

"Oh, it will happen for sure," the older one assured me, folding his arms and smiling confidently at me.

"Watch out for the guys who just want you for your money," I was warned by the younger one. His lips were cracked and his breath smelled stale of dehydration from his observance of Ramadan. I had to laugh about his comment. My money, hah — I'm a thousand-aire. Being wanted for my money might actually be refreshing considering that in the States, my savings were considered chump change.

The train pulled into KL Sentral, the main transportation hub for this thumping metropolis of 7 million. I rode the escalator into the mass of chubby brown people to find a taxi to my AirBnB rental. This bustling station was my own version of Ellis Island, my golden door — I entered Malaysia as the wretched refuse from America's teeming shore.

The first order of business was that nature was calling. I walked toward the men's room before getting into a taxi and noticed a few wandering eyes spying me from the bench outside. A couple of men sprang to their feet to follow me to the urinals. I stood there looking to my left and then to my right to see the glowing eyes set in dark faces, eager to have a look. Guys on either side reached out to me and welcomed me to their country in the only way they could. It was good to be back in a place where at my age I could still turn heads, even if only at a urinal. Though I knew this was likely not going to be where I would find my dream man, the auditions had officially begun.

Take me Malaysia. Take all of me.

CHAPTER 16
AUDITIONS

I checked into my semi-crappy apartment, a descriptor befitting many an apartment building in Kuala Lumpur. This particular crappy high-rise was the pink moldy one full of Arab men in Bukit Bintang, which I think doesn't narrow it down either. I had a hazy view of a stadium and the LRT — the decrepit "rapid" transit train that rattled its way by every few minutes below my balcony. The air quality made it impossible to see more than half a mile away and difficult for me to breath without a mask. Sumatra was burning I was told, clearing its pesky rainforests to make way for something more productive: palms trees for palm oil to satisfy the world's insatiable appetite for fried snack foods.

I arrived in my new home city and was faced with the enormous task of making a good life for myself here. Where to begin? I started with one of those geo-social apps that got me here in the first place. I let all the boyfriend prospects I had been chatting with in the intervening months know that I had arrived. I liked that there were potential romances brewing in my life at all.

One of the first realizations I had about my new home was that shopping malls define Malaysia. The mall is the only place you can walk around without being vanquished by the heat, humidity, traffic noise, and air pollution. They're the only place you can't drive a motorcycle in, so other than the ubiquitous piped-in, cheesy, pop remix music, they're a lot more peaceful than the insanely noisy and dangerous streets.

Coming from my American crunchy granola background, I see shopping malls as a last resort. A mall is where you go when you need a suit or a new pair of suede shoes. But in Kuala Lumpur, the mall is the town square, the village market, the meeting place, and the playground where you let your kids run free. Everything and everyone is at the mall. If you're not at a mall, you're a sad, pathetic, loser and people will pity you.

KL is in fact an interconnected maze of subterranean parking garages and shopping malls — much like a Habitrail for humans. You can walk from one end of the city to the other entirely without ever having to expose yourself to the harsh outdoor elements. With the hot, smoky air outside that gave me a perennial cough, the malls seemed like a godsend but I knew my tolerance for mall life was going to be short lived.

Naturally, I met my first new friend in a mall. Desmond was a handsome, well-dressed, educated Chinese man about my age who seemed practical and knowledgeable about all things Malaysian. We met online and had been chatting for months before I arrived.

"Welcome to Malaysia," Desmond said clinking glasses of highly overpriced white wine. Our meeting had the tension of a date. We were sizing each other up: are you boyfriend material or just a booty call? Conversation was stiff with Desmond. Like many Chinese, he covered up any nervousness by giving me rapid-fire advice before I even finished my question. I was in need of advice and someone to hold my hand, and Desmond turned out to be just the loyal and dutiful friend to do it. After wine and dinner, he drove me back to my place and before he let me out, he warned me about young Malay guys.

"You must be very careful with the Malay. They are very drama," he told me leaving off the 'tic.' He further elucidated the race-based profiles of Malaysia: "The Indians are tricky and the Chinese are all about the money. And no one likes the Arabs. Just be careful here."

I closed the door to his car and headed to the lobby where I waited for a ridiculously long time before getting on a hot, crowded elevator packed full of Arab men. I started to understand the term "Arab shower" as I noticed a very potent mix of body odor and perfume. It was partly a turn on to be jammed in with all these hunky guys. But they were all shouting and gesticulating wildly in a tiny elevator. I dodged flailing hands with phones in them. I got off at 14 and stumbled to my room, ready to collapse from jetlag.

True to jetlag, I lay down at 10pm exhausted and woke up fully refreshed at 1 am, ready to start the day, so I texted Bibi that I was in town. I knew he was a night owl and in fact he said he was nearby having a bite to eat in Jalan Alor and could stop by. I went down to the gate to let him in only to find that he was on a motorcycle. Bibi was a young Malay guy so if I took Desmond's advice to heart, I was going to be having my hands full of drama tonight. Hey, bring it on, I thought. It's better than the crickets of my dating life in America.

Bibi is a 23-year old Muslim electrician who happens to be gay. In Malaysia, this means he leads 2 lives — the dutiful life his family and co-workers expect. Then there's the secret gay life which means that the minute he is behind closed doors, little Malaysian Clark Kent turns into sexual Superman. His shirt bursts open revealing his rippling muscles and his x-ray eyes undress me on the spot. This is going to be a fun bout of jetlag. It *was* fun…until it wasn't.

There's something odd about men, not just Western men, but men the world-over. The minute they've had their orgasm, they do one of 2 things. They either throw on their clothes and run as fast as possible for the nearest exit, or worse — they stick around and reveal a little too much about themselves in a blathering post-orgasmic stream of consciousness that would bore even a psychotherapist. Bibi did the latter. The minute he was done with "business" the emotional outpouring began, followed by the needs. Then the demands and expectations. If you have no one to talk to about your secret desires in this country where gay sexuality is so suppressed, when you *do* find a sympathetic ear, you want to fill it. Fill it to overflowing. And that's just what he did.

Bibi is one of 5 kids living at home in a not-so-nice neighborhood of KL. He learned to be an electrician to have a marketable skill. But he really wanted to be a kept man. He instantly volunteered to find me an apartment for us to live in. Yes, he said, "us." He would do the shopping and cooking and we would have a good life together.

"Bibi, I just met you. I can't live with you. I don't even have an apartment yet. I would want to get to know you first," I pleaded.

"Now you know me. You are good person I can tell. I am good person. Take good care you. I good cook. I make Malay food for you. I keep the other boys away from you and protect you. You need protection in this city."

Oh dear. Not only was he insinuating himself into my life, but as chief cook and cock-blocker, he was going to keep me under lock and key.

"Bibi, I just need to get to sleep. It was good to meet you," I told him restlessly indicating that it might be time to go. Soon. I turned on all the lights and the music off.

"You don't want me. I thought you good person. You bad

person. I give you my body for nothing." And he stepped into his work boots and stormed out slamming the door behind him. I watched him speed off into the night on his motorcycle. I've spent enough time in Thailand to have become accustomed to this kind of drama and hunger. I felt sorry for Bibi — more than I've felt sorry for Thai guys who exhibited the same behavior. In this country, unlike in Thailand, I fear that he really *is* alone and will have no one to talk to. His religion will put the finishing touches on his personal freedom, and he'll be stuck leading a double life of illegal drinking and quick sexual encounters that scare away the very men he wishes will protect *him*.

Desmond was right twice already in just a few hours. I came to respect Desmond's words that night and appointed him my personal touchstone. Still, to round out my racial profiling, I needed to find out for myself how the Chinese are all about money and how the Indians are tricky. I couldn't wait!

My first full day in KL was spent looking for an apartment. I found someone willing to rent a room for a month — an Indian guy. Ooh baby, I thought, let me see how tricky he is going to be. In chatting with him through AirBnB I revealed that I might be dating a Chinese guy thinking maybe there was some possibility that things would heat up with Desmond. The minute he read that, he canceled my booking and took his profile off of AirBnB, effectively stranding me, and then he tried to keep my deposit. I called the Chinese landlord of the apartment I was currently in to see if I could stay an extra week. He told me that because it was a last-minute booking the price was going to be higher. All I could think was that Desmond nailed it with the stereotypes. In short order, I had gotten the Arab undesirability, the Malay theatrics, the Indian slipperiness, and the Chinese ruthless capitalism.

After much hand-wringing and sweaty days spent zipping around the city with Desmond to see apartments, I finally found a place in a brand new high-rise. It was so new we had

160

to take the shrink wrapping off the doors. A young Chinese couple would be my landlords. We met in the apartment to sign the papers making my residence in Malaysia semi-official. I was living in the country on a 90-day tourist visa so there was a date stamp on my stays which meant I had to leave the country briefly and return to have another 3 months in Malaysia.

This was the first time I'd ever lived in a high-rise. I was perched on the 15th floor with a small view of the city and a grand view of the 50-meter frangipani lined pool. The apartment was essentially a 450-square foot gray and white box with a sliding door and balcony at one end. The kitchen was so tiny that if you opened the refrigerator door, you were stuck in the kitchen. The place was furnished with 2 barstools, 1 card table and chair, 1 small red plastic lamp, and a bed. This is characteristic of Malaysian Chinese interior design: spare, white, and cheap, yet this was considered a fairly swanky place on embassy row at 2,500 Malaysian ringgits per month (about $600 USD). This would be my showcase apartment for the "auditions." I signed a 3-month lease.

The floor was a glossy, brilliant white that showed every speck of dirt, every eyelash, and every black pubic hair. In light of how many Asian men I was auditioning for the position of boyfriend each week, I spent half my time going around picking up their wiry black hairs with a moistened fingertip. I was astounded by how many black hairs were actually visible on the floor considering that Asian men for the most part tend to be hairless. I became slightly paranoid that my next candidate would come over and upon entering the apartment would shriek, "Oh my god, look at that pubic hair on the floor. I'm leaving."

After the lease-signing, Desmond came over and joined me for a glass of wine. We sat on the bed listening to some jazz from my laptop, watching the sky flashing with lightning. I opened the slider to get the full effect of the bolts of electricity crackling through the night sky and the thunderous booms echoing off the surrounding high-rise apartment buildings. The noises seemed end-of-the-world loud. Then a monsoon drenched the city, the palm trees strained in the wind and the pool actually formed waves. I felt a long way from America but not a long way from home. Perched on the 15th floor in a concrete canyon like a peregrine falcon, I would swoop out each day hunting for a mate. I had nothing of my former life but my laptop and a few articles of clothing. I neither felt homesick nor did I miss any material items I left behind. I came here for a purpose and now I just had to find him.

CHAPTER 17
BUNNY HAS TWO DADDIES

*B*unny has two daddies is not the opening line of a children's book about gay rabbits. Bunny is a doughy Malay nurse with a taste, no, an *appetite* for older white guys. He is what we might call a potato queen, and for Bunny, the more potatoes in his diet the better. I'd been chatting with him for a couple months before I finally met him in KL. I think Bunny thinks that I'm going to be daddy #3 and I have to disabuse him of this notion.

I meet Bunny for lunch at a Malay food buffet called a "mixed rice" in the makeshift food court in an alley behind my apartment building. We each survey the steam trays full of vegetables and meaty looking things soaking in red pools of oil. The fetid stench of belacan (fermented shrimp paste) permeates the air. It all looks incredibly spicy and like I would need a bottle of antacids for dessert. One thing I'm sure is that there will be no pork — Muslims are "halal" and that means no pork, no alcohol, and no dogs (for pets). Already I'm liking Malaysia, coming from a nation where barky dogs are coddled as family members with more rights and better health care than a lot of people.

Bunny and I fill our plates with heaping piles of the mushy food served with white rice. The total cost is 4 ringgits each — about $1. I pick up the check in a fit of extreme largess and we take our plates to a plastic table under a tent and sit looking into each other's eyes before eating. Bunny gives me a look that he's about to do something he might be embarrassed about — something I couldn't possibly understand. That's when he starts playing with his food with his fingers. He mushes it around and around and takes a big handful of food and shoves it into his mouth with one big push. I sit in some hybrid form of horror and amusement. Is he eating like this to impress me? Does he have some sort of social disorder that causes him to revert to being a child playing with his food and eating with his fingers? I watch him in silent disbelief for a couple minutes. He flashes a big, goofy smile full of mushy food and then unrepentantly shoves another fistful into his big moon face. His eyes dart from side to side as he knows what I'm thinking.

"What in *god's name* are you doing with your food, Bunny?"

"I'm eating," he gulps, telling me with a sheepish glow on his face.

"Well, umm, thank you very much. That was abundantly clear to me, Bun dear. You know, we in the West have these pesky little things called utensils. Why are you not using them?"

Bunny is not a person of many words, but a person of many faces. With the variety of comical facial expressions he produces at any given minute, he is like a pudgy, shaved head, bug-eyed, Muslim, Asian, gay, male version of Lily Tomlin. His face on the verge of laughter now relaxes me and makes me laugh. In fact, I start laughing out loud at his chimpanzee-like eating habits. But then I notice a group of business men in tight suits walk over and do the same. They all sit down on the plastic stools and start mashing food into their mouths with their fingers. They're talking about fixed indexed annuities and shoveling fistfuls of chicken and okra into their faces. It's a bit like being in a group home for autistic kids.

How did I miss this fascinating custom on my first visit to Malaysia? Bunny takes a moment to explain to me that this is a Malay custom and not at all considered impolite or déclassé. I want to try it myself but I don't trust the cleanliness of my hands and so I remain the only person in this outdoor restaurant to use a fork.

Over lunch Bunny tells me that he has a boyfriend in Australia and a boyfriend in England (each in their 60s). He has had them both for years. Neither of them knows about the other — sort of a gay spin on the Muslim belief that each man can have 4 wives.

"Bunny, why didn't you tell me you already had 2 boyfriends when I asked you out on a date?"

"You didn't ask," he replied with a guileful look while wiping his greasy fingers on some toilet tissue.

Bunny tells me he has just been thrown out of his home when his mother discovered some porn magazines under his bed. Islam and homosexuality do not mix, so they heartlessly gave him the heave-ho. I felt terribly sorry for the poor guy. On the other hand, Bunny has 2 hubbies who send him money and plane tickets so I think maybe he can squeeze a rent stipend out of them and get his own apartment.

For an Asian, being thrown out of the family home is about the worst fate that could befall one. On the contrary we in the West count the days until that glorious moment

165

when we are free from our parents. Why would a gay man want to live with his Muslim parents anyway? I tried to convince Bunny that it might actually be a blessing. Living on his own, he could leave his porn magazines and dildos all over the apartment with impunity. His eyes got moist as he was still raw from the eviction. Though I appreciated Bunny and his struggles as a gay Muslim, I had the distinct feeling he and I wouldn't be going any further than just lunch. I told him that I didn't want to be the latest acquisition in his harem.

"Why didn't you tell me you wouldn't date me if I already had 2 boyfriends," he asked before we parted company.

"You didn't ask," I told him, and we laughed and hugged goodbye. The auditions continued.

CHAPTER 18
AND THEN THERE WAS IZ

A couple days after Bunny, I met a guy named Izuan who sent me a note on PlanetRomeo saying he'd like to meet me. He was particularly intrigued that I was a singer. He texted that he sings with the London Gay Men's Chorus and was staying at the Corus Hotel in the city center. We made a date and I threw on my light blue seersucker hot pants and my little orange girly backpack. This is not a look that is extremely popular in a Muslim country, particularly on the "Curry in a Hurry" bus that pulls up in front of my apartment on Jalan Ampang.

The Curry is a broken-down blue bus with doors hanging open that comes slowly through the stifling traffic with its horn trumpeting like an elephant. It arrives and departs in a big cloud of filthy diesel smoke with gears grinding at each change. A woman stands at the door yelling out destinations I can't understand. I run up with my 1 ringgit in hand. She snatches it from my fingers and beckons me to hurry up and jump aboard so that we can sit in traffic. I climb on and shimmy down the jammed aisle hoping to find a broken seat or a greasy strap to hang onto. All eyes are on me in my tight shorts that were cut about 4 inches too short by Tu the Thai tailor in Chiang Mai.

I'm feeling a bit like Sasha Baron Cohen in his movie, *Bruno* when he's in hot pants in Jerusalem — only for *him* it was a stunt. For me this is my only pair of shorts. There's something I love about the Curry in a Hurry, which I need to point out is not its real name. I can't tell you what the real name of the bus is because the marquis on the front is so covered in soot that it's unreadable. It is completely packed with Indian and Pakistani people, 90% of whom are men who may be a little deodorant challenged and exist on a diet of curried everything. They ride in this un-air-conditioned bus holding onto the straps overhead with perspiration steam rising up from their armpits. The whole bus does indeed smell like the curry lunch buffet at the Passage Through India restaurant — only it smells like curry that was tucked under someone's arm and left to molder for a day or two. The bus ride is a 25-cent immersion in all that *isn't* American. At times in Malaysia, especially in the myriad malls with Ace Hardware and Red Lobster, it's hard to make the distinction between East and West. But on the Curry, there's no mistaking that honey, you sure ain't in Kansas. Except that you have no idea where in tarnation you really are — the bus is so crowded and the windows so dirty you can't see where you are. I have to use the GPS on my phone to navigate and tell me when to jump from the Curry.

I step out in front of the hotel where Izuan is staying in the phallus-like shadows of the Petronas Towers. Magnificent shade trees attempt to calm the traffic of Jalan Ampang. I take the elevator to his room and knock on the door. Izuan greets me with a big smile and a warm hug as if we have known each other for years. Izuan is Malay which means of course he's Muslim but somehow his religion has not defeated him, partly attributed to the fact that he left Malaysia for London years ago. He was just back visiting his family and had a couple days to catch up on KL life. Enter me, the guy in seersucker hot pants.

"What on earth are you doing in K-Hell?" he asked me revealing his pet name for the city. "Gay tourists don't come to KL and for good reason."

"Why, I'm looking for love, and I think I'm going to find it right here in KL," I tell him with as much innocent conviction as one can muster at a hotel door on a booty call. I was starting to sound like a dirty Dorothy.

He laughed and slapped his thighs. I didn't find it amusing. Then his face sobered up a bit. "Really, you're *serious?* What made you choose KL? You know this is a Muslim country, girlfriend!"

I explained to him my pan-Asian quest for a boyfriend and how I had had the yellow bus epiphany which was starting to sound too much like the yellow brick road. I told him how I struck out in the rest of Asia but Malaysia seemed like the place where I would hit a home run. I also told him I wanted to find someone musical, bright, sexy, and charming. I was describing Izuan. I could see him chewing on the corner of his lips perhaps out of concern for me about to be gobbled up and spit out by KL or maybe it was some poignancy that he had moved away and so it was surely not going to be him. But it might have been.

"Hey, do you know *Over the Rainbow* by Harold Arlen? He is a millennial and so I had to ask but of course he did. We sang a bar or two together in 2-part harmony.

We spent the afternoon in bed laughing and singing. Izuan is a wiry, thin, sharp-witted, and yet sentimental guy — not unlike me. He put on a tight, red singlet and with me in my light blue hot pants, we set out for a walk to scare up some dinner. We ended up where most people in KL end up — in a food court in a mall. We sat with each other and pushed our food around looking a bit longingly into each other's eyes amid swarms of chubby people and the roar of the food court.

After dinner, we went for a walk through the park behind the mall where there is a nightly show of dancing waters timed with classical music shot through with a disco beat. The colorful waters jet high into the air with the steely Petronas Towers looming overhead. Tourists from all over the Muslim world come to enjoy the spectacle. Izuan took my hand, pulling me in for a kiss right there. It was not a long, lingering kiss, but there was no mistaking that it was a kiss on the lips. This simply isn't done in Malaysia or any Muslim country. I have seen signs in parks that say, "No indecent behavior," with a picture of a man and woman kissing and a big X over their faces. They didn't show a man and a man kissing so perhaps that's not considered indecent, and hey, the Bangladeshi guys walk around holding hands as if they were lovers. (Men holding hands in *friendship* is permitted. But if love or any tender affection is involved, then it's forbidden.)

Izuan and I crossed the line that night and were being downright indecent and I was loving it. His fearlessness was an aphrodisiac for me. I felt safe with him — this was *his* country after all. He could speak the language to fend off any heckling or could produce the right amount of cash to bribe away any police action. I felt my heart racing with romance and the fear of being arrested for a simple moment of passion in this magnificent if cheesy setting.

We walked back toward his hotel and stopped in at a Johnny Rockets for an ice cream sundae. Somehow it seemed romantic in a corny American way. We sat across each other holding hands while employees lined up and sang a little song out of tune while I fed Izuan my cherry. He bit off the fruit and rolled it around in his open mouth before swallowing it and licking his lips in slow motion. He fluttered his eyelashes at me and shoved a spoonful of cream into my mouth. I gulped it down and we both laughed at the scene we were making. We were cruising for a caning with our irreverence. The danger

170

was intoxicating.

After messing up Johnny Rockets' mainstream values we called it a night. I kept a toothbrush in "girly bag" for break-through moments like this. We spent the night wrapped tightly around each other in his hotel room on his last night in town. Over breakfast I found myself choking back tears knowing he was leaving so soon.

"Oh no, don't do that. Don't you get me started, mister," he begged me, and then *his* eyes starting welling up.

"I can't help it, Iz. I've had a wonderful (checking my watch) 18½ hours with you," I snorted. "I came here to find *you* and now you're leaving. Damn this! First Ash and now you." My face was flush with the heat of a curry breakfast and the tears.

"Ash? Who's *Ash?*" he wanted to know. "Look, you can come visit me in England if it doesn't work out for you here."

"Well, I just got here, and I want it to work out *here* but who knows where life leads." I explained.

"Yeah, I guess." He went silent and we sat looking at each other over our unfinished breakfasts.

We said goodbye that afternoon as he left for the airport and I went on with my quest for love, face to the wind. He jumped into a taxi while I went back to my pool and lay out under the sun watching the clouds gather for the afternoon monsoon. I rolled off the edge of the pool into the water, exhaled all my air and sank to the bottom where I could sob and no one would see. I came so close with Izuan. Perhaps he was the harbinger of something big headed my way. Or maybe meeting him was just a spiritual poke in the eye to snap me out of my ridiculous, self-indulgent fantasy of finding a boyfriend here. I wondered if I should just go back home with my tail between my legs.

I dried off and went back to my little white box in the sky, hung my bathing suit on the line, and made myself some dinner in my tiny kitchen.

171

CHAPTER 19
GET YOURSELF A GOOD ONE

*B*eing a gay white person in Malaysia gets you membership into a club — a sort of underground network of other intrepid homos who know a thing or two that went over the heads of the rest of the gay tourists who come to Southeast Asia on sex holidays. Really no gay man in his right mind comes to Kuala Lumpur — why would you? The few gay bars are like shuttered speakeasies under the threat of crackdown. You must be in the know in order to find them. The very few gay foreigners I met in KL were there because they had a Malaysian partner who couldn't leave his mommy.

Desmond thought it a good idea that I meet his English friend, Tim, who lives with his Malay boyfriend, Ajay. Tim is a retired entrepreneur in his 60s and Ajay is a microbiology professor in Borneo. They share Tim's lavish apartment on the weekends when Ajay can sneak away from his parents to nurture his secret relationship. Tim is an informed if not particularly refined guy. He reads the papers and watches the news and spouts bold opinions about everything in a Bill O'Reilly sort of way. He's typical of many expats from Britain who have figured out how to up their standard of living by moving to a poorer country. And they will be happy to tell you every detail of how they got their penthouse apartment, their trophy boyfriend, and about their trip across town in their late model European sedan to save 50 cents on tomatoes at the Chow Kit wet market.

This is not why I came to Malaysia. I came because the men were warm and hospitable and eager to connect. On that subject, Tim has a few choice things to say and he says them to me in a loud voice in a café in Pavilion Mall in KL. We sit alongside "the catwalk" — the open-air corridor in the mall where the gays who are brazen enough to make themselves visible, parade with their buddies and lovers. It's as close to a gay ghetto as you'll find in Malaysia.

"You are a white man and as such you must get yourself a good one," Tim tells me waving his wine glass in the air while aggressively eyeing the young men passing by.

"A good one? A good one *what?*" I asked, knowing full well what he meant.

"Look, the odds are in your favor here," he leaned in uncomfortably close to me and didn't lower his voice. I felt specks of his spit hitting my cheeks. "You can have any man you want in this city, so make sure you get yourself a good one. Yes, you must." He nodded at me finishing his wine.

I didn't even attempt to straighten out the twisted ethics of that statement. Where does one begin with people like Tim? His words did make me keenly aware of the indelible mark of the British on this place. The reason I can speak to everyone today, the reason there is a rail system, the reason they think "homely" means cozy (not ugly), is because of the British occupation of what they once called British Malaya. Their involvement goes all the way back to 1771 and ends in 1957 when the country gained its full independence from England and Malaysia became a sovereign nation. In Tim's eyes though, Britannia still rules the waves. How could I possibly respond to the millennia of British imperialism and entitlement?

"Well, we'll see, Tim. Maybe *they'll* get themselves a good one. Maybe I'll be lucky enough to be the one for someone special. I'll check back with you," I told him. My romantic naïveté didn't captivate him.

Tim began quibbling with the waiter over the price of his 2nd glass of wine which was supposed to be half off at happy hour even though he ordered it after happy hour expired. The quibbling turned to yelling.

"I am *not* happy!" he shouted, red in the face and slamming his fist on the table causing my beer to splash. "This is unacceptable and I will not come back here again. Very unhappy indeed!" The wait staff retreated to the front desk. I saw the hushed discussions among the Bangladeshi and Filipino foreign workers. There was lots of pointing at the bill and then a representative came back with a revised bill. I marveled at how some Westerners can insist on something and press their issue until they get their way. I felt soiled sitting across from him.

CHAPTER 20
OUTREACH FAIL

*Even if you fall on your face,
you're still moving forward.*
— Victor Kiam

After several weeks of chasing the vision of the yellow bus, I found myself longing to connect with locals in a meaningful way. I wanted to get involved in the community, but how? There were scant few places to find any sense of well-formed gay community as the government puts the kybosh on any organizing. I had heard about the Pink Triangle Foundation, Malaysia's community-based HIV/AIDS organization and thought that it might be a good venue so I signed up for the training to become a safe sex education counselor and outreach worker.

PT Foundation sits beneath a rundown gay sauna hidden from public view in a moldy concrete building down a dark alley in a sketchy neighborhood that used to be the red-light district of Kuala Lumpur. It's not by accident that anything serving the gay community must be tucked away in some hidden corner, banished from public view. PT's location is reflective of the country's view of homosexuals as deviants, outcasts. But being that it's Asia and not Saudi Arabia, gay lives and organizations are simply ignored and not really dealt with in any decisive, punitive way. The government will cut off funding but they won't raid the organization and shut them down. It's soft homophobia — the Ronald Reagan kind — the kind I grew up with in America in the 70s and 80s.

I had the joy of seeing institutionalized homophobia in America dissolve almost entirely in my lifetime. We in the US went from leading secret lives in the shadows to being granted all the rights of first class citizens in a stunningly short period. Here in Malaysia, it is like stepping back in time about 40 years. The government will not allow condoms and safe sex literature to be distributed at saunas that cater specifically to gay clientele because that would identify them as gay organizations which then makes them illegal.

PT Foundation's solution is to train its own version of SEAL Team 6 — a task force of gay men who visit the gay saunas clad only in towels, armed with bags of safe sex kits, information, and a signup sheet to get tested for HIV. Our goal is to get condoms into men's hands, knowledge into their heads, and themselves to a testing site immediately. In theory, it's a very powerful grassroots technique. The reality for a foreigner in a sex club tasked with getting the message across was something entirely different.

Sex clubs in KL are known as "saunas" because they offer traditional steam rooms — if you feel that the outside air isn't enough of a steam bath already. In fact, there's not a lot of sauna-ing going on. Instead there's a lot of hanky-panky going on in dark rooms and hallways. This is the workplace of the highly equipped and trained PT Foundation safe sex outreach worker and tonight, ta da, I am one!

My first assignment is at Chakran Traditional Massage Therapy, the notoriously seedy sauna in Brickfields, where the red-light district now lives. The sauna is on the 2nd and 3rd floors of a nondescript concrete storefront on a street where whorehouses are marked by glowing red entrances and bossy Chinese pimps sitting outside touting the services of women. To call this neighborhood dark and depressing is an understatement. Rats scurry before me as I enter the building and go upstairs to introduce myself at the front desk.

"Hello, my name is David and I'm here from PT Foundation…"

"Here's your towel and a key," the officious guy behind the desk cuts me off before I finish my introduction. He hands me a threadbare towel with holes in unfortunate places. "You must wear the towel only, no street clothes allowed."

I check my clothes in a locker and put on my towel which looks like Charlie Brown's Halloween ghost costume. I grab my clipboard and safe sex kits and practice my lines: "Hello, would you like a safe sex kit? Hi, I'm David from PT Foundation. Hi, it sure looks like you could use a condom on that, would you like one? Would you like me to put it on for you?" I embellish my routine as I go up one more flight of stairs to the center of action.

Suddenly I get a little nervous when I have to put my pitch to the public. I approach a group of men clustered in a dark corner. All I can see is the whites of their eyes and teeth. I hear them chatting in a language that I don't recognize but I'm sure it's something from the subcontinent. I approach them with the caution of an African safari tour guide.

"Hi, I'm uh, well, hey, can you, would you, um…" I fumble around with my papers and my baggies of condoms and lube and then I drop my pencil in the dark. I bend over to find it and at once feel a warm hand on my ass. I reach for my pencil and grab someone's ankle. Oh no — this is turning into a disaster. It's not like I'm unfamiliar with the territory, it's just that I've never had to be in a sex club with a clipboard and an official agenda. Finally, I pull it together and clear my throat.

"Hey guys, would any of you like to take a safe sex survey?" This is when everyone walks away as if I had just farted. Wipe out! Total outreach failure. What about my cachet as a white person? Being the buzz kill safe sex preacher trumps my skin color and I'm roundly dismissed.

I lick my wounds and pull myself together and head back to the locker room figuring that I might fare better on the periphery rather than in the trenches. I pounce on each person as they enter the locker room. Nearly everyone ignores me as they have one thing on their mind and I assure you it isn't answering my safe sex survey.

One guy eyes me up and down as I approach him. "Hi. Would you like to take a survey and get a safe sex kit?" He doesn't answer but lifts my towel and takes a look at what's underneath. He likes what he sees and goes for it and I stand there with my clipboard, waving my pencil in the air, rendered completely ineffective.

Through the entire 3-hour shift, I found only 3 guys willing to take my little survey. The ones who responded were all middle aged Chinese professionals — the only ones who spoke enough English to answer my questions. This particular sauna is popular with foreign workers from Pakistan, Indonesia, and Bangladesh. I simply couldn't find a way to penetrate that population sector. Ahem.

On the way back to my apartment I pass through KL Sentral, the Grand Central Station of KL, to catch my train. I walk through the swarming masses beneath giant banners for cell phones and luxury apartment buildings. Everyone is in a hurry as they're heading for trains, buses, and to the mall. I walk into a bathroom before I catch my train and at the urinal bank all eyes greet me. These men are not relieving themselves, no, it's Saturday and this is date night for the desperate in a Muslim country. No man will go home untouched tonight. Unable to wedge myself in at the urinals, I turn and walk out. A few guys zip up and follow me into the central part of the massive station. They've made note of my seersucker hot pants and my tangerine backpack and so there's no escaping into the crowd — I will be followed wherever I go tonight. I slip into a 7-11 and pick up a 100 Plus isotonic drink to refresh myself and I notice I'm being tailed.

Heading out toward the center of the terminal with my refreshing lime drink, I sense that someone is coming a little closer. A swishy gay guy does a "drive by" which means he doesn't slow down at all but bends the arc of his trajectory so that he gets uncomfortably close to me, makes eye contact, looks me up and down and then licks his lips as he passes. He disappears into the crowd and then within a couple of minutes, he orbits by again, this time coming even closer. I get another chance to see him lick his lips slower and in an even more lascivious manner. Thank you so much, now my life is complete.

Then a person of very short stature with a high forehead comes by and looks up at me. I look down expecting he will either be asking for money or we will soulfully exchange glances about his unfortunate predicament. Instead, he leers at me and flicks his tongue at me while lifting his eyebrows repeatedly in a flirty gesture. This is starting to seem like a circus sideshow. I am somewhat amused and a lot creeped out by it.

I take the escalator up to the 2nd level toward the mall. Two guys follow me up. I turn around and head toward the down escalator just to be sure they're following me. Yes, in fact they are. Now I'm starting to see this as a fascinating social experiment. Let me see who will follow me to the bathroom. I walk down to the one where all the guys were standing at the urinal. The escalator guys are in hot pursuit. They walk in and one goes to the stall and holds the door open. He licks his lips and gestures to me with his head to join him. Not a chance buddy, this is a Muslim country that canes people for such offenses and besides, hooking up in a toilet in Malaysia isn't exactly what I would call pursuing my romantic vision.

The bases are loaded at the urinals. Guys from Pakistan in traditional robes stand there waiting. Sikh men with beards and turbans stand there. Effeminate Malay guys stand shoulder to shoulder with Chinese businessmen and Indian cab drivers. It's the United Nations of peepers. Maybe I should hand out safe sex kits at the urinals.

I squeeze in to take my place as the sole representative of the Caucasian race. That's when it gets ugly. A little grab fest ensues as the men start getting aggressive and I start freaking out. I'm too new here to know the danger signs and how far this can go before the police will start hauling people off to jail. I bolt out of the bathroom and head for my train, ending my evening of scratching KL's vast underbelly. The more oppressive the society it seems, the more developed the underground sex scene is. Sexuality is, after all, entirely irrepressible and infinitely mutable.

I escape through the turnstiles and stand on the crowded platform panting and waiting for the LRT train to my neighborhood. My linen shirt is soaked in the armpits. Fans sweep across the crowd circulating hot humid air. Nothing about this is pleasant, beautiful, or natural. The train pulls up and hordes of people push in before letting passengers out. I stand a head above and a world apart from my home land of order and cleanliness. Suddenly I feel very, very out of place.

CHAPTER 21
SCHOOLMARM

*S*ummarily deeming myself ineffective as a safe sex outreach worker, I was still looking for some deeper way to get involved in Kuala Lumpur. One afternoon in the elevator, I met an American woman who lived next door to me on the 15th floor. She told me about a volunteer opportunity to teach English and gave me the contact information. I gave them a call.

Another American woman answered the phone at the United Nations office. They were looking for volunteers to teach refugee kids who had fled political and religious persecution in the Chin State of Myanmar. The position would be with the United Nations High Commissioner for Refugees (UNHCR). The refugee families were living in KL awaiting resettlement in the US or Australia, stuck in political limbo for years. They were Christians, an untold number of whom lived in the rat-infested slums of Pudu in the heart of KL.

After getting all the intake papers signed at the UN's outpost, I was sent to the Zotung Refugee School to meet the kids and start teaching once a week. But what do I know about teaching English? I came to this volunteer job with absolutely no knowledge of teaching and even less patience for kids. The UNHCR had absolutely no budget for anything. Nothing for books, paper, or pens. Nothing. Anything I needed I had to buy on my own. I borrowed some surplus workbooks from Cynthia, a teacher from the International School whom I would be taking over for. I shadowed Cynthia one Saturday afternoon at the school and then the following week I was on my own. I've never been so unprepared for a task as potentially demanding and important as this.

I've also never been a lover of children, frankly. To quote Fran Lebowitz, "Children are the most desirable opponents at Scrabble as they are both easy to beat and fun to cheat." Hmm, maybe I should get a Scrabble board. I amuse myself with seeing how many derogatory names I can come up with for kids. Off the top of my head, let's see...crotch nuggets, crumb snatchers, ankle biters, linoleum lizards, muff monkeys. I'm about the last person on earth who should become a teacher. But the UNHCR was desperate and I was in need of something more soulful to do than booty calls. So, I was in.

Finding the Zotung School was half the battle. I got off the train and started walking in the wrong direction. The whole neighborhood of Pudu is a series of ugly concrete shop lots that are nearly indistinguishable from each other. After wandering for a half hour in the tropical sun, I started becoming delirious and then I got hopelessly lost texting Cynthia for some help. The school essentially has no address — it's just a doorway in a nondescript building with a motorcycle mechanic on the ground floor. A motorcycle blocks the rusted metal door that opens into a damp and unlighted staircase with a broken banister that is leaning dangerously over the stairs and tied to the wall with a rope. The place smells like sewage and moist concrete. I can hear reverberations of children's voices echoing in the stairwell so I must be in the right place. I push open a hollow core door that is covered with years of grimy handprints.

Suddenly I'm face to face with a dozen kids who push back

their chairs and jump to their feet, "Good morning teacher!" they all yell at the tops of their voices in perfect unison. What could I do but smile? I take off my hat and proceed to fall in love with them. I have no idea where to begin, so I walk to the front of the class and put down girly bag and pull out some workbooks. They watch me in silence.

"OK, class, I am Mister David." Can we say that together?

"Teachuh David," they all yell it back. The sound is deafening. Hmm. Teachuh. Close enough, I'll take it.

I ask them to introduce themselves one at a time and write their names on the board. I try my best to memorize their names: Tamwa Oo, Hang Thung Lia, Jun Cheung, Sanpi, Miriam, Elee, Joel, and Dim Dim. All I remember is Dim Dim, a tiny girl about 9 years old with little red bows in her hair. She flashes a big, slightly mischievous smile at me and then writes her name on the board as Dim2.

"Class, today we are going to play some games," they all cheer. "But first we are going to do some writing and vocabulary," and they all groan. "I want you to write a few sentences to tell me your name, where you are from, if you have any brothers and sisters and what you want to be when you grow up."

It's a miracle that they understand. This obviously isn't the first English class they've ever had. I go around and check their papers which are earnestly being written with varying degrees of English proficiency. Hang Thung Lia wants to learn the guitar and be a music teacher. Tamwa Oo wants to be a dancer. Dim Dim wants to be a violinist.

I had 8 students when I started. Over time a few of them were resettled to Melbourne and Oklahoma. Four students remained my core for the duration of my time in Malaysia. Because of the attrition, the class became more intimate and afforded me the chance to get to know the children well.

Each week I would prepare my lesson plan over breakfast, designing my curriculum and coming up with my "word of the day" that would inspire them to look up the word and write something on the topic. I felt like a pastor coming up with my sermon as I would make the word of the day relevant to their situation, current events, geography, or just sometimes a moral lesson. One week it was "respect." They would write about who they respect and why. One week it was "progress" and they wrote about where they wished to make progress and what they'd already accomplished. It prodded them to work with past, present, and future verb tenses.

I would work with them on their vocabulary and their writing skills. We would do group readings shouting over the kids in the next room and the noise of motorcycle revving in the garage below. Then we would do "fix this" where I would write something like, "I like eat vegetables." And they would have to shout out the fix. "Yes, it needs a 'to.' And what is 'to?' A preposition, right! Can you name any other prepositions?" Then we would play a game at the end of class like Charades. They loved these interactive games the most.

Teaching these kids became the dreaded highlight of my life in Malaysia. Getting there was taking my life in my hands as Malaysian vehicular traffic does not yield to pedestrians. I would fend for my life on every street crossing. I shared the precious few sidewalks with parked motorcycles, giant rats, and dripping air conditioners. Overflowing dumpsters smelled of rotting food.

The school itself was downright disgusting. The mere smell of it made me want to vomit each time I entered. The toilet was a hole in the floor with a bucket of water next to it for spooning into the hole. I've seen some funky toilets in Asia, but Zotung's toilets topped the list. The 2 classrooms were hot and humid, noisy from the elevated freeway just outside, and occasionally full of fumes from bumper-to-bumper traffic. Not to mention the infestation of giant cockroaches. Alright, I mentioned it.

A few times in the middle of my lesson, a cockroach would come out from under the file cabinet toward my sandaled feet.

I tried to contain my horror. One of the boys would jump up and rescue me by taking it away in his closed fist. He would let it crawl on his arm like his pet, and then usually torment the girls tossing it onto them. The class would erupt into chaos. I found it amusing, adorable, and revolting all at the same time.

After class, I would retrace my precarious steps in the searing tropical heat toward the Pudu LRT station. On my walk to the station I would evaluate myself: today the Charades were a success but my word of the day failed. The reading assignment was difficult with different abilities. Their writing doesn't seem to be improving, but they surprisingly loved the "fix this" exercise.

I get on the rattling old train and take a side-facing seat on the slick metal bench. The doors slam shut. I keep my eyes on the stops and check my phone to make sure I know where I am. I comically slide toward the front of the bench at each grinding stop of the train. I change at Masjid Jamek station alongside the massive, ornate mosque, negotiate my way through a sea of black haired people rushing through the underground passageways. I get on the LRT that takes me to Jelatek station where I disembark and walk along a noisy highway with no sidewalk. Motorcycles with no mufflers tear by me so close I feel their hot wind.

An hour after leaving school I am finally back to my apartment exhausted and sweaty, my nerves shot. Perhaps a couple percentage points of my hearing is gone. I recuperate at the pool with a sandwich and then fall asleep for a nap. Teaching leaves me feeling drained and yet virtuous inside. The cool waters of the pool wash away the grime of the school, the streets, and the train stations. I wonder if my students ever swam in a pool, or swam at all. Maybe they swam across a river to get to Malaysia.

Living in a poor-ish country, with millions of seriously impoverished migrant workers from all over the subcontinent and southeast Asia, you begin to see how enormously privileged and sheltered Americans are. It is starting to sink in after a month of living in KL, that life is indeed hard here. It can kick your ass and leave you wrung out and irritated. I dread the thought of teaching at the Zotung Refugee School. I don't want to get out of my pool, out of my air-conditioned box, and face the commute, the heat, the smell. Then the faces of the kids haunt me. They write to me in their exercises about how happy they are at the school and how wonderful it is to live in KL. I can only imagine what they fled if they think Pudu is beautiful. I think of them jumping up to greet me when I walk in, how they stand and shout at the close of class, "Thank you teachuh! See! You! Next! Week!" I find it both heartwarming and heart wrenching, and so I keep going back week after week not sure who is getting more out of the deal, the kids or me.

One week I walk into the class and no one stands up to greet me. My entrance goes completely unnoticed. I am surprised and curious about the lack of good cheer which normally brightens the dismal setting. Joel and Hang Thung Lia who are best friends, normally sit next to each other with their legs and arms thrown over one another in boyish affection. Today they sit a row apart ignoring each other. HTL has his head down on the desk, Joel stares ahead with a blank look on his face. The girls don't greet me either. What's going on here, I wonder? I ask the boys if they had had a fight. They shake their heads no. I ask the girls if the boys had had a fight. They also shake their heads no.

"Then what's going on," I ask. "Why is everyone so unhappy today?" No answer. At their core, they are Asian and negative emotions are considered unnecessary and counterproductive. At my core, I'm Californian and awkward silences must be examined, negativity delved into to find resolution, and perhaps a movie made. A psychotherapy modality and book on the subject will be forthcoming.

Occasionally when teaching, I've found it necessary to ditch my lesson plan and go with the flow to address what's needed by the students in the moment. Today was one of those days. So instead of launching into metaphors and similes, I wrote on the board, "WORD OF THE DAY: MOOD/MOODY."

"Does anyone know the meaning of the word 'mood?' Let's say it together — it sounds like 'food.' 'Mood.'" No one repeated the word with me. I was bombing like a bad comedian on stage.

"OK, Dim Dim, look up the word and read me the definition, please." They remember a word more if they look it up themselves. She did as I asked. Then I wrote some moods on the board for them: "Sad, Glad, Mad, Happy, Excited, Angry, Bored."

"Hang Thung Lia and Joel, please move back to your normal seats." They complied. "Now, I want you to write a paragraph about what your mood is today and why." They silently set about writing. I watched the pencils wiggling and the lip-biting as they scrutinized their papers. Then I asked to see what they wrote hoping that I would get some insight into the strange silence. Curiously, they weren't shy about sharing their papers with me.

Hang Thung Lia wrote that he was feeling lonely because his girlfriend doesn't want him anymore. He used the word "lovelorn." I couldn't believe he used that word. Clearly, he had done some research into his broken heart so that he could articulate it. He also wrote that his phone died. Jeez kid, double whammy, no *wonder* you're so glum! For kids today, phones are almost more important than friends. They are the conveyance devices of attention, love, and some connection to the outside world — especially for *these* kids who are so cut off by their poverty and undocumented status.

While the others were still writing, I sat down next to the lovelorn one and looked him in the eye (which I later learned is confrontational in Chin culture) and said, "You know, Hang Thung Lia, feeling lonely and sad is OK, it's a normal part of life. And sometimes you will feel pain in your life. Just remember that you have your friends here and they will be your friends even without your phone and girlfriend." He braced himself with his arms around his chest and writhed a bit. I am guessing about 35% of what I said made it through the language barrier. Still, if he heard the words 'sad is OK' and 'friend,' he got the message.

Hang Thung Lia is the oldest in the class and his bruised heart and lost phone had a sort of emotional domino effect on the class. His retreat to the back of the room to sit by himself cut him off from his best friend and cuddle buddy who seemed lost without him. The girls, most of the time, deferred to the boys. Their papers didn't reveal anything. They were just "holding the space" for the boys. I didn't try to explain what *that* meant — some things just don't translate.

At midpoint in the class I went around the room and asked for each of the students to tell me in one word what their mood was now. I got the usual "Happy" and "Glad." But when I got to Hang Thung Lia, his mood was, "Happy on the outside, sad on the inside." Nat King Cole couldn't have said it better.

Hey, *progress*...last week's word. Somehow just for him to write out his pain seemed to help him, and relocating him back with his buddy re-engaged him. Being the English teacher seemed to also mean playing guidance counselor, an even more rewarding perk of the job.

However, my teaching at Zotung was decidedly book-worm-ish. Over time my writing assignments and "word of the day" were beginning to bore even me. The kids seemed to be languishing and instead of paying attention in class, they wrote notes and checked their phones. I didn't quite know how to wrest them from the throes of abject boredom in my class, so I consulted my books as a bookworm does and came up with some more assignments.

Then one day I walked into class to find 2 new teachers from England had taken over the adjoining classroom to teach the younger kids. They had battery operated Bluetooth speakers and iPhones. They even brought a guitar. They had the kids standing on their chairs singing songs and clapping along. It was hard for Miss Schoolmarm to conduct her dull class with all the commotion of the super-ESL teachers next door doing the Hokey Pokey. They were putting their left feet in and their left feet out and shaking them all about. At one point, I wrote the word "ROWDY" on the board and had the students look it up. I was unamused and secretly envious of this teaching duo who could motivate children with just a few props and a lot of chutzpah that I was clearly lacking.

I went home that day feeling like a total failure, ready to quit. I failed at doing safe sex outreach work and now I'm failing as an English teacher. Clearly, I didn't have the training to teach like the others nor the charisma to excite children to jump to their feet and sing songs, and I really, really hate the Hokey Pokey. What good is the Hokey F-ing Pokey going to do for them when they get resettled? Wouldn't they be better off knowing their past participles and subject verb agreement?

The following week I went in expecting to be further humiliated by the Up With People ESL-ers, but they weren't there. The classroom was silent. The kids were just sitting there without a teacher. I, however, showed up and wrote my word of the day on the board: "COMPASSION." I had them write persuasive letters to someone they know who smokes to please stop smoking. I had them read books and identify the 5W's and the H: Who, What, Where, When, Why and How. As a nod to the ESL teachers on speed, I offered a game of Charades and a fake chat show where we would interview each other. Jun Cheung operated an imaginary camera while Tamwa Oo interviewed Dim Dim.

"Welcome to the chat show, Dim Dim. Where are you from?" She held the water bottle slash microphone to her mouth. They traded roles and brought in the boys to interview them. And then they insisted on interviewing me.

I began to feel more comfortable in my schoolmarm skin.

Perhaps the biggest lesson I taught was the one I taught to myself about just showing up in all my dullness with nothing in my magic bag of tricks. Being there for the kids, week after week was enough.

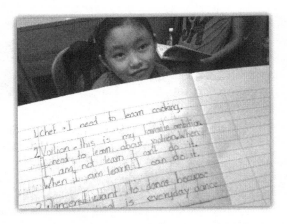

One morning, I asked the students to write out their "wish lists." I collected their writing afterward and found myself having to choke back tears. Here is some of what I received from them:

"My name is Dim. I'm 10 years old. I want to play violin and I need a violin but I don't have one. I need to buy. I don't have money. When I grow up I can buy a violin but now I'm young but I want to learn now. I need violin lessons but I can't afford them. Some people have a violin. I can't learn without one hear. I'm really really like a violin."

"My name is Hang Thung Lia. I come from Myanmar. I have two brothers and I don't have any sisters. I want to play guitar. I need to study a guitar. I think one day I will become a music teacher."

"Hello. My name is Tammy. I want to learn to dance and I need study and learn dance lesson. I don't know how to dance

but I want to learn. Sometime my lovely sister teach me how to dance but she doesn't teach base...I cannot do without Jesus...So I need to pray to Jesus. I believe someday he will give me answer."

"Crotch nuggets" might be a fitting description for spoiled brats in America complaining that they don't have the latest iPhone. But that epithet doesn't describe these kids who have nothing and still find their dingy school beautiful. They are virtually undefeatable in the face of terrible circumstance. I couldn't tell them that no one is listening to their wish lists. I couldn't tell them that they may never get resettled and if they do, they will be miniature misfits in a land of giants, cleaning Walmart stores on the night shift in Oklahoma.

They've taught *me* a thing or two about courage. Courage to leave their country and start over. Courage to be happy with what they have even when it's so little. Teaching these kids gave me confidence to share what little talent I have.

I'm not Jesus and maybe I don't have the ability to grant them their wish lists, but I show up and I listen. In a place that mostly ignores and exploits them, that's maybe not such a small contribution.

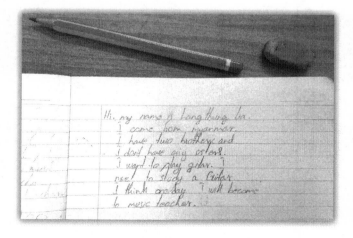

191

CHAPTER 22
GOLD MINE IN THE KENARI

What happened next only happens once or twice in a lifetime if it happens at all. I received a note on PlanetRomeo from a 27-year old Malaysian-Chinese guy named Chuan who spoke about his love for classical music and noticed that I was both a classical singer, pianist, and clarinetist. He wrote about his piano and violin studies. Hmm, this was highly unusual, I thought, tapping my fingertips together. Never in my travels in Southeast Asia has anyone approached me with that level of sophistication. I was intrigued though I was really hoping to meet someone closer to my own age, not someone even *younger* than Sebastian. He was just asking for a date so I didn't hold his age against him. The only catch was that his profile photo showed him looking angry and brooding. Nonetheless, after a bit of chatting, we arranged for an outing to see a dance performance at the Kuala Lumpur Performing Arts Center.

A cultural date promised to be refreshing relief from my increasingly sketchy auditions for a boyfriend — things were getting very weird, surreal even. I was lured into a public meeting with one guy who lead me on a wild goose chase telling me where to meet him in a mall. First by the escalator but he wasn't there. Then on the 3rd floor but he wasn't there either. Suddenly he said he was behind me and told me to turn around and look, but there was no one there. He texted that something urgent had come up and to meet him at the Starbucks and of course he wasn't there — the guy was obviously mental and was toying with me. In addition, I had a couple of guys go AWOL on me after a first date. One claimed he got food poisoning from the dinner I made...which I also ate. I never saw *him* again. Another one texted how much he enjoyed our date and then disappeared off the chat apps until I heard from another American friend he went out with, that he missed me and wondered what happened to *me*. I was confounded. Finally, a drunk guy nearly date raped me when I showed up at his apartment. I had to force him off of me and run for the door.

I was starting to see KL as a town full of hungry hunters and lone wolves, many who have gone a bit crazy under the weight of Islam. And what about *me?* Each time I'd click the door closed on another "audition" I'd think, hmm, chalk one up for the Rump Ranger, but boy, that really didn't hit the spot. Then I'd order up another one like one orders a pizza for delivery. The ability to attract was wearing thin with the attendant realization that booty calls were not sincere attempts to find what I came to Malaysia for. They were only quick fixes to the loneliness of starting a new life in a foreign country. Those dates were what I call "empty calorie sex," and sometimes you just want to pig out on that pizza delivered to your door. You want to put your face in it and smear it all over yourself and devour the delivery boy too. But the growing emptiness was not getting filled by this doorbell trade.

My upcoming date with Chuan warmed my heart. If nothing came of it, at least I will have gotten to see KLPAC and a dance performance, and I might have a new friend with our love of classical music in common. I dressed in, you guessed it, my seersucker hot pants paired with my nicest linen shirt, sprayed on a little cologne — the sign of a *real* date. He texted me that he was arriving shortly and to come down. I ran to the elevator with girly bag flopping on my back. I half expected no one to be there considering what a Mad Hatter's ride I'd been on lately. But he was there in his beat up tin box of a car called a Kenari. I could see him smiling and he rolled down the window to greet me. "Come, come. Get in." It was the first I heard of his hybrid British/American accent. I got in and looked over at him. My heart leaped. He was absolutely glowing, unable to contain a big smile. He had big lips, huge teeth, batwing eyebrows and the thinnest slit for eyes I've ever seen on an Asian person, almost like a cartoon caricature.

"Wow, you look so much better than your profile picture," were my first words to him. I was relieved Chuan didn't look anything like that picture. I noticed he was playing Bach's unaccompanied cello suites as we took off from the driveway into the hellish traffic of KL. The little car bounced around corners and hopped over potholes. I was impressed with his driving ability to engage in first date chitchat while commanding the Kenari like a fighter pilot.

"Why did you come to Kuala Lumpur?" he asked as most people do.

"I came to find love," I told him, already bored with having answered that question dozens of time. But this time, with Chuan, the answer was received with curiosity and delight. Telling various cab drivers, security guards, people in the market, would elicit a response akin to putting a steaming turd in their hand. The dirty looks I got were astounding. I think an American guy telling someone in Asia that you came here to find love may just be the wrong thing to say. My tender quest for love gets lost in translation and here's what they hear: "I came here to find girls to sell into sex slavery." Thus, I gave up telling people the story of the yellow bus epiphany and just told them I came here to teach English. With Chuan, I wanted to say, "I came here to find *you*."

We got to the performing arts center and found our seats toward the back. We sat with our legs painfully close. I couldn't help obsessing about this. All that was happening on stage seemed to mean nothing compared to the heat of his leg getting nearer mine and our elbows touching on the armrest. Eventually our legs met confirming that this was indeed a *date,* not just a friendly outing. Afterward we had some dinner at a mall and went back to my apartment. I put my hand on his knee while he drove. He didn't seem to mind but when we stopped at traffic lights, he took my hand away so that neighboring cars or police wouldn't see.

Back at the apartment I told him, "Chuan, I want you to know that I really have enjoyed our evening together. You're a very special guy but I don't want to jump right into bed, OK? I'd like to go a little slower than most guys do on a first date." He seemed agreeable to that. Since I didn't have a sofa in the little white box in the sky, we sat on the bed, not *in* the bed

I put on some favorite pieces of music, and he told me about his dying piano that he left at his mother's apartment while he was away for years in Singapore and Shanghai. He told me he would bring his violin next time so we could try to play some duets with the clarinet. He explained how he had left China to return to KL to give it one last try. A relationship was paramount for him and after several months of dating, he had given up on Malaysia. He was waiting for his work permit for China to come through. Then he would return to Shanghai to continue his career as a high-end hair dresser with Toni & Guy.

My heart kind of sank. Oh god, not another Sebastian who would leave in a short time and break my heart. Again. Can't I ever get my timing right? He reassured me that his departure would be months from now. We said goodnight after quite a few kisses and then he was gone. I wondered if I would hear from him again.

Indeed, I did hear from him. He wrote to me before he even got to the parking garage. And then again once he was home. We chatted feverishly by text as one does with a millennial, and within a couple days we had another date. This time we had a daytime date at a park in Kelana Jaya at the end of the LRT train line. He knew I couldn't stand being stuck in traffic so I took the train for an hour to meet him. We spent a lazy afternoon by a garbage strewn lake wondering if we would get mugged by some of the nefarious looking men who circled around the shore. The park was surrounded by highways buzzing with muffler-less motorcycles.

"Chuan, what about this is pleasant?" I asked with my head slightly cocked.

"Hey come on, we can walk on these rocks — it's a Chinese reflexology labyrinth. It stimulates your feet. Grandma says it's good for your organs."

"This is good for you? It hurts *my* feet. Hey, what about lunch?" I asked.

"Let's go to the mall!" he suggested with enthusiasm trying to excite me.

"Ugh, the malls. Is there anything else to do in Malaysia other than go to a mall? I'm going to call it Mall-Asia." I laughed feeling so clever and witty.

Thus began the dynamic of our budding relationship. He comes bearing endless enthusiasm for small pleasures and I mow it down.

"Isn't there a funky café or restaurant in an old colonial building that we could go to? Malls are so soulless." My words seemed not to curb his excitement. But they didn't seem to change the course of the afternoon either.

"There's a great Thai restaurant in the 1 Utama mall. Let's go. It's only 15 minutes by car." To me that meant it's only 15 minutes if it were 3am. But 15 minutes in KL during

196

the daytime means up to an hour stuck in traffic and 15 minutes whirling around a hot maze-like parking garage in the bowels of a mall. Of course, we sat in traffic and of course we whirled around the hot parking garage until I was nauseous. The mall was a mall like any other with its sameness of stores and loud Muzak.

Chuan it turns out is a foodie and an amazing chef with very high standards for cuisine. The Thai restaurant he chose was excellent and maybe, maybe worth the traffic and parking garage hell. That night of our 2nd date, we went back to the white box in the sky and spent the evening together — a real sleepover — a sure sign of something significant.

In the morning, he jumped out of bed, threw open the fridge door and surveyed my stores. He pulled out some bread, some berries, eggs, and spices. After a few minutes of whisking and chopping, he was serving up French toast with berry compote and a tropical fruit salad. This boy not only knew how to cook, he knew how to please. A sleepover and berry compote — Chuan meant business.

When he left, he asked if we could exchange wrist watches. I gave him my corroded Timex and he gave me his very fancy Swiss Army watch. He texted me from work how excited he was to be wearing "hubby's watch." Did he just say hubby? I re-read it to be sure. *Yes,* he called me hubby after only 2 dates. There were at least 2 ways of looking at this: 1 is that he's crazy and going too far too fast; 2 is that I came here to find love and now I met someone who's onboard, so why not just let it happen?

On just the 10th day of knowing each other, he wrote a text to me: "I love you. Ever since I met you, the empty space in my heart got fulfilled." I wrote back, "Oh don't make me cry. Am at the gym and the equipment will rust." He was moving very fast, and it was all I could do to keep up with him and let this unfold at a breakneck pace. Chuan was why I came here and I would be stupid to shrink away from his affection.

Then one day things went awry in the burgeoning storybook affair. He spent the night with me and we were awakened by his mother's angry texts. "Son, I know what you're doing and it's very disappointing," she wrote at 1:30 am. She speaks to him in Cantonese but writes her terse texts in English.

"Wow, Chuan, your mother is quite meddling, don't you think? You need to set a boundary with her — you're not a child anymore, right? She needs to keep out of your personal life. I mean, Chuan, she's still calling you fat pig in Cantonese and you're 27 years old. No, that's just wrong."

He explained how his mother found his diary years ago and confronted him on being gay. While she had somewhat accepted his sexuality in the intervening years, she seemed to be in denial now and was backpedaling. I found her to be wildly intrusive and took to Chuan's defense, remembering all too well how Sebastian's mother tried to destroy our relationship telling him he should visit their town's pastor for "reparative therapy." It would seem that I'm on a mission to corrupt mother's sons all over the world.

The issues with Chuan's mother were brewing mostly out of my sight. The next date we had, he simply didn't show up. I sat in the little white box watching heinously bad Malaysian TV shows waiting for Chuan. He never came. I texted a few times and didn't hear anything back. Another one AWOL, I thought, and my heart began contracting back to its normal size. By the end of the evening I was furious for being completely stood up and went to bed having ended the relationship in my mind. Back to the auditions.

In the morning Chuan wrote to me that he felt bad and wanted to come over.

"No way," I wrote, "If you stand me up with no explanation, it's over. I won't put up with being treated like that. Not by you. Not by anyone." I went on and on until he pleaded terrible sorrow for having done that to me.

"Well, you did stand me up and you destroyed my trust, so I'm not going to see you again. Chuan, it's over." I wrote to him.

"Please let me have another chance," he wrote.

"Nope. I need my alone time to collect my thoughts. I'm going out this evening anyway. Goodbye."

"I want to come and swim and workout at your place. Will you join me?"

"Nope. I'm going out. Go ahead but I don't want to see you. So just use the pool and you can leave the garage and apartment key I gave you under my door when you leave." There were more texts but I turned off my ringer and refused to read or respond to them.

When I went for the door to go get the Curry in a Hurry to head downtown for dinner, I noticed a note stuffed under my door. I suspected it would be with the garage key. There was no key, just the note written sloppily on a napkin that said, "All I know is I can't stop thinking about you." I thought it was either sweet or the beginning of an ugly stalking affair. He didn't seem to get that no meant no. Maybe the meaning of "no" got lost in translation. Or that as an Asian uncomfortable with saying no, he couldn't even hear the word when I used it? I shook my head and rolled my eyes not knowing what to make of this.

Note in hand, I looked over the balcony and saw him at the pool, 15 floors below. He didn't see me. Alright, I have to head this off. I stormed down the hall to the elevator and jammed the pool button. I stomped over in my seersucker hot pants, threw down girly bag on a lounge chair. There's nothing like a spurned white guy in hot pants and a gay lover's quarrel in a Muslim country. He saw me coming and hid behind a frangipani tree as if I wouldn't see him standing in his bikini behind the narrow trunk.

I started walking over and he kept inching around the tree attempting to remain hidden. I stopped, feeling suddenly sorry for him. There was something wrong with this dynamic. It was the dynamic of me scolding my childhood dog, Tippy. I yelled at her for peeing in the house. Then she peed more cowering from me. Wait, I'm not Chuan's master and he's not a dog. Could I maybe lighten up a bit?

"Chuan, can you come out from behind the tree, please?" He stepped sheepishly into full view but didn't say anything. I was admiring his bikini for a long moment before I refocused on my anger. Wait, what was I angry about?

"Look, I'm going out to dinner to have some alone time. I hate that you stood me up last night but let's talk about it later, OK? You can let yourself into the apartment. There's food in the fridge if you feel like cooking. I'll be back in a few hours."

"Hubby, I'm sorry," is all he said.

"You'll be there when I get back?" I asked, looking back.

"Yes, Hubby. See you later. Be careful on the bus, watch your wallet."

As I waited and waited for the Curry to belch its way out of the haze toward me I pondered the possibility of being with Chuan. I mean *really* being with him. I thought to myself, he's a really good guy, but maybe he's a little needy. OK he's a *lot* needy, so what? Like I'm not? Maybe he needs an older man to fill the void his father left in his life so he can stop being a mama's boy and become a man. Maybe I need *him* to fill the void left in my life by Sebastian (and everyone else I've ever met) so I can stop being a sniveling crybaby. Jesus, we're all just running around filling each other's voids, aren't we? It's amazing how much gut-wrenching soul searching one can do while waiting for a bus in Malaysia.

Yeah, Chuan stood me up, but he apologized and he didn't give up on me when I gave up on him. Perhaps it was time to introduce him to Tim, because I think maybe, just maybe, I got myself a good one.

CHAPTER 23
MALL-ASIA, MOTHER OUTLAW

here's something special about experiencing a place when you're in love. It has a way of rendering the mundane in candy colors — and Kuala Lumpur needs a strong prescription of rose-colored glasses to make it palatable. The reality of my new life was that when Chuan was not with me, I would be on the Curry in a Hurry with people staring at me in my hot pants, or walking in the searing heat with my parasol with people staring at me, or wandering the maze of malls with people following me into the bathrooms. On a date with Chuan, we would be in his car, adding a little comfort and ease to my day even if it meant sitting in traffic. At least we would be holding hands and listening to Bach without my entourage of onlookers.

My apartment was situated in the middle of KL's worst traffic-choked street and wedged between a mall and some embassies surrounded with concertina wire and high walls. To get to the mall on my own I had to actually walk out in traffic and step gingerly around puddles big enough to be navigable by canoe hoping not to get splashed by a bus. There was no place to go for a pleasant walk except maybe down to the pool which in the months since I had moved in became populated with Saudi families who were loud and destructive. I no longer enjoyed my pool time if I had to share it with 7 bratty kids yelling over the top of me, jumping on the lounge chairs, and tearing limbs off the frangipani trees.

Chuan worked part time at a hair salon in the Park Royal Hotel, so I would often take the bus downtown to have lunch with him at an old mall across the street. I would sit in the lobby of the salon watching him make women beautiful. I liked seeing his joy as he combed out long hair, spinning the client around, and blow drying her. He seemed to take great pride in his work, enjoying having me watch him while his co-workers gossiped about the white guy with the orange girly bag.

After his appointment, he shakes off the hair and we cross 4 lanes of screaming loud traffic without a crosswalk, run up the stairs to the top floor of the rundown Sungei Wong Plaza. He leads me to an un-air-conditioned, charmless food court. Dozens of booths vending steam trays full of mushy food are set out for the lunch crowd. Patrons dine beneath ceiling fans circulating the hot, stale air. "Now, what is pleasant about *this?*" became my mantra. And Chuan tirelessly found something I would like.

"They have great eggplant with garlic sauce at this place, come on, I'll show you." He leads me there and helps me to order. He is right, the eggplant *is* good. "Hubby, after lunch let's go to the store on the 3rd floor — they have a cheese grater there that you need for your kitchen." Having grown up shopping with his mother in this massive, multi-leveled mall with low ceilings, he knows exactly where to find anything we need. "Then we can go to the Chinese optical shop and get you some new glasses."

There was a profound sweetness in his wishing to show me his KL and help acquire everything we needed for the apartment. Chuan was adopting me, tucking me under his protective wing. He knew I was overpaying for produce at the malls, so he took me to the Chinese "wet market" of Kepong to stock up. The market is a massive open air one where thousands of little Chinese ladies in flip flops push through crowds with their plastic bags filled with fresh veggies. These wet markets are not for the faint-hearted, however. At the entrance, you hear the screaming of chickens being slaughtered. There's a frantic cluck, cluck, cluck as the bird is yanked out of a cage and then the pained squawk as its neck is bent back and slit in full view of passersby. The bird is then thrown into a plastic barrel where it flaps uncontrollably bleeding to death. I couldn't take my eyes off what I had seen in PETA documentaries about animal cruelty.

"Hubby, come on, let's go," Chuan beckons, leading me into the bustling crowds in search of the perfect pineapple and some dragon fruit.

"I think I'm not going to eat chicken anymore," I muttered inaudibly.

The grunge and noise and smells of the market all seemed to be mitigated by Chuan's steady guidance. He noticed that the prices would jump up as I walked through. Any item I inquired about was suddenly twice the price. Then they saw I was with Chuan who would insert himself at the counter and say a few magic words in Cantonese and the price would be reduced.

He would inspect the dragon fruit. "These are the Thai ones — no good. Get the Vietnamese ones." Then there was the fish section of the market. It was like a grisly version of Les Poisson scene in *The Little Mermaid* when the chef is chopping the heads off fish to the horror of the little crab watching. Fish heads and scales were flying into the air with every whack of a meat clever. Blood ran down steel tables and into gutters beneath my feet. Guts were being slung everywhere. Bulging eyes and squiggly things lurch out of buckets on the ground. Rats scurry under the tables scouting for food bits. On this field trip to the wet market I learned one thing: wear a dark t-shirt and closed-toe shoes. My white shirt and sandals were splashed with fish juices.

"Oh, Hub, you have to try these noodles!" and Chuan took me to a table in the middle of the noisy market where we sat down on plastic stools with little old uncles and aunties slurping up their chicken and noodles. I had become weary from the relentless assault on the senses that is Asia, but Chuan's excitement shot some enthusiasm into me.

I appreciated that the other diners at the table kept to themselves and didn't ask me what I was doing at this market. They just stared over their steaming bowls at me without smiling. Being the only white person in the village, I was viewed with suspicion, not delight. Surely, I was up to no good or something went really wrong with my tour bus and I ended up here splattered with fish juice.

The ride back to the apartment was once again spent stuck in a thunderstorm and traffic. I learned to get a newspaper before getting into the car so I could distract myself as we reverse spiraled our way out of parking garages and into the jams. I would be lost in the newspaper reading about Malaysia's corrupt government and the prime minister's notorious financial scandal while Chuan drove.

"Hey, did you hear that your Prime Minister fired the attorney general who was prosecuting him on corruption charges?" I would read Chuan the headlines aloud. "Says here the Malaysian ringgit is taking a nosedive against the US dollar because of the 1MDB scandal. Good for me, my rent just went down, but that means inflation is coming for imports."

I was learning how to deal with Malaysia — just stay "checked-out" as much as possible. "Hubby, go dormant!" was a sign that a heinous traffic jam was ahead and rather than bitch about it, I could simply pick up the paper and be gone. Unfortunately, what I was reading in the paper wasn't any less irritating than what was zooming on the road around us or stuck in front of us. I was getting the real feel for Malaysia — choked in traffic and scandal — and wasn't sure I was liking it. "Hey it says here in the paper that the 'Malaysian dream' is to get out of Malaysia." Chuan was silent.

To embrace Kuala Lumpur is to embrace 2 things: the automobile and the mall. Chuan has an extraordinary ability with both. He can navigate the crazy tangle of roads that grip KL as well as the warren of shopping malls that basically *are* the city. I'd rather be on my bicycle, and to me, a mall is a mall is a mall. In the US, a mall was the last place on earth I would go and only when I was desperate to find some item I couldn't find anywhere else. To Chuan, each mall was a playing field rich with opportunities for socializing, bargain hunting, and eating. I could blindfold him and he would be able to tell from the smells and sounds which mall we were in. To him the smell of Famous Amos cookies meant the ground floor at the old Sungei Wang mall. The smell of Cinnabon meant 1 Utama mall. The smell of fresh paint and loud 40s jazz coming from the ubiquitous tinny speakers meant the Putra Mall aka "The Mall" unlike the other malls which were not called "The Mall."

And this is where my righteousness begins. If I stay in any place long enough to scratch the surface and see beyond what the tourist or short-term visitor sees, I begin to see its shortcomings. There's a time period in which a place is amusing or at least interesting in all its grossness. Then there's the point of no return and once I have crossed that threshold, an indignant, self-righteous, expat American emerges. I had not yet gotten to that point but I could feel it coming and the malls were working my last nerve.

"Is there anything else to do in KL except go to the mall, Chuan?" I would whine.

"Well, yes but it's just not that nice. Remember, you don't like the heat and the rats, so a mall is a good option for you. Hey, they just opened the new Putra Mall with a movie theater on the top floor. Wanna go? They used to have a roller coaster inside. I wonder if it's still there." He had a good point about the heat and the rats but I was thinking the Amalfi Coast of Italy would be a better option.

"But, but…it's still a mall. I can't stand spending another evening wandering around in a mall, Chuan. Malaysia has torn down all its beautiful heritage buildings and buried its history with shopping malls and parking garages! What's wrong with this country? All people want to do is shop."

And so we spent another night in exotic Malaysia at a shopping mall.

Meanwhile, Chuan's mother and I were like lovers in competition for our beloved. She continued to text us at the most inappropriate moments as if she had a 6th sense for coitus interruptus. Chuan worked out his issues with her, negotiating 3 nights a week at her place and 4 nights with me. The nagging texts and calls stopped.

However, Chuan felt it was time for me to meet her, so I took the train out to the town near their apartment and they picked me up. All I had to wear was my hot pants and I was sure she would complain about them behind my back. I stood waiting in the rain for them to arrive at the station. The car pulled up and she was in the passenger seat — *my* seat. I mustered a smile to greet her, "Hello Mrs. Choy," and got in the back seat shaking out my umbrella.

"David, I like that you have your umbrella. You are prepared, la. Very good, la," she told me. "La" is added to the end of a sentence as a local expression meaning anything from "dumb shit" to "OK" to "yeah."

"I was a boy scout when I was a kid and so I like to be prepared…" I said trailing off realizing this goofy anecdote meant nothing to her. She smiled and nodded silently. When she smiled, her eyes became even narrower than Chuan's. I was amazed she could see at all. His mother is actually a very pretty woman, and she attempted to be gracious when she was addressing me directly. The problem was when she turned to Chuan and started speaking in Cantonese. I once overheard her trashing me on the phone. It sounded something like this: "Dim da gong da fum big age difference." The last 2 or 3 words of her sentences were always in English and, I was sure, aimed at me. I heard more, "Ying ma tim gai la gong big mistake." She was warning Chuan that white people were calculating and they will change their minds on you. This is my new mother outlaw.

"It's part of our culture for the Chinese mother to bad mouth the son or daughter-in-law," Chuan explained. This vetting of the newcomers didn't make me love Chinese culture any more than I already did.

"But we're not even married, Chuan!" I protested.

"Oh, she's just thinking ahead."

When she *did* speak to me it was to assess how practical and savvy I was with money, "Hey, David. How is your graphics business doing, ah? You have savings, ah?"

"I just keep my life simple. No mortgage. No car. No kids."

"Good for you, thinking of your future, la. You must teach Chuan to be responsible," she told me with a wink. I didn't tell her that I have hardly any work anymore and that I don't have much savings either. Framing me up as the paragon of financial responsibility...really? I might carry an umbrella but look at me — I'm a 50-year old in hot pants moved to Malaysia to find love. I thought about telling her how much her son's ass would fetch in the human trafficking market to see what she thinks of *that* for responsibility. But that might actually get me 2 thumbs up, "Yes, my son's ass worth lotta money. You should see his brother," I could hear her say.

I felt sorry for Chuan's mother, actually. Her husband took his life many years ago leaving the family marooned and without any financial stability. In addition, she's a cancer survivor and all this in a country with little or no social services for the elderly. Her older son moved to Hong Kong to pursue his career as a chef and hasn't yet sent money home to her.

She makes ends meet by delivering vegetarian dumplings to restaurants, an ambitious but tiring task for a woman in her 60s. As a result, she understandably clings to Chuan for dear life. Chuan's cheerful demeanor is her emotional buoy, just as he had become mine, in what was turning out to be a challenging country to live in.

Chinese filial piety dictates that children will take care of their elders without question. Chuan's lust to get out of Malaysia and his brother's pursuit of his career in Hong Kong both conflict with their inherent obligation to put their mother's needs first.

As a result, Mrs. Choy could only see me as someone who would take something away from her, not add anything to her life. I tried to find some compassion for her in spite of her trashing me to Chuan.

Before we parted company that evening, she gave me a plastic bag containing some of her dumplings to eat later. I took this as some form of olive branch and so I made modest attempts to be kind to her in spite of her ingrained homophobia and dislike of anyone vying for the attention of her son. Her homophobia comes from being raised behind the bamboo curtain of a Muslim country which censors everything objectionable, even heterosexual kisses, from TV and movies. I guess I couldn't blame her for this gap of knowledge.

Her dumplings were delicious — I carefully opened one, untying the string binding the handmade bamboo leaf wrapper. I examined its handcrafted beauty and the triangular shape filled with millet and beans. Then I smashed it in a bowl, poured milk and cinnamon on it, and had it for my breakfast — a truly unforgivable culinary offense to the Chinese.

CHAPTER 24
CROSSING THE RUBICON

*M*y lease in the little white box in the sky was running out and I needed to find a new apartment. I was ready to commit to a year's lease but not at the place I was currently in. I wanted a place where I could go for a walk, someplace nearer to transportation other than the Curry in a Hurry. And I wanted a place that the Saudis had not yet invaded. I spent my days searching for apartments — a great way to learn a city and its transportation systems.

I found one place in a modern high-rise in a Chinese neighborhood near the Putra World Trade Center. The apartment was a 1 bedroom unit on the 29th floor with a jaw-dropping, panoramic view of the city with the Petronas Towers as the centerpiece. I signed the papers based on the view alone. Twice as high, twice as big, and with a legendary sky pool on the 37th floor, the new place seemed like a major upgrade from the humble white shoe box. The wood floors meant I wouldn't spend my days picking up little black hairs off the white floor.

Chuan and I packed all my stuff — a few bags and a couple suitcases — and we were off to the new place. We rode the elevator up, opened the door, and for the first time we saw the view at night. It was truly magnificent. The entire metropolis was shimmering and blinking like a toy city below us. We watched the toy trains go by the river at the base of the building. This place gave me a renewed sense of life in KL. I thought to myself, "I think I can make this work. No, yes. I can do this. This is gonna be great!"

"Chuan, we could put the piano over there," I said pointing to the left wall.

"Really? A piano?"

"A home isn't a home without a piano," I said, pulling him in for a romantic embrace. He started jumping like a fruit fly.

"Let's go to IKEA and get this place furnished tomorrow and then go take a look at pianos," I told him.

We kept the rooms dark and the curtains open that first night as we settled into the bed and made love feeling like lions perched high on a hill. We slept with towels for sheets and t-shirts for pillow cases, but we were together at the top of the world.

The first time I heard Chuan play piano was at a piano store in a mall. He sat at a 6-foot grand for sale and played Beethoven's Pathétique sonata from memory — no small musical feat. I was stunned by his ability. Whenever he played, wherever he played, the whole store would stop what they were doing and listen. Passersby would peek in at the door. There really was no choice in the matter — we had to have a piano for the new apartment so we went to his favorite dealer, played several pianos and selected one particular upright and arranged for its delivery.

Chuan took a full-time job at L'Oreal as a corporate trainer so that he could stay in Malaysia to be with me instead of moving to China as he had originally planned. But his job meant I would have weekdays to myself. I set out to get to know the neighborhood near our new building. Unlike the last place, this one had a real neighborhood including a massive Malay wet market complete with the requisite rats and goat's heads lying around on the ground with their tongues sticking out. It was a market of horrors like all the rest but now I was on my own to explore and shop there. If prices were inflated because of my skin color, then it was up to me to negotiate them down or pay the asking price.

Chuan would go off to work in the morning, and I would go out exploring before the day got too hot. I got to know the restaurants and some of the locals in the various shops. I found a local Indian booze store where I got my 6-packs of dreadful local beer and an occasional bottle of hooch that might very well have been denatured alcohol. I got to know the vegetarian restaurant, and the Indian place that had food so hot it would burn me at both ends of my digestive tract. To get to my UN teaching job, I could walk along the filthy river full of trash, jump over the crazy biting ants, say hello to the guy pooping in the river, and be with the kids in less than a half-hour. Who could be happier?

But give me a couple weeks in a place and no matter how nice it is, the contented familiarity unwaveringly turns sour. As I began to notice the neighborhoodliness of the place, I also began to notice how it could be better, like for instance if people didn't park their cars and motorbikes on the sidewalk, then there might actually be a sidewalk on which to walk. It was after all called a sideWALK, not a sidePARK. And come on people, is it really necessary to throw your garbage on the street and poop in the river? I mean, really, there's a garbage can and a public toilet right next to you and you still have to do that?

A month after moving in, there were torrential rains and the Gombak River overflowed its banks. When the water began to recede, it revealed a colorful miles-long quilt of plastic bags embedded in the railing alongside the river. That was some measure of just how much garbage was flowing down river at any given moment, and that was just the river. The muddy path to my building from the LRT station was littered with bottles, cans, candy wrappers, and Styrofoam. I found it all revolting and took matters into my own hands. I would bring a bag with me on the way to, or from the apartment and I would pick up as much garbage as I could along the way. Chuan was slightly horrified to see me doing something so undignified as picking up trash. He could also see I was turning into the self-appointed decency police.

Locals found it unnerving to see an aging foreigner stooping to pick up garbage in their own country. Some people thanked me, others just thought I was some sort of foreign nutbag. I think some people really believed that white people shouldn't have to do this kind of dirty work. For me it was partly to set an example for others and partly to just clean up my own backyard. I would pass some business people on their way to work and I would make sure they witnessed me picking up the garbage. I would mutter something insulting like, "Filthy people, can't even respect their own country," loud enough for everyone to hear. I would pick up cigarette butts and hand them back to the person who threw them on the street.

I would chastise people standing on a bridge over the Gombak throwing their candy wrappers and potato chip bags over the edge. "Hey, stop that! Respect your country. Use the rubbish bin," and I would point it out to them as if they'd never used one in their lives. They never, ever confronted me back — they just gave a dumbfounded look and on rare occasion apologized. That was the real prize: an apology from a local to a foreigner for trashing their own country.

When I had the chance to discuss this with more vocal people I would bring up the subject, "You know the problem with Malaysia is that it will never become fully developed as a nation because the people act like troglodytes still living in the countryside. They refuse to be more civilized. They poop in the rivers and trash the streets. No one will take this country seriously on world stage like they do Singapore." That comparison always stings the Malaysians because they are border countries and in fact used to be united, but Singapore evolved rapidly and Malaysia lagged behind. Way behind. Singapore is now a world class city-state, and the only place in the world to outlaw chewing gum to keep the streets clean. To spit or litter will get you caned. If you pooped in a river you'd probably face the death penalty in Singapore.

One night I crossed the Rubicon of righteous indignation and almost didn't come back. I had read about the corrupt police of Malaysia where one can bribe oneself out of almost anything. Unlike America where you make your payment to an attorney who can get murder charges dropped if you have the money, in Malaysia, it's more organic. A cop stops you, does a quick racial profiling with impunity, and then if you are not the favored race, puts his hands out to receive a bribe, also known as "coffee money." Perhaps it works in suppressing crime — no one likes to be stopped and shaken down even for $20. As a white person in Asia though, I may complain about the price of food being hiked up in the markets, but I also enjoy a certain immunity to some of the infractions that locals would be subjected to. One night, though, I lost my immunity and would get a closer look at the penal system from the *inside*.

Let me first tell you what characterizes a "bad day" in Kuala Lumpur. A bad day is comprised of wading through wads of trash on the path you just cleaned up yesterday on the way to the LRT station. You pass the guy squatting in the river and have to look at a turd hanging out of his ass. Cars and motorbikes try to run you off the road but because the sidewalk is blocked you have nowhere else to walk. You finally get to the LRT station and then you walk up the stairs because the escalator is broken. After you've gone through the payment turnstiles and paid, you find that the trains aren't running. You stand on the crowded platform in 92-degree heat with 90% humidity shoulder to shoulder with people who have never owned or used a deodorant stick. Giant fans overhead only blow more body odor molecules up your nose. You get to smell the various body odors of the subcontinent. Mmm, that man on your left is from Bangladesh, a nice pungency fills the space around him. The man to your right is Indian and smells like a nice spicy onion cake — but you're feeling a little peckish and an onion cake just now would fill the bill. The one in front of you is Nepalese and is sharing his unwashed security uniform with you — it is the essence of fresh Limburger cheese. It's an all-you-can-smell buffet right here on the LRT platform. This is what you call a bad day in KL. Thank you all *so much* for doing your part.

Unfortunately, this hypothetical bad day was in fact happening to me. Unattended Malay kids were running around screaming, shoving, and knocking people dangerously close to electrified tracks. A long announcement comes on the public-address system to explain the delay in Bahasa Malayu, a language I failed to learn in high school. Then the English portion follows which says, "We apologize for the delay." That's it? I look around and ask various people if they could explain what's going on. Everyone looks at me as if I just told them their mother is a whore. I leave the platform and the gate agent doesn't know what's going on or when the next train might be.

"Train finish," he says, waving his hand in the air like the Queen of England.

"What's going on? Why no train?"

"Train finish," he repeats.

"I heard you the first time."

"Finish," I have come to learn, means closed, done, baked, broken, and complete. And it is often said with that hand waving gesture and sometimes in conjunction with the Indian head bobbing thing. It's actually not an easy set of motor functions to perform — kind of like patting your head and rubbing your stomach. But the gate agent manages to do it. He is a government employee and has done his duty.

I exit the station having to pay the fare for the ride I didn't get. Being that it's only 25 cents, I'm annoyed in principle only. But my plans for going to a jazz performance are ruined unless I can get a taxi. However, it is rush hour and as I descend the staircase from the LRT I can see the long line of red tail lights fading off into the haze. This means anywhere I go tonight I am going to have to walk, and walking in KL means taking your life into your own hands. No one but no one walks in Malaysia. If Malaysians could drive their car or motorcycle from the sofa to the fridge, let me assure you, they would. Walking is for losers and wide-eyed tourists who don't know any better.

Still, I'm determined to get to my jazz concert so I chart my course along a major highway with bumper-to-bumper traffic fouling the air. I begin by walking around the line of motorcycles on the sidewalk and into the line of stopped traffic. Tail pipes blow their exhaust onto my bare legs. I put a handkerchief over my mouth and my ear buds in and soldier on. I am hating everything about this, the heat, the humidity, the foul air, the noise, the insult to pedestrians. I put on Beethoven's 7th Symphony which gives me a sense of boldness as I walk this disgraceful path.

I get to a place where someone parked a big, black SUV on the sidewalk which forces me to tippy-toe alongside it or step into the oncoming traffic which has now started moving. Suddenly I am Phillippe Petit walking between the World Trade Center towers, teetering not with a fall to my death 102 stories below but with becoming the hood ornament on someone's Perodua. This is when my indignation reaches a fever pitch and I do what any self-righteous American would do — I reach into my pocket for my keys. I'm gonna learn that SUV driver good! With my keys in my left hand and Beethoven blasting in my ears, I dig the key into the side of the shiny black van and drag a nice line along the length of it. I go up and down to make it clear that it wasn't just some shopping cart. The curvaceous line makes my defiant act pretty too, which is important for me as a graphic artist. I'm sure the artfulness of my vandalism will soothe the owner when he discovers it later. Over the Beethoven I hear the sharp zipping noise as my key drags along from taillight to headlight and I continue on my merry way feeling smug and empowered for having taught someone to never park on a sidewalk again.

Apparently, I wasn't the only one who heard the zipping of key on car. Within seconds something hot and heavy and squishy lands on my back to tackle me. It sure ain't girly bag and it's not Daron, the pipsqueak Chinese guy I met in Brickfields. No, it's a 200-pound Malay man hitting me and yelling at me.

"You scratch my car! You scratch my car! Why you do that?" He takes swats at me while yelling. Drivers stuck in their lanes roll down their tinted windows to see what's going on. A taxi pulls over and the driver jumps out to see the white guy in hot pants get his ass kicked by a Malay guy with fire in his eyes. I am not sure if he's going to help me or if he's just there as a spectator.

"Why you scratch my car?" he demands.

"Because you parked on the sidewalk and you force aunties and little old ladies to walk in the traffic. That is wrong!" I figure I might as well let him have it.

"You don't like, then you call the police and I pay the summons if I break the law. I am calling the police on you now. Don't move! Don't. You. Move," and he points at me while fiddling with his phone and speaking in Malay to the police. I duck behind a row of hedges and realize I need to immediately hide the evidence. While showing that I'm not moving, I take off girly bag and jam my keys into the bottom of the bag beneath my sweater while the guy is examining his car.

"Police coming. You pay for this!" he yells from behind the

car. My work is done. I made my point and hid the weapon. Now I just wait for the consequences. The police show up within 3 minutes — an amazing occurrence for such an ineffective bureau. The officer is a woman in uniform with a black tudong tightly framing her face. She listens to the Malay guy's angry accusations and then asks me for *my* story. I realize that I am going to have to deny everything or I will end up being jailed, caned, and deported.

"I'm sorry, officer, I was walking and listening to music and this guy started attacking me thinking I scratched his car. Why would I scratch his car? He's a bit crazy, don't you think?" I imagine that only about 30% of that made it through the traffic noise and the language barrier.

"Come with me. We go to police station now," and she gently led me by my arm down the street and onto the overpass and into the police kiosk beside the road. We passed many people staring at us. I faked a haggard sense of relief for the passersby, like I had been robbed rather than the reality which was that I was being apprehended for a crime.

The police woman put me inside a small office where a couple officers were smoking and filling out forms. They asked me for my passport and questioned me. Then they brought in the victim. He came right over to me, stepped on my sandaled foot and pushed me against a wall, yelling at me in Malay. He had me pinned and the officers just stood and watched. Putting the perpetrator in direct, face-to-face contact with the victim was an ancient form of justice. I commended them for that except that my Morton's neuroma was hurting and some guy was spitting mad in my face. I was fearing for my life, and didn't know what would be next. I was sure my actions would disappoint Chuan — this was not a dignified situation to be in.

"Get him away from me, he's crazy!" I yelled. No one did anything. For them, this was some form of settling a score against white people and they were going to let him have his way with me. I yanked my foot out from under his shoe and pushed away from him. I demanded they keep him away from me but still they did nothing. They didn't laugh or take any delight in his tormenting me but they didn't stop it either.

After a few minutes, he was asked to leave and the officers told me they would take me to another station. I was escorted un-cuffed to the back seat of a patrol car. We drove with the flashing lights on to another station where I was greeted by a man in a jumpsuit carrying an automatic rifle who would escort me into the building.

I sat inside the quiet lobby for 45 minutes waiting for something, but unsure exactly *what* we were waiting for. A drunk person was brought in and strong-armed into the back yelling all the way. My escort with the rifle sat next to me texting and occasionally looking at me and smiling. I wasn't sure what this meant. Was he excited that he got to guard the white guy — perhaps a rare treat? At one point, he asked me to stand up for a selfie with him. Who was I to say no and deprive this guy of his pleasure for having captured me. We looked into his phone lens, both did the thumbs up and smiled with him showing off his rifle. Click. Who knows where *that* photo ended up. I wanted a copy for my blog but I didn't know how to engineer that.

I asked him if I could use the toilet. He escorted me with his rifle to a large bathroom and stood guarding the door while I used the urinal. I was beginning to enjoy the security of my captor. He took me back to the lobby and waited beside me until another patrol car picked me up and I was driven to a 3rd building — the *headquarters*. On the way, the driver interrogated me asking me why I would do such a thing.

"Why you scratch his car? Come on. You just come to Malaysia. Enjoy your time here and stay out of trouble. Don't make problems for everyone, OK?" I didn't respond.

I was marched up the stairs to a big open air room with 3 officers sitting at rusted steel desks with ceiling fans slowly circulating their cigarette smoke. There was a bureaucratic silence about the place. All the furniture and walls were yellowed with nicotine stains.

I was shown to a seat next to a desk with an officer wearing lots of service decorations on his uniform. He spoke perfect English, "So tell me why did you scratch his car?"

"Here's what happened. I was walking alongside his car and all of a sudden, he jumped out and started to hit me. I think he's a little crazy. He has anger issues for sure. Don't you think so? I don't have any keys on me. What would I have scratched his car with?" He asked me to empty my pockets and I took out my phone and my handmade paisley handkerchief.

The officer smiled and agreed, "Yeah I think he's angry and we're going to have a hard time proving you did it. But we are waiting to review the closed-circuit TV from that area. May I look in your bag, please?" Finally, I was getting the respect that I really didn't deserve — chalk one up for white privilege. I offered him girly bag. He seemed slightly amused that it was orange sherbet colored. He held it up and showed it to the other officers who smirked. Then he opened it up and looked in. I was sweating like a whore in church and trying to look calm. I distracted him a bit with chit chat.

"Have you been to the States? Lots of Malaysians like to go to Las Vegas. It's not far from where I live. I live near the Grand Canyon. Have you heard of that? It's one of the 7 wonders of the world." I talked while he was fishing around. Please, please, please, let my keys remain buried in the bottom. If he finds the keys, my goose is cooked, I'll be caned and sent back to America with bloody butt cheeks.

He didn't find the keys so I offered one possible solution, trying to be helpful while also revealing the plaintiff's offense, "Maybe it was my wrist watch that scratched his car. You know he was parked on the sidewalk and didn't leave much room to walk along the side so maybe my watch scratched it?"

He asked to take my watch and he disappeared for a conference with the victim and another officer. They left telling me they needed to inspect his car. Then they returned and had yet another conference at the end of the office.

Chuan who was with his mother that evening had been texting me wondering what I was doing. I took this moment to write him back: "I'm at the police headquarters. Everything is OK. I'm not hurt. More details later."

"OK Hubby, let me know if you need me to come and get you," was his text response. I was amazed how calm he was. But he knew this was coming and though he didn't know exactly what I had done, I could tell he wasn't surprised, either.

The officer returned with my watch and said, "You're being released. We can't prove that you scratched his car. The CCTV didn't reveal anything because it was dark. So, you are free to go now." I didn't breathe a huge sigh of relief. That would reveal that I was guilty and had just gotten away with something. Instead I unpacked one more bit of theater and shook my head in mild disapproval for the inconvenience of having been attacked and detained.

"And I was on my way to a jazz concert. What a night! I had heard KL is dangerous at night, and now I know," I told the officer.

"Yeah, you have to be very careful. Where is your wife and where are you staying?" he asked me in a not-accusatory way. He was just curious.

"Oh, I'm not married. I'm staying near the PWTC. Where are we now? I've been to 3 places. I'm not sure where I am and not sure how to get back to my apartment...I mean my hotel." I didn't want him to know that I was living here on a tourist visa.

"Not married at your age? Tsk, tsk. That's terrible — traveling all alone. You know it's dangerous out there. I'm going to arrange transport for you." He made a call and then we waited. In the meantime, the victim was brought around for one more swipe at me. He stood over me seated in my chair next to the friendly officer.

"You go back to your country. You lie to me. You scratch my car. Why you did lie to me? You are terrible person!" I looked away to avoid eye contact with him knowing full well that he was right. I lied and I was a terrible person for scratching his car. We had a couple things in common that night — we both broke the law and we both learned a lesson. He was escorted out of the building.

Two officers arrived to drive me back to the apartment. They were the same officers who drove me earlier only this time they seemed friendlier since I had been officially exonerated.

"Where from?" the driver asked flashing a warm smile.

"America," I told them. They seemed delighted.

"Where you go in Malaysia?"

I told them I had been to Malacca and Pangkor Island, and the officer in the passenger seat lit up and turned to me, "I from Pangkor! Very nice place. My home." I appreciated his sweetness and the desire to connect.

"Yes, very nice place. Very nice," I said, even though I had been there and saw that the beach was covered with garbage and the streets overrun with noisy motorcycles. I hated Pangkor Island but for the purposes of getting back to my apartment, I lied. Again.

The driver pulled into a late-night traffic jam, put on the flashing lights and gave a couple blasts of the siren. The traffic parted and we cruised toward my apartment. With lights dancing off the buildings, we drove past the Indian booze store and the vegetarian restaurant. I felt special tonight in a very perverse way.

I told them to just drop me in front of the Putra Mall — where my evening's adventure had begun. They obliged. With an ironic twist, they both turned from the front seat, smiled and shook my hand and wished me the best for my holiday. I thanked them and said goodnight.

I stepped out onto the side of the road and watched other pedestrians looking at the foreigner getting out of the patrol car. I wondered what they were thinking. I pulled out my phone and called Chuan.

"Hubby, you won't believe what just happened."

"Oh, yes I would. You scratched a car, didn't you?" His voice was calm and knowing.

"Yep. And I got attacked, arrested, and then released. And they just gave me a police escort home. I can't believe it."

"I knew this was going to happen. I'm glad you're OK, though. Do you need me to come and comfort you?" he asked sweetly.

"No Hubby, thanks. I am just gonna go up to the apartment and have a drink and calm down. I'll be fine and tell you all about it tomorrow." I dug my keys out of girly bag and looked at them with a wicked half-smile. Some black paint remnants were stuck to the end of the apartment key. If I had not hidden those keys well, I would have been in jail tonight awaiting the stroke of the rotan in the morning. Instead I stood at the window with my double bourbon on the rocks looking at the blinking city below. I got a view behind the scenes of Malaysia that most tourists would never get. I escaped the police without a bribe, in fact the whole evening only cost me 25 cents. Perhaps this could be a story for the Lonely Planet Malaysia guide on how to have a cheap night on the town including a free ride home.

CHAPTER 25
FALL INTO WINTER

Autumn in Southeast Asia is like every other season, it arrives almost unnoticed. Mid-November in America is when the holiday season is kicked off with the arrival of the first request for year-end donations. Ironically, here in this Muslim country, Christmas has already begun. Giant Christmas trees appear in malls. The tacky Christmas music that I had hoped would be banned by the Muslims is cranked up high to get everyone into the spirit. Women are seen in hijab posing for pictures with Santa. Creepy robotic elf displays bob their heads and lift their beer steins. It's a white, Western, Christian drinking fantasy in the snow for dry, Muslim, Asians living at the equator. This wintry spectacle in Malaysia makes even less sense than Christmas in America. I stand in Pavilion Mall watching the little Muslim kids going to sit on Santa's lap to tell them their wishes in Malay. I wonder what they're wishing for. More government privileges?

But what about Thanksgiving? Now *there's* a holiday I enjoy which, of course, is completely unheralded in Malaysia. There is really no specific harvest time to celebrate since it's growing season all year round and eating some strange, large bird from America is virtually unheard of here among locals. Not wanting Thanksgiving to go uncelebrated, I teamed up with a group of expat Americans from the International School of Kuala Lumpur. Cynthia and her husband Scott agreed to host the dinner at their palatial apartment if I agreed to take care of brining and roasting the turkey.

About 20 guests showed up that Thursday evening, and Chuan got to have his first experience of this American tradition complete with everyone sharing a personal story around the dinner table. One guest shared her family's tradition of listening to the 1967 recording of Arlo Guthrie's *Alice's Restaurant*.

Chuan and I debriefed in the car afterward. "Hubby, it was all mushy food, and what's up with that *Alice's Restaurant* thing?" he asked. I tried to explain to him the tradition of mushy food and how much he'd appreciate not having to chew if he didn't have teeth like many of the pilgrims. However, there was no logical explanation for *Alice's Restaurant*.

"Just chalk that up to Americans being eccentric. Not everyone listens to that at Thanksgiving," I assured him.

"Alright, well, I'm not sure Thanksgiving is going to be an important holiday for me. I don't get the cheesy grits thing, either," he told me. I laughed because I really liked Scott's cheesy grits.

Chuan was amazed how friendly and welcoming this group of Americans were. "Well, Americans *are* mostly friendly people. But, Chuan, all those promises of 'we'll have you over soon' and 'you're so fabulous,' and 'be my best friend forever' — don't believe any of it. Tomorrow they will be sober and you'll never hear from any of them again." This of course, turned out to be entirely true. He felt a little betrayed when no one returned my emails to try to connect another time or come to our housewarming party. I've just come to expect grand albeit flimsy professions of affection from Americans. I'd put up with almost anything for some turkey with stuffing and cheesy grits.

"Look, the only thing Americans export any more is entertainment. We dance and sing in traffic jams and make the world feel good about their bad circumstances. We inject cheese into things. We make chicken waffle flavored potato chips. We are a creative country, but we are not an earnest people. Just enjoy Americans in the moment and then let them go," I pontificated, high from several glasses of champagne.

Thanksgiving while special for me, was a bust for Chuan, but Christmas was just ahead. Malaysian-Chinese families do celebrate *that* holiday. I offered to make Christmas dinner at my apartment and Chuan invited his mother and brother and his brother's wife. In my tiny kitchen with 2 small stove burners and a toaster oven, I was committing to Christmas dinner for 5 and a chance to impress the "relatives" with my culinary skills. I was a bit nervous knowing that Chuan's brother was a professional chef, Chuan was an amateur chef, and Chuan's mom doesn't really like Western food. I promised not to do cheesy grits. Instead I did 3 sessions in my toaster oven: roasted chicken, roasted root vegetables, and potatoes. We all sat around the small white Formica table with the sparkling quilt of the city as seen from the 29th floor. They could hardly take their eyes off the view.

"David, you must come to Kepong and go to my favorite vegetarian restaurant, la. Very good vegetarian food. Very good," his mother said.

"David, how did you make the fennel gravy for the vegetables?" his brother asked. It seemed that they were embracing me as some sort of addition to the family — at least that's how it appeared at the table. What followed in the months ahead was something entirely different. Maybe we Americans and Malaysian-Chinese aren't so different after all with our grand professions of friendship.

After dinner Chuan played a little Beethoven on the new piano. Then we all said goodnight with awkward hugs. Chuan drove his mother home, and I took some of the leftovers to the cats in the garage on the first floor.

When I first moved into the building, some fierce mama cat with her boobs dragging gave birth to a litter of kittens. I felt sorry for the tiny creatures, and watched them one by one disappear to who knows where. But one kitten remained — a little black one with white paws. We became best friends and I had him over often — the lone Malaysian kitty and the lonely American with promises of kibble — promises I delivered on.

I would feed the cats in the garage in spite of the signs

posted saying not to. "Boots," as I called him, came up in the elevator to my apartment for some snacks, slashed at me when he was done, and then indicated that it would be kind of me to push the elevator button for him. I put him in the elevator, pressed "G" and stepped out hoping he would know to exit upon his arrival back in the garage. He figured it out because he was in the garage waiting for me the next day. I would feed him a little handful of food from my backpack, and he would walk me half-way to the train station. There at midpoint to the station, along the filthy river, we would say goodbye, and I would be on my way.

Then one day Boots was not in the garage to greet me or follow me to the train station. I don't know what happened to him. All the cats had disappeared. I suspect the building's security guards rounded them all up, put them in a pillow case with a rock, and threw them into the Gombak River behind my apartment. I walked to the train station every day hoping to see him come bouncing out of the tall weeds that grow along the river. I never did. Boots' little bag of kibble sat on my shelf molding.

CHAPTER 26
AN EARLY DEPARTURE

Thy fate is the common fate of all,
Into each life some rain must fall,
Some days must be dark and dreary.
— Henry Wadsworth Longfellow

Kuala Lumpur is a tough place for tender flesh — vulnerable creatures don't last long here. I returned to the apartment one morning after my swim and walk up the 29 flights to find a text from the headmaster at the Zotung Refugee School: "Hi, teacher David. I am sorry to say you Hang Thung Lia, your student was crashed by car at around 4:00am and died. He went out together with his friends around 3:00am and happened accident, I think, resulted from being drunk with his friends not to be able to cross the road. Sorry, teacher."

I struggled to find my breath. I wasn't exactly sure from his text what had happened but I was fairly certain that "died" meant he had been killed. I called the headmaster and he spoke rapidly seeming to be on the verge of hysteria. A calm mind might have been able to parse his gibberish, but in my own state of near-hysteria, I only understood about half of what he said. He did, however, confirm that one of my favorite students, Hang Thung Lia, had been struck by a car in a hit and run accident near Berjaya Times Square. He was running from a gang that had attacked and robbed him and his friends. The driver of the car fled the scene and by the time the police arrived, the 14-year old boy was dead — crumpled like a piece of garbage on the roadside. There would be a memorial at his home the next day followed by a service at their church in Pudu, and I was invited to attend.

I forwarded the text to Chuan who was at work. He called me back immediately. I couldn't speak as I paced around the apartment wailing at this tragedy. As an undocumented immigrant, no justice would be done and I would never find out anything more about his death than I could squeeze out of the broken English of the headmaster.

I got on line and contacted the other teachers and some of my friends in the US and Hong Kong. We raised 1,700 ringgits to help pay for the boy's funeral. This was about a month's income for that family. When he got home from work, Chuan and I drove down to the Indian flower market in Chinatown to buy an arrangement for the boy's family. We stopped by Cynthia and Scott's apartment to pick up their donation. Cynthia, who was also Hang Thung Lia's teacher, was so destroyed she couldn't even come down to the car. Scott handed me an envelope and gave me a big hug.

Hang Thung Lia was an on and off again good student who would disappear from time to time. I was told by the headmaster that he liked to drink and was a bit wild. Nothing wrong with that I thought, while outwardly expressing my professorial concern. When I first met Hang Thung Lia in class, he was inattentive and listless — he clearly had some chip on his shoulder — and I frequently had to prod him to pay attention. I would go over to him and put my hand heavily on his shoulder. He knew that meant to put away the phone and focus on his lesson. His shoulder bones were like a bird's.

Over time we made peace with each other. He came to life in my class. In fact, he flourished. In spite of his being the bad boy among the students, he was usually more advanced and excelled in pronunciation and writing. A few weeks before his death, he won the Word of the Day contest and gift bag I had put together as a prize for the one who remembered the meaning of the most words I had thrown at them. Two weeks ago, he was finally able to pronounce "with" properly (unbelievably challenging for Asian tongues) before everyone else. He sat at the front of the class clutching his gift bag, smug for having done it.

The day of his funeral, I met my students at Zotung. They were all waiting silently outside the school with their headmaster. I got out of the car and greeted the sullen bunch before walking to Hang Thung Lia's apartment. We made our way through squalid, rat-infested alleys strewn with rotting garbage. Joel took on the task of carrying the bouquet while the other kids plugged their noses. A toddler came out of a building to see the flowery entourage going by, waddled over to us and hit the flowers with a big smack. Some petals fell off the bouquet. What was *that* about — just some random anger from a baby? We got to the family's apartment building and walked up the unlighted staircase to the apartment to find dozens of pairs of shoes outside the door and the hushed voices of people mourning. We slipped off our shoes and went in.

Hang Thung Lia's mother was over the top distraught and walked about the apartment wailing and reciting his name, not unlike I had done in my apartment the day before. The sounds of her worn-out voice drowned out the babies making cooing noises. I greeted the father (who was actually the stepdad replacing his deceased biological father) and handed him the envelope of money from the teachers and friends in America. The parents didn't speak any English so the school headmaster translated to him the amount that I brought. He began to weep and grabbed onto my shirt, soaking the front of it while I hugged him.

I felt somehow shy about letting loose my own feelings. I wanted to wander around the house screaming with the mother. I felt some need to keep myself composed in front of my students, but If I had to do it over again, I would have just let myself grieve uncontrollably with her.

The students and I sat quietly on the floor of their apartment as they had not a lick of furniture and no air conditioning — it was hot and uncomfortable with so many people in attendance. They may not have had a fan but what they did have was a palpable sense of community and love. It seemed like every Burmese person in the neighborhood filed in and out to sit with the family for a spell. After an hour of sitting on the floor with my students, I suggested we go out for a walk and get some food before going to the memorial service at their local church. When I stood up, the mother came over and broke out of her wailing spell and said, "Thank you teacher, thank you," and held onto me. She hugged and petted the flowers and kissed the plastic wrapped picture of her son she had been holding tightly against her chest.

I took the students out for lunch and a breath of hot polluted air. We ordered noodles with fish balls at an outdoor table by the road side near the church. Joel was Hang Thung Lia's best friend and curiously silent since we gathered at the school. His half smiles belied some pain. I was surprised that he could smile at all but what does a 13-year old know about the finality of death?

He stared down at his bowl of noodles and played with them with his chopsticks, without taking a bite.

"Joel, you're not eating your lunch. Why are you not eating?" I asked a few times and didn't get a satisfying answer until I put the words in his mouth for him.

"Too painful?" I asked.

"Yes, too painful," he said nodding his head. I was sure Joel would be hit the hardest as he came to the memorial

231

without anyone — no siblings or parent to hold his hand or comfort him. In the last class I had had with him and Hang Thung Lia, they were best buddies goofing off and laughing. Joel is perhaps protected by his young mind and this will all mean more to him years from now or better yet, he will have completely forgotten it. I wish I could.

After lunch, we went to the church for the memorial which was packed with hundreds of community members and a line of wreaths at the front. My bouquet was placed on a chair with "Saya David" written on it. I felt so esteemed to be part of the display, to be welcomed into this community and called the lofty title of teacher. They had no idea how much of a kid-hating curmudgeon I was and how unprepared I was to teach. They also had no idea how fond I had grown of these kids and how broken my heart was sitting there as the only non-Burmese person come to pay his respects. I stood with them as they sang songs and a sermon was read. I didn't understand a word but in grief, all that is necessary sometimes is one's presence.

The memory of Hang Thung Lia still haunts me. I miss the way he used to pivot on the balls of his feet pretending to hold a microphone like a rock star. He loved to blurt out in the middle of class, "Everybody dance now!" — a line from C+C Music Factory. He would say it from the back of class and I would collapse out of my schoolmarm persona, laughing out loud and then the whole class would erupt into laughter.

I'm so sorry he never got to be the music teacher he wanted to be and that he was run over like a rat on the brutal streets of Kuala Lumpur — a poor refugee without a country. His death will go unnoticed by any official measures, but I for one will always remember the skinny little hunchbacked kid who made me laugh. Nobody is dancing now.

CHAPTER 27
LOVE IN THE TIME OF DIARRHEA

*C*huan and I took a road trip north to Penang for business. He had become the hair color expert of Malaysia, teaching his special techniques to salon owners all over the country. On our way, we stopped for lunch at some roadside food stalls. He went for the Malay food and I wandered from his side to the Indian food stalls because I am an adventurous eater and I like to take risks. Let me restate that. I *was* an adventurous eater. For years, I had been eating street food in Thailand, but I had been duly warned about eating street food in Malaysia by doctors and even Malaysians.

How could it be so different, I wondered — they're border countries, after all. The voice of naïveté has spoken once again. The difference in a nutshell is: foreign workers. In Thailand, the restaurants are run almost entirely by Thai women, and their cooking traditions, standards, and hygiene practices originated in Thailand — handed down from mother to daughter for generations. In spite of how dirty Thailand can be on a street level, the people themselves are obsessively clean. In Malaysia, however, the restaurants are largely staffed by foreign workers from Bangladesh, Pakistan, and India — countries notorious for being hygiene challenged.

I ordered my Indian food that afternoon and I got a little more than I had bargained for. Within a day, I started feeling bloated and nauseous. "Look, Chuan, I can't see my junk anymore," I proclaimed looking down at my distended belly eclipsing any view below the waist. I looked like a very hairy woman in her 3rd trimester.

Then came the cramps and the diarrhea. Of course, I thought it could just be traveler's diarrhea and it would pass. It didn't. After several days of worsening conditions, and a rising fever, I treated myself with Ciprofloxacin — a drug one should never be without in Southeast Asia. The medication seemed to stop the diarrhea and quell the fever, but I still wasn't feeling 100%, so I went for a visit to the hospital near my apartment for some lab work. Being the earnest patient that I am, and being that I didn't feel like pooping in a cup in a hospital bathroom with people waiting outside, I decided to bring along a yogurt container with a sample for them. Hooray, how thoughtful of me. I packaged it up in a little bag and carried it like Little Red Riding Hood with her basket of baked goods. Except mine was a bag of diarrhea and I was going to the Indian hospital.

I set off along the trash-lined river path behind my apartment that leads to the hospital. Then I saw the guy I often see squatting with his butt hanging over the river. The bacterial irony of this was not lost on me. It's not rocket science that if you shit in your water you are going to get sick. We've know this for centuries but somehow that message hadn't made it here. I gave my thumbs up to the guy pooping in the river and I went on to the hospital to deliver my sample to the lab.

A couple days later I was at the gym working out and my phone rang. It was the Damai Service Hospital calling.

"We need you to come in immediately." Yikes that sounded scary.

"Come in? Why, what's going on?" I asked stepping off

234

the exercise bike.

"You've tested positive for typhus," I was told by a nurse.

"Typhus? You mean *typhoid fever?*" I asked.

"Yes, and you must come in for a doctor's consult," she told me.

I went back to the hospital and they handed me the lab results. Next to "*S.* Paratyphi B" it said "antigen POSITIVE." Really, anything positive in a hospital is a negative. I found it chilling just to see the words. Nearly a quarter of a million people die from the disease annually. Untreated it has a 10-30% fatality rate.

"How does one get it?" I asked.

"Food or water contaminated with feces," the rotund Indian doctor explained. He told me that it was good that I had already taken Cipro and that I had dodged a bullet. *Again,* I thought.

All I could think of was, where could I have gotten this? Chuan and I rewound the last few weeks. "Remember we saw that guy cooking at a food stall reaching into his pants to scratch his butt crack and then pulling his hands out and chopping vegetables?" he said.

"Yeah and what about the guy we saw at that food stall in Brickfields — remember he bonked a rat on the head with a pan, picked it up by the tail and dropped it into the sewer and continue cooking without washing his hands or the counter?" I recalled, my voice accelerating.

"Yeah, and the rats we saw crawling in the food stall storage bin when we were on our way to the Indian booze store!" Chuan added. And what about all the hair I kept finding in my food? How many times did I sit down to a meal with Chuan and as I dug in, I'd see the long wiry strand of someone's hair poking out of my gravy?

"Got another one, Chuan. Hmm. This one is curly. Let's see if we can find the cook with curly hair and give this one back to them." He wasn't amused because he knew I might very well do that.

All the hygiene horrors of recent months were playing back in my head trying to trace the point where the little critters might have entered my system. One never knows *exactly* where these invisible demons come from but some form of this lapse in hygiene might have gone on at the food stall on our way to Penang. The hand you don't want to shake is also the hand you don't want cutting your veggies. From that day forward I would only eat my own food or food prepared in a reputable kitchen. Chuan went one step further to say I should only eat in Chinese places because the cleanliness standards are higher. My Malaysia was getting smaller and smaller.

This however, meant I would be cooking more at home. And that meant I had to brave the markets for ingredients as there were no real grocery stores open near my apartment at that time. There was a big Costco sort of food warehouse nearby…that would be if Costco had dim lighting, no air-conditioning, and smelled like dead animals. I poked my head in to look. Palettes of food were stacked to the ceiling and forklifts whizzed and whirled about. I wandered the aisles until I came to the nuts and legumes section. The large bags of almonds at half the price of the fancy grocery stores looked enticing until I noticed the teeth or claw marks on the nuts. Those were not tine marks of whatever hulled them, I thought to myself, so I passed on them.

Ah, but look at this — macadamia nuts — my favorite, and priced at only 5.79 ringgits per package, such a *deal*. Much in need of a little nibbly indulgence, I bought a bag. My stomach grumbled all the way home where I couldn't wait to rip open the package and crunch myself into mono-unsaturated bliss.

I washed one nut because you can't trust packaged food items here to be clean. (Packaged doesn't mean ready to eat, it means someone sealed it in plastic.) I bit into my "macadamia nut" and it turned out not to be what I thought. It was not unpleasant tasting, though. Could they be large hazel nuts? I was curious what in fact they were since the package was unlabeled and they were so cheap. Whatever they were, they must be locally produced so I texted a picture to Chuan, my font of local food wisdom, for a quick identification and waited for his answer.

He wrote back that he didn't know what they were called but they were not really *eating* nuts per se, but rather used to flavor a curry. To me that meant they're still edible even if not for the purpose of snacking. I decided to roast them and salt them. After about 20 minutes, I pulled them out of the oven and nibbled one. Tasty. Let me have a few more. OK, not bad. Let me have a small handful. That's when my stomach started to tighten and churn. The churning quickly led to cramps and then I started feeling feverish. Oh dear. I texted Chuan telling him that I wasn't feeling well after eating the mystery nuts.

My condition worsened as I grew pale and started feeling dizzy. To distract myself, I tried to watch a documentary on the BBC called *Filthy Cities*. Up came scenes of foul tannery waste and beheaded bodies being chucked around revolutionary Paris. All too familiar to my life in KL, this imagery was not helping with my burgeoning nausea.

Chuan went on the web and did some research and within a few minutes he wrote back that the nuts were called "candlenuts" (aka "kukui nuts") and are toxic when eaten raw. Oh crap!

I called him immediately crying that I had poisoned myself and would soon be dying. I was going to die alone in the apartment watching *Filthy Cities* — a total disappointment to my boyfriend for not having been more prudent about food choices. If I was going to poison myself, I wanted it to be an intentional act and with something more historic like hemlock or something more dignified like a fistful of Seconal pills paired with a nice bottle of Malbec. There would be nothing dignified about finding me dead in a pile of my own candlenut spew.

I quickly looked up candlenuts on the Internet adding

the keyword "fatal." Although toxic, nothing came up about them being fatal, and the antidote was simple: coconut water. This seemed like some sort of local witchdoctor wisdom and that I might have to toss some virgin into a volcano, rattle a saber, drink the pure water from a young coconut and then my health would be restored.

Chuan is nothing if not an efficient problem solver. Within 20 minutes he had left his mother's apartment, gone to the grocery store, wrangled up some fresh coconuts and was turning the lock on the door to find me prostrated in front of the toilet bowl with a rainbow palette of chunks flying out of my mouth and nose. I sat on the rug in front of the bowl feeling sort of proud for having heaved out all the nuts plus my homemade mung bean stew. Chuan tore open a coconut like only a local can do and I sucked its water from a straw. Remarkably (and without virgins or a saber) the clouds in my stomach parted and the sun came out again. The color returned to my face. I was cured and now just needed to get the mung beans and carrots flushed out of my nose.

"Aw, Hubby, you're my big man baby and I am not going to let you get into any more trouble," he said, wiping vomit off my face. Chuan once again saved me from the many perils of his country. Thus, it became his role in my life in Malaysia to be my chief problem solver and leash holder. After the car scratching, the typhoid, and now the candlenut poisoning he was reluctant to ever let me go out of the apartment alone.

The imbalance of care seemed more evident than ever. Other than consoling his occasional nightmares of ghosts attacking him in his sleep, and my making him dinner after work, I didn't have much to offer Chuan in the form of comfort.

He and I spent our months together doing simple things like taking our pastel crayons and paper to the Titiwangsa Lake Gardens park. We sat on a blanket by the lake drawing while flicking ants off our legs. His drawings were abstract,

238

mine more realistic. Chuan always wanted to visit the horses stabled near the lake. I told him how in Tucson there were horse farms near my place and that often I would see them riding on the bike path. His eyes lit up.

"Hubby, could we get a horse in America?" he would ask me as if he were a kid.

"Yes, sure. Of course. We could keep it in the courtyard at the townhouse in Arizona. The home owners' association allows for 2 pets and the CC&Rs doesn't say anything about horses."

Saturday nights, we would go to a jazz club. Sundays, we would sleep in, make a big breakfast and try to find something — anything — to do that didn't involve a shopping mall, parking garage, and traffic.

This meant getting out of KL as often as possible. So, we took trips to Penang, Malacca, Bali, and marine parks in the South China Sea. Every place we went was crowded, polluted, and painfully hot and humid. For these reasons, I stopped wanting to go anywhere in Southeast Asia. I found myself dreaming of open space and quiet. I longed for the feel of cool, dry air that didn't come from a box on the wall.

I introduced Chuan to Ken Burns' documentaries of America's national parks. On the big screen TV in the living room we watched scenes of Yosemite's snow-covered mountains and the pristine lakes of Glacier National Park. He fell asleep while I sat on the sofa wide-eyed and missing America.

CHAPTER 28
CHICKY CHICKY,
SHAMPOO SHAMPOO

Somewhere in between the food poisonings, the air pollution, and the homophobia I came to the conclusion that I'd had enough of Malaysia. Chuan and I sat down and had a long talk about it.

"Look Chuan, I don't think I can keep doing this. How many more times am I willing to be sick. I just finished my 3rd case of food poisoning in Malaysia and I've had a hacking cough from the haze almost the entire time I've been here," I pleaded.

"Well, I just started my job and I don't want to leave it right away — that wouldn't look good on my résumé. I need to stay another year."

"Oy! Another *year*? And then what? Where are we going to go? You could get a tourist visa and be in the US for 6 months at a time but then where would we go?" I got a little panicky that maybe we were not going to be able to stay together.

"Hubby, the most important thing is that we be together," he told me, "I want to be with you forever." We agreed to stay in KL for another year, but I warned him that I was going to have to spend some time in Thailand eating clean food and being around smiling people once in a while. He agreed and said he would come with me for holidays. Thailand was back on the table as a possible place for us both to settle. It would be close to home for him, and Thailand for me had already become a second home. Now that I wouldn't have to deal with dating capricious Thai guys, living there seemed more feasible.

But a year is a long time when you're stuck in your apartment afraid to go out, *warned* not to go out. My life became confined to the 565 square feet of the apartment with the extraordinary view. I played the piano, practiced clarinet, read the paper, and had dinner on the table for Chuan 4 nights a week. I woke up with the call to prayer at around 5:30 each morning to work with my American graphic design clients in the middle of their afternoon. Then I went back to bed and woke up again late morning for a swim, a workout, and a brisk plod up the 29 flights. It was a functional existence, but I felt like I was under house arrest.

Chuan would take me out of the apartment in the car, much as he takes his elderly grandparents out to the market or for a meal. With Chuan by my side, I was protected from pathogens, lecherous lip-lickers, and motorcycles on sidewalks. He would safely deliver us to a mall where we would dine at a restaurant of his choice on food that was not likely to have me riding the porcelain bus home. He would follow me into the bathroom and fend off the looky-loos.

"Stop looking at my boyfriend's penis!" he would yell at the guys who would follow me in and stand next to me at the urinals.

"Chuan! Shhh. I don't mind if they look," I would scold

241

him. I enjoyed the attention even if it was admittedly a bit of a sleazy pleasure.

"Well, you have your fun then, I'll meet you back at the car."

"Wait, don't leave me," and I would run after him zipping myself up trying to catch up with him in the crowded mall.

"Let's do something fun, huh? I'm tired of going to shopping malls. Let's go on a trip to Bali. What do you think?"

"Hubby, I have a job and can't just leave."

"I'll plan the trip and we'll go when you can take some time off, OK?" I told him.

We went home and arranged our flight and hotel — Bali here we come. On the day we were to leave, we were on the train heading to the airport when we received a text from AirAsia that the volcano Mount Rinjani near the Denpasar airport was spewing ash, shutting down all flights into and out of Bali. Bali here we don't come.

"Great, now what are we going to do?" I asked Chuan. "Maybe go somewhere else? You have the time off from work, we're all packed and ready to go. Might as well."

We got to the ticket counter and with a quick spin of the globe, they re-booked us on the next flight to Borneo. Borneo sounds exotic, I thought. Let's do *that*. It was that random. We rushed to make a hotel reservation and within an hour, we were flying to Kota Kinabalu in the East Malaysian state of Sabah — home of orangutans, cloud leopards, and kidnappers. Before we took off, I sent out a text to a few friends that we had to divert from Bali to Borneo and my phone started buzzing back with warnings about being kidnapped by Philippine pirates. I immediately did a search of the US State Department's website. There I saw a warning for US citizens to stay away from Sabah. Sigh. Erupting volcanoes, kidnapping pirates — you know, you just can't plan for everything, can you?

We arrived and checked into our hotel room right next to the airstrip and spent most of the weekend taking the airport shuttle to downtown restaurants, keeping ourselves away from kidnappers.

Our first night, we set off to find seafood in town. As we exited the van in front of the seafood restaurants at the dock, a slightly netherworld kind of guy with bug eyes steps up to me, looks me in the eye like Peter Lorre and says, "Chicky chicky tonight?" I somehow thought he was working for one of the competing restaurants and was offering me a chicken dinner.

"No thanks, we're going for seafood," I told him with a confident smile and pointed to the fish restaurant.

"Hubby, he was trying to sell you a prostitute and you told him you wanted seafood? Chicky chicky means *girls!*" We both burst out laughing. I looked back and the guy had a bemused look on his face. I felt hopelessly naïve.

We sat in the restaurant and ordered our grilled shrimp dinner watching boys aiming their laser pointers at jets taking off from the nearby airport. I sat there horrified knowing that their pranks could temporarily blind a pilot.

"You know in the US, that's a federal offense. You would go to jail for up to 5 years," I told Chuan. Now on a short leash, I returned to being simply an observer, not the grand corrector of all that's wrong. The plane will have to crash and Malaysia will have to deal with the consequences itself. Police woman has turned in her badge.

We took a snorkeling trip out to a nearby marine park. Going on a snorkeling trip in the South China Sea means not just the chance to see the garish colors of tropical fish, but also to observe more outlandish mainland Chinese fashion. Two Chinese women boarded our scrappy snorkeling boat in black lace cocktail dresses and high heels. Nothing says "snorkeling trip" like a cocktail dress and heels on a small boat being buffeted by rough seas. We watched the ladies leave the boat when we arrived on the island and dine in a restaurant on shore, still wearing their life preservers. In fact, none of the Chinese tourists ever took off their life preservers, as if to say, once on land you could still drown at any minute.

Chuan and I sat après-snorkel in a beachside café marveling at the Chinese obsession with capturing selfies and wefies on their phones. They stand with the phone on a stick pointed at themselves cycling through a range of poses and fake facial expressions, sometimes pinching the air overhead to generate the optical illusion of pinching the person a hundred feet behind them. One group of life-jacketed women stood at the water's edge while the other conducted them in their poses. Left hands up, ladies. V-sign now. Chin to right shoulder, knees together. Now pivot. Other side. Let the wind catch your hair, that's right. Work it for the camera.

They saw us laughing and mimicking their posing, but our spying on them didn't deter them at all. We all laughed together but they didn't quite get that we were in fact laughing *at* them, not *with* them. None of this had anything to do with the bounty of marine wildlife swimming just a few feet behind them. We watched as they waded into the water with extreme caution, one slow step at a time occasionally followed by a squeal and a mad dash back to the shore. What was it, I wondered, that grazed their legs sending them into hysteria, a plastic bag maybe?

Chuan and I took off with our fins and swam beyond the boundaries of the marine park into the South China Sea. We followed schools of slender silver fish darting one way then the next. We watched orange and white striped lionfish twirling around rocks. I spotted my first shark ever — a 4-foot blacktip reef shark. Chuan crunched my hand and groaned through his snorkel when I pointed it out to him just about 20 feet off in the blue green waters. We popped our heads above the surface to confer.

"Scared scared," he said not letting go of my hand.

"It was beautiful! I'm so thrilled to finally see a shark after all these years of snorkeling. And could you please release my hand?"

The shark took no interest in us and we continued back

to watch the Mainlandia show on shore while we sipped coconut cocktails and I uncurled my scrunched fingers.

We dodged the volcano, escaped being kidnapped, and didn't order chicky chicky for dinner. It was a weekend of what we *didn't* do and then it was back to KL — back to the 565 square feet of my cushy jail cell for my one-year sentence.

I planned our next escape: a weekend drinking trip to Langkawi, the Malaysian island where all the sinful delights of Malaysia are sold duty-free. It would be a weekend of boozing and gorging ourselves on chocolate.

We dropped into Langkawi, a vertical air insertion via AirAsia, the no-frills airline that promises cheap fares, no legroom for long-legged Caucasians, and the guarantee that someone's Malay child will be kicking the back of your seat for the entire flight. In that regard, the airline delivered its promises.

I was seated a few rows away from Chuan where I would endure my beating on my own. First it seemed pleasurable, like a flying massage chair. That's it, massage each of the lumbar vertebra starting at L5 and working up to L1. Nice. I wondered if I would need to tip the child. Then came the violent kicking and the tantrum. One of the drastic differences between Malay child rearing and Chinese child rearing is that basically there is nothing off limits for Malay kids. They may climb on the sculptures and touch the artwork at a museum, they may scream and yell in a fine restaurant while their parents are face down in their phones, and they may kick the shit out of the airline seat on a plane — this time, mine. I roll my eyes. I look at the people on either side of me and roll my eyes in their stone faces. I'm getting no response and without anyone to complain to, I'm not sure I will be able to keep my lips zipped as is my promise to Chuan. "Don't make a scene" is the pan-Asian way to handle every crisis and now that I'm in Asia I have to do as they do.

Rather than stand up and scream at them, I decide to reach through the gap between the chairs and grab the leg of the offending kicker. I feel the soft tissue of a baby's leg that is now being restrained by my hairy white claw. I feel the other leg still kicking my chair. Hairy white claw digs its nails into the baby's calf. Then the kicking stops. I expect now to hear the wailing but it doesn't come. This is the difference between Asia and America. If I did this in America the child would be hysterical, the flight would be landed at the nearest airstrip and an air marshal would drag me from the plane in handcuffs. Not here. I look back and the mother is playing a video game on her phone completely unconcerned by the hairy white claw with a death grip on her child's leg. The kicking stops then starts again. The hairy white claw reaches through once again and this time yanks the leg a little bit to shock the child. There's a moment of stillness and then the kicking starts again. Mom is now looking out the window oblivious to the trauma her child is being subjected to.

Finally, I can't take it anymore and I stand up and yell at the mother.

"Your child is kicking my seat. I want you to stop it, NOW!"

Chuan looks up and sees me yelling and rolls *his* eyes. Is he rolling them at me or at what I must be going through?

The mother looks at me sheepishly and says, "Solly." And then the kicking continues with a vengeance, unhampered by the mother. I ring the call button for the flight attendant which in AirAsia means absolutely nothing. The flight attendants would not get up off their jump seats if someone brandished an axe and started hacking at the cockpit door. So, I just get up, push my way to the aisle and re-seat myself after a brief sotto voce conference with Chuan. People around us are texting and talking on their cell phones mid-flight, seat belts unfastened at landing. They routinely get their luggage out of the overheard compartment while we are still taxiing. For some this might be their first flight ever. Did I just see someone attempting to throw their paper cup out the window?

After this short flight on ScareAsia, we're in Langkawi ready for a mid-morning bender at the duty-free stores. Langkawi Island sits off the northwest coast of the Malay Peninsula, near Thailand. Once a beautiful island, it is now overrun with tourists like us on their holiday drinking sprees. We make some attempts to go to the beach which has about 3 people per square foot. The beach is covered with garbage and boats. Drones buzz past our heads threating to get tangled in our hair. What we really want to do is stay in our rooms and enjoy a bottle of prosecco with shots of chilled Jägermeister.

After our nap, I popped a cork of bubbly so that it shot off loudly over the Muslim neighborhood below the hotel balcony. The cork landed with a loud bonk on someone's tin roof in the dry kampung (village) announcing that it was party time for the non-Muslims. We proceeded to get in-our-cups drunk in our hotel room. Chuan, like many Chinese, will light up red after just one drink. His eyes and ears glow devilishly crimson as his blood alcohol level rises. This "alcohol flush syndrome" comes from a genetic deficiency the Chinese have that leaves them intolerant of alcohol. While I can disguise my state of drunkenness with some breath mints and the stabilizing help of a stationary object such as a wall, Chuan can't. Nonetheless we set out for the town like a couple of sailors on shore leave when we run into his boss, Randall, in a restaurant. Now Randall is extraordinarily good-looking and even in my most sober of minds, I might not be able to contain my lascivious thoughts. But this is Chuan's *boss,* I tell myself, making a real effort to not give this tall, thin, chiseled Chinese man the once-over. Then I notice his grapefruit-sized biceps and his pointy little nipples poking through his tight white shirt. Chuan introduces me to him, and I teeter forth to shake his hand, and have a look at his heaving chest. Oh, god, I'm really just a gay version of Donald Trump talking to this man's chest. Being that this is Langkawi, I can only hope he's in a similar inebriated state and can't intuit my thought balloons which are saying terribly unmentionable things that will get Chuan fired. It turns out he's gay, too, and a manager at L'Oreal — I guess that shouldn't have been a surprise but frankly my brain wasn't firing on all 4 cylinders in that moment.

Extricating ourselves from that situation before it gets out of hand, we make our drunken way down the street to a highly-regarded restaurant called Champor-Champor, known for its diva chef and her genius with spice. We fling open the door while I'm still saying the name over and over "Shampoo-Shampoo," and laughing out loud about how truly brilliant I am with word play. Then we see the woman. *The* woman. She stops in her tracks to eye us down.

Divas are usually very accomplished, fierce women who scare insecure straight men and entrance gay men. I look back at her and give her a look of "I'm not afraid of you so bring it on, Diva Chef. Let's see what ya got." We fall into our rattan chairs, and she comes to our table to greet us and drop off menus. I have no idea how to read even English at this point so my glowing red boyfriend will take care of ordering. I look into the woman's eyes and we glare at each other with something between admiration and extreme distaste. I am going to tame you, Mrs. Shampoo-Shampoo, I tell her with my eyes.

A timid young man comes to take our orders. He disappears into the kitchen and with much yelling, banging, and steam coming out of the door, he begins piling our table with delectable food. Chicken bathing in creamy sauces with cones of saffron rice piled next to them. The smell is beyond beyond. I take one creamy, nutty, spicy, sweet bite and I nearly pass out from the flavor that just envelops my entire being. I want to swim naked across a lake of her coconut curry sauce, finding refuge on her islands of moist potatoes, sipping her blended fruit drinks under a bok choy tree dripping with her light oyster sauce.

I am astounded, no, *dumbfounded* by her culinary artistry. She leaves me a quivering, drunk pile of burping flesh at the table of her restaurant. I didn't tame her at all. She tamed *me*.

"Wow, Chuan, was that spectacular or what?" I asked knowing full well that Chuan always tempers his responses and will say something like, "not bad" with a down-turned grin — the Chinese are hard to please. He acknowledges the food with a nod while slurping down the last bit of yellow curry.

"Well, I'm going in to the kitchen to tell her what a genius she is," and I march off to the kitchen. I throw open the louvered doors and see her standing at the butcher block. She looks up at me with a meat clever in her hand and a face that says, who dareth enter my lair?

"Madam," I say, with my head making a big drunken circle and then bending into a deeply pretentious bow until our eyes meet, "You are the *grand dame* of spice," and I pull out of my bow, pivot, and walk out. I glance back to wink at her and she has the biggest ear-to-ear grin of deep satisfaction on her face. She was speechless either from hearing somebody speak in such a ridiculously florid manner or she was simply basking in the accolade.

Back at the table I whispered loudly to Chuan, "Hubby, I just told her she was the 'grand dame of spice.' I can't believe I said that. Seriously, I told her that. What a pompous thing to say."

He just shook his head in shame. "I'm going to need a shorter leash."

The next day we took a break from boozing and hired a private boat for a trip to an even smaller island off the coast of Langkawi. There we attempted to go snorkeling but there were no fish to be seen. So, we watched tourists feeding chicken skin to white bellied sea eagles knowing full well that chicken isn't really a part of an eagle's diet. But this is

Malaysia and ecology be damned if you can get tourists to pay money to feed them.

Getting bored with sitting on the beach watching some dad stuffing his cigarette butts into the sand while his daughter made sand castles, I went for a walk to investigate the monkeys. Chuan told me to avoid the monkeys at the end of the beach which for me is like saying, don't watch that train wreck. How can I *not* go see the cute little monkeys?

"What's wrong with these monkeys? I've been to Thailand. I know monkeys. The monkeys won't hurt you," I told him.

"Don't do it, Hubby, they're vicious, evil monkeys," he warned me as I stubbornly took off to see just how evil they really were.

I got within 20 feet of a lady monkey with her nipples sticking out of her fur. She had close-set topaz eyes and tufts of hair fanning out from her cheeks. She looked so adorable.

"Hello little monkey, aren't you adorable. Hey, we're only a few genes away from being related. We share 96% of our genes. If you had only 4% more human genes, you could be an intelligent human being and go on Jerry Springer."

It was then that I noticed several other monkeys coming toward us to join in the conversation. Oh look, a whole family coming to say hello. I continued talking to them, "Oh hello family of monkeys. Wuja wuja wuja wuja." That's when all at once, their cute little faces erupted, turning inside out bearing huge fangs and hissing violently at me. I freaked out and ran screaming toward Chuan with a band of vicious, evil simians chasing me down the beach.

"Why you did that?" Chuan was on his feet yelling at *me*, not the monkeys.

"I didn't do anything. I was just talking to the one with the boobs saying she could go on Jerry Springer if only she were smarter. She didn't appreciate the irony and went ape shit on me." I started laughing about the "ape shit" comment of which now I knew the derivation. Chuan remained silently mad at me for risking being mauled by the evil rotten beach monkeys.

"I can't let you out of my sight. What if one of them bit you?" he said, admonishing me.

I calmed myself down by picking up some trash on the beach on the way back to the boat. I carried some baby's dirty diapers at the end of a stick like a white surrender flag. The metaphor was real — I had pretty much surrendered. How would I ever get out of Malaysia alive and without monkey bites all over my ass?

Malaysians love when a tourist picks up the garbage that they shamelessly left on the beach and then waves it around for them to see. I photo bombed through a group of Malay girls doing their group portrait — them with their selfie stick, I with my diaper stick. They seemed unamused, containing their laughter no doubt until I was out of sight. Not me, though. I thought it was hilarious and giggled my way past them. In fact, I laughed so hard I dropped the diapers. They stood silently watching me wondering how far I would take this charade.

I picked up the diapers and dumped them off at the trash bins, circling back to the place where the dad had jammed his cigarette butts in the sand. I picked several of them up and then went to where his little girl was playing in the sand and handed them to her.

"I have a little gift for you," I said. "Open your hand. Here you go. These are your daddy's. He left them in the sand and I'm sure he will want them back." She and her mother looked at me with that same look I always get when I shame people for doing something so obviously wrong in my little righteous book of global stewardship. How do you respond to that — do you thank the person? Do you apologize? Do you fight for your right to litter?

I wonder what went through their heads and I wonder where those cigarette butts ended up? Putting them in the garbage bin often means they get burned in a bonfire anyway, but I didn't stick around long enough to find out.

CHAPTER 29
SUPREME DECISION

The US Supreme Court has ruled that same-sex marriage is a legal right across the United States.

*I*t was the summer of 2015 and hopefully my last summer living in Malaysia. A year had transpired since I'd been away from the United States and about as long since I had seen a blue sky or been able to eavesdrop on a conversation. I was beginning to feel like a ghost of another kind in a place where I may be considered exotic but also unapproachable.

I had become an expat for the "4G" reasons: guns, god, greed, and gluttony — the ugly aspects of America. Living in Malaysia I had really only eliminated the guns portion of my discontent with America.

Malaysia is a very religious country evidenced by the call to prayer which emanates 5 times a day from every mosque; it's just as gluttonous evidenced by the prevalence of McDonald's and KFC depicted on practically every bus, subway car, and street corner; the gluttony and greed are more "soft indictments." People are gluttonous and greedy the world over, thus every country starts with a baseline of 2Gs, except maybe Bhutan.

In the end, the only real reason to stay away from the US remained the guns. Gun deaths are an extreme rarity in Southeast Asia. According the United Nations Office on Drugs and Crime, in 2006, the US logged 9,960 homicides by firearm; Malaysia logged only 64. Gun ownership in America in 2010 was 27,000,000; in Malaysia: 370,000. Having been one who was shot at in America, I'd say the gun presence was palpable.

However, chalk up an extra "G" for Malaysia that America doesn't have in spades: germs. Having been constantly sick in Malaysia, I would conclude that it is indeed a more germy country than the US. What are my chances of being shot versus getting sick? I'd say it's more likely I would get some virulent tropical disease and buy the farm sooner than I would get shot at a second time in the US.

That left the US and Malaysia tied with 4Gs of undesirability each. The tie-breaker was the L word — the reason I came to Malaysia. Love was keeping me in Malaysia. Perhaps there was somewhere else we could go and eliminate some of the Gs and keep the L? We considered Thailand and were still chewing on the idea like a piece of tough jerky — we could sort of live in Pai or Chiang Mai. But what about the intense heat and the burning season when they set the rice fields ablaze making it virtually uninhabitable? And what would we do for culture? Malaysia has the Malaysia Philharmonic and the KL Performing Arts Center. Pai has the reggae festival and Songkran — the big water gun festival where people get ear and eye infections from being sprayed with tainted water. Thailand is a little too much folly. Malaysia is just a little too sober. We talked about traveling all year round — he would cut hair and I would do my computer work. We would be on the run chasing good weather, good vibes, and cheap happy hours. Chuan and I stepped together into this muddy quagmire of indecision — wanting to go *somewhere,* to find the sweet spot between folly and sobriety, but not sure just where in the world that would be.

Then came the game changer. It was the morning of Friday, June 26 in Malaysia and I had been reading online that the US Supreme Court was expected to hand down their decision that day regarding marriage equality in the Obergefell v. Hodges case which would grant or deny same-sex couples the right to marry under the Fourteenth Amendment to the Constitution. Chuan was just waking up and I poked at him to get up and get ready for work.

"Hubby, wake up. This is a big day in America for gays. It could be our lucky day."

"Grrrr. Let me sleep," he groaned and rolled over, never taking much interest in politics, no less, *American* politics. And never before coffee.

"No, really, Chuan, we should be listening to the news today. This could be *big."*

Typical of most days, he had his oatmeal breakfast at the tiny white table in our tiny white apartment in the clouds. After, I walked him to the elevator, looked both ways to make sure no one saw and then kissed him goodbye.

"Let's go to the jazz club tonight, OK? We can get a pizza there and stay for dessert and see if we hear from the Supreme Court."

"See you after work. Bye," he jams the elevator button and the doors close on our morning as he plunges 30 floors into the garage.

My days in the towering apartment building are admittedly dull. If I am not teaching at the United Nations school, I might be giving a tutoring session to Zahirul and Taysif, the Bangladeshi boys who worked in the rooftop restaurant by the pool. Today I don my swim suit and go up to the 37th floor to say hello to them. They aren't at work yet, so I swim a few laps in the sky pool taking in the magnificent view of the entire city. Barn swallows circle overheard in the mornings and evenings. I stand at one end of the pool with the waterfall massaging my shoulders while looking out at the tangle of streets, trains, and skyscrapers of the city, dominated by the Petronas Towers gleaming like steely corn cobs through the haze.

I can't deny that I enjoy this — the warm waters, the million-dollar view, the thrill of swimming in midair — and all just an elevator ride from my apartment. This is my village of 1,100 apartments, and this is my swimming hole. I especially enjoy when an afternoon monsoon drenches the pool and green spider webs of lightning strike the spires of the surrounding buildings. I dangerously stay in the pool plugging my ears for the crash wondering if I will be fried to a crisp in the next flash. Nature overpowers man in those moments in this city that seems to have lost all association with the natural world.

The Bangladeshi boys arrive poolside for work wearing their striped dress shirts and black pants, casting a wave and a smile in my direction. I swim over and ask them if they want to do a quick English lesson for a fruit shake. They get me the drink and say they'll take the lesson tomorrow morning in the lobby. Deal. I haul myself out of the water and dry in the sun and sip my pineapple shake with an umbrella in it. Six Arab boys appear with their hookers and booze bottles. Their loud voices and cigarette smoke precede their actual arrival next to me where they trip on my lounge chair and start yelling and gesticulating wildly over the top of me. Malaysia has become a playground for idle Saudis. Boys are sent away to Kuala Lumpur with the presumption that they are going to school in a Muslim country where they will retain their religious piety when in fact they are on the rooftop committing all manner of haram. They are as rich, sexy, and repulsive as any college frat boys in America would be.

The Arab miscreants' arrival signals my departure. I finish my drink and yell to the diminutive and well-mannered Bangladeshi boys, "Don't forget your notebooks and text me if you're going to be late!" I slip into the express elevator and retreat to the quieter and decidedly less fabulous 4th floor pool. I walk past the Carrot Café restaurant that just opened in the lobby. I notice they changed their slogan from "Feel the Test" to "Feel the Taste" after I laughed out loud and pointed when they were installing the sign. They corrected their grammar with a piece of plastic and some tape. Now the slogan is simply illogical unless you figure that a lot of people eat with their hands in Malaysia. To them maybe the food *does* feel tasty. It gives me a vindicated chuckle and I head to the pool to do my laps.

At the 4th floor pool I can swim in peace without the fabulous view, without the throngs of people with cameras. I can swim undisturbed...until something is dropped into the pool from a high floor apartment. Today it's a water bottle from the 22nd floor. I count the floors up so that I can later call Chandran, the building security potentate to report the incident. The velocity of a water bottle dropped from that height could at least knock me out if not kill me. The boys who threw the bottle cackle looking down from their balcony as they release little bits of paper to the wind. Chandran will tell me with his warbling Indian accent and head bob, "Yes Boss, we take this very seriously and will handle this with the utmost concern." He will do nothing.

A posse of younger Arab boys (the ones too young for hookers and booze) assembles here and starts building a diving board by stacking the pool furniture and begin doing belly flops in the pool — right in my swimming path. The Nepalese security guards walk past noting the cluster of chairs but do nothing. They will chase me out of the gym for wearing flip flops but stacking lounge chairs and jumping off of them seems to be outside their purview of concern.

"Excuse me!" They look around to see who I'm yelling at. "Yes, you. Would you please not jump right in front of me while I'm trying to swim laps?" I plead with the boys from the middle of the massive pool.

"No English! No English!" the chubbiest one yells back at me with his arms flailing in the air and his belly fat jiggling. I motion with my hands that *I* swim in this small lane and *you* can have all the rest of the pool. He looks at me with defiance and continues doing his belly flops. I swim another lap and he flops aggressively right in front of me. He surfaces and the water clears his face matting his long eyelashes together. I go after him.

"If you jump in front of me again I will drown you. I will drown your ass right here and now," I tell him holding his arm. I take liberties with my threats since he doesn't speak English.

Then in perfect English he says in a very whiny voice, "Drown me? You're threatening me? What did I do to deserve that? You better not drown me, I'll tell security."

I can't help but laugh. Everything about this is wrong — the aggression, his lying, and my threatening him. Not to mention how he's going to tell security if I drown him. Just my being here is wrong, I concede, and I towel off and leave for my walk up the 25 flights to my apartment. I could leave this, I tell myself. I won't miss the errant youth of Saudi Arabia. Yeah, I could definitely leave this place.

My walk up the stairs is my daily meditation. It's one of the only places I will never encounter people or motorcycles. Malaysians would rather die of starvation in their high-rise apartments in a power outage than to use the stairs, so I am guaranteed that I can completely clear my head in silence. I start out full of anger at Saudi families for dumping their brats at the pool ruining one of my few daily pleasures. By the 10th floor I note that I have 19 floors left to resolve whatever it is that troubles me.

The Supreme Court decision comes to mind. What if they declare marriage equality tonight and grant me the right to marry Chuan? Are we ready for marriage? Would I be willing to move back to the States and live as a married man? By the time I reach the 29th floor I have my answer.

Back in the apartment, I shut the door on all external irritants. I hang my bathing suit to dry, fix myself some lunch, read the local paper and check my watch — it's still the middle of the night in America. I put the air conditioner on high and start watching a documentary. Soon I will jam in my earplugs for a long nap waiting for Chuan to come bouncing through the door. It's Friday afternoon and he gets to leave work early. I'm excited. We'll be going out for jazz and pizza tonight.

But first there's a knock at the door. I pause the movie and peek out and see the Indian guy from the end of the hall. I open the door slowly.

"Yes, how may I help you?"

"Hello sir, I would like to know if I may have the pleasure to know your Wi-Fi password?" he asks with his thick marbles-in-the-mouth Indian drawl.

"Oh, hmm. Why don't you have your own internet account? Your apartment is a bit far to receive the signal, no?" I ask suspiciously not wanting to have my bandwidth gobbled up by some guy downloading porn. Worse, I didn't want to have him sitting outside my door with his laptop listening to everything about our lives. I invite him in to discuss the matter and show him to the table. He sits down admiring the view. My back is to the large screen TV I had just been watching some sinking ship documentary on.

"I am new here to building. Account soon but problem is waiting list," he tells me, his head ticking to the left.

"Oh yes, I had that problem. It took me 6 weeks to get my internet when I moved in. Sure, you can borrow my password," and I wrote it down for him.

"Where from? You live here with wife? How much you pay for apartment? Where work? How much money you make?" The usual sequence of prying questions has begun.

"No, I am not married," I enter the ring with my routine answer but in the comfort of my own home I decide not to hide my sexuality this time.

"I live here with my boyfriend," I revealed to him expecting he would get it and shut up.

"No wife?"

"Nope."

"Not married?" he continues in disbelief.

"No. Not married."

"You live here alone?"

"No, I live here with my Chinese boyfriend. My wife is a *man.*" I tell him folding my arms defensively and stubbornly. I'm willing to do this all afternoon if I have to. I will let him ask me until he gets that I am a bona fide homosexual and there is no vagina living in this house, not for me to enjoy, not for him to enjoy. Fortunately, I didn't have to engage in this tedious conversation all afternoon because something wonderful happened at the perfect moment.

While he's drilling me with his questions, the idle TV screen behind me goes into screen-saver mode which I have set to my Flickr account revealing a fine art nude photoshoot I did with 2 men in Paris the year before. My Indian neighbor is getting perhaps his first view of men's nipples, buttocks, and erections in giant, widescreen, high-definition. It's like a gay porn drive-in movie right there in my living room. There's only one person watching this feature presentation, and I'm watching *him.* I wonder if I should get him some popcorn. My eyes begin to sparkle as his eyes grow wide and the color drops out of his face. It seems he has stopped breathing. The questions about my supposed wife just trail off into silence.

He gets up and excuses himself taking the Wi-Fi password. He doesn't shake my hand goodbye and then he runs down the hall back to his apartment. He moved out the next week without saying goodbye or thank you.

259

At 4:30, just as I am waking from my afternoon nap I hear the elevator ding and Chuan's key turning the lock. The door opens and he bounces up and down with excitement running over to me for a happy weekend hug. This is our sweet routine that makes me smile from my head to my toes.

We have a little rest and catch up on our day. He tells me of the horrible traffic and the co-worker he hates. I tell him of the Arab boys at the pool and the Indian guy with the screen saver porn. Then we dress up for dinner. I put on my long black pinstriped skinny pants, my Liberty Print floral dress shirt and a spray of cologne. We grab our phones and we're off into the evening traffic jams bound for Alexis, the jazz club, for drinks and dinner.

I'm finally released from the cage and Alexis is my place of refuge. It is KL's own Rick's Café Americain. Emerging from the chaos of the streets, we part the thick black curtains that hide the entrance to the darkened jazz club. There might as well be a secret password at the door as this modern-day speakeasy features local and international jazz bands and discreet cocktails for the Malay who are forbidden from drinking. The tables are lit with candles, and the stage has a glossy black grand piano with a blue velvet backdrop. Someone named Sam might as well be seated at the piano playing *As Time Goes By*. Tonight, we are dining at the bar as all the tables are occupied.

"Chuan, do you have your BBC alerts on vibrate just in case we hear from the Supreme Court?" I ask him with a certain nervous anticipation. He pulls his phone out of his pocket, checks it, and we sit at the bar to order a pizza.

I'm busy trying to explain to the cook behind the bar how I would like my pizza. "Can you make it a little smaller and thicker rather than big and thin like a cracker?" He cuts half of the dough off and makes it smaller.

"No, no, no! Put that dough back. I don't want a *tiny* thin crust pizza, I want a thicker pizza." He doesn't understand, so

I go behind the bar to show him which raises the eyebrows of all the staff — this just is not done. I can feel Chuan bracing for yet another clash of the cultures when I see him pull his phone out of his pocket. I stop and watch him. I know it's time to be hearing from the Supremes. He reads the notice and holds the phone up to me to come and look. His face is emotionless. Oh no, I thought, they've ruled against marriage equality.

I drop what I'm doing with the pizza and return to the side of the bar I belong on and read the BBC alert off his phone. "The US Supreme Court has ruled that same-sex marriage is a legal right across the United States."

My breathing is heavy and tears fill my eyes. All that we as gay people have fought for is now at our fingertips. The freedom to live together as first class citizens in my own country is now a possibility.

"Chuan, you know what this means, don't you? The Supreme Court is the final word. We can move to America if you want. You could get permanent residency," I say.

"Yes hubby. Did you tell them you want your arugula on the pizza *after* the baking or before?"

"Chuan! This is HUGE! This is the game changer. We have full federal rights of immigration. We could get married and you could get permanent residency in the States now," I start getting irritated that he's not getting the gravitas of this moment.

"Yes, Hubby, I know. Let's talk about that later, OK?" he calmly pleads with me to drop it.

"Well, would you like to come to America to live?" I ask him not wanting to wait until later.

"Hubby, I told you we're going to stay together forever and if you want to move to the States, then we are going together."

I sit back on my bar stool and sip from my drink knowing that if my pizza comes out right, I will have gotten everything I have ever wanted in my life. My pizza comes out just perfect, and I eat it while reading Justice Anthony Kennedy's majority opinion for the court out loud to Chuan. I can barely get the words out without choking up:

"No union is more profound than marriage, for it embodies the highest ideals of love, fidelity, devotion, sacrifice, and family. In forming a marital union, two people become something greater than once they were. As some of the petitioners in these cases demonstrate, marriage embodies a love that may endure even past death. Their hope is not to be condemned to live in loneliness, excluded from one of civilization's oldest institutions. They ask for equal dignity in the eyes of the law.

The Constitution grants them that right...it is so ordered."

The band takes the stage and for the first time in a long time, in a dim little gin joint half way around the word, I feel a sense of pride as an American. If the only reason to stay in Malaysia is Chuan, and if he's willing to leave, then maybe it's time to go home.

Coincidentally, on the way home from Alexis, we passed by a massive new billboard advertising the latest Apple iPhone and featuring a panoramic photograph of the desert at sunset near my home in Tucson. I couldn't believe it.

"Chuan, look at that!" I yelled, pointing as we zoomed past it. "That billboard — that's *Tucson!* I know where they shot that picture. It's not far from the house. What are the chances of us seeing a billboard of Tucson here in KL of all places just as we're thinking about moving there? Isn't that amazing? You know, they say there are no coincidences, whoever 'they' is," I prattle on.

"Yes, Hubby, I'm driving."

CHAPTER 30
PARTING GLANCES

I didn't propose marriage to Chuan that night though I did think about it. When you've lived your whole life as a second-class citizen, it takes some adjusting to realize that we have been granted all the rights and privileges that everyone else has always had. It's like when a chicken raised in a cage is set free and then stays in the cage. Really, I can get married now? Even the word "husband" feels so foreign on my tongue. I found it hard to believe that my husband could have the right to a green card like every other spouse of an American citizen.

That evening I watched the White House being lighted with rainbow colors. No, no, no. This can't be happening — when did America become so progressive? I was in Thailand watching on the BBC when gays were suddenly allowed to serve openly in the military. Each time I've returned to the US, my status as a gay man has gone up a notch.

To marry or not to marry became our elephant in the room. Should Chuan come to the US on a tourist visa and see what he thinks of America or should we apply for a fiancée visa, get married, and *then* apply for permanent residency? We tossed these questions around for months. Chuan joked that every time I got down to tie my shoelaces, he thought I was going to propose. He never said what his answer would be.

In the end, we decided to go for the tourist visa. Applying for a fiancée visa put too much pressure on us to get married after only a year of being together. Marriage seemed premature. Chuan would go through the ridiculously scrutinizing process of getting a B2 visa but then would have the right to visit the US at any time for the next 10 years. He submitted bank statements, letters of reference, property deeds and pay stubs. If he got his visa, I promised him a grand tour of Arizona, California, Oregon, and then a trip to Florida to meet my parents. After all *that,* if he was still interested in living in the US, then we would go forward with marriage and a green card.

The day of his interview at the US embassy, I was like a nervous expectant father. I taught at Zotung that morning frequently checking my pocket to see if he had texted me. Finally, on the way home from my class, Chuan texted me that he had had his interview and that he was granted his visa. I called him right away.

"Congratulations, Chuan! That's such good news."

"I'm coming to America! Yay, yay, yay! But Hubby, the woman who interviewed me asked me where I would be staying. I told her I would stay with you and then she asked if you were my boyfriend. Everyone at the counter could hear, so I told them that we were just friends. I didn't want everyone in the embassy to hear that I'm gay."

"Wow, that's so invasive. Especially in a Muslim country. They are trying to test you to see if you have 'intent to reside' in the US," I explained. "Welcome to America. Customs and Border Protection can make your life miserable."

That night we began watching documentaries about the US. I started him off with *American Experience* on PBS. I was trying to get him familiar with what he could expect in America and how we became the country we are today. I bribed him with popcorn, but by the time the wagon trains set out across America, he was sound asleep on the sofa.

The air pollution in Malaysia was reaching an all-time high in 2015. The "haze" was so bad that from the 29th floor, I couldn't see the ground. I had to wear my face mask to go to the garbage chute down the hall.

I texted my American expat teacher friend Cynthia to ask her if she would rather be gunned down in fresh air in America or have her purse snatched in the smog of Malaysia? Her answer: "Be gunned down in fresh air...just saying." My thoughts exactly. I'd rather face all the disappointments of my wacko country than to not be able to breath the air.

My lungs simply couldn't tolerate the smog and I developed another lung infection which gave me a hacking cough like a heavy smoker. Chuan, the master of home remedies insisted that if he hit me hard on the back, it would dislodge some of the gunk piling up in my lungs.

"Take a deep breath, Hub, and when you are exhaling quickly, I'll hit you on the back."

I breathed in and when he hit me a moth ball sized wad of green goo came flying out of my mouth and landed on the white tile floor. We both looked at it like it was an alien hatchling. I got closer to it and poked it to see if it was alive. It stuck to my finger. It was the consistency of rubber cement.

In the morning, I made breakfast for Chuan and gave him his face mask to wear on his way to work. "The pollution index is at 184 today: DANGEROUS. Do you want the red, green, or white mask?" I asked.

"Hmm. Which one goes with my outfit?"

"Your mask and shoes should match, so take the white one." He strapped on the mask and off he went to the elevator. I quickly sealed the door gap with a towel. That morning I did some research on air pollution in Asia and found the chilling statistics in the *New York Times* that 4,400 people die *every day* in China from pulmonary diseases attributed to air pollution. I looked out the window at the smog, and promptly booked my return flight to the US. I couldn't wait any longer for Chuan. I had 115 days left of this house arrest and was not sure how I would make it through.

Moving away from a place is like dying and being allowed to attend your own funeral, only worse because you have to be there for the un-fun parts like getting rid of furniture, cleaning out the fridge, and the junk drawers. The fun parts are the farewell luncheons, the free drinks people buy you, folks coming forth to say goodbye, and the friends sending the crying face emoticons. These are the same people who normally are too busy to see you, who, had they made time for you during your tenure in this place, you might not have moved. Leaving is a chance to take stock of your life and see where you might possibly have had an impact or made a difference in someone's life, even in a small way.

Take for example one of my main pet peeves in life: unconscious use of resources, wastefulness, and littering. I've complained bitterly about Asia's reckless use of plastics. How many times have I purchased an item and handed the cashier my own bag only to have them put my items in a plastic bag anyway. And then when I say, "No! No plastic," they put the new plastic bag in my re-used bag. Now I have doubled my own bag population and not for lack of trying. I simply cannot get my message across in Asia. Not in concept. Not in practice.

But the other day something miraculous happened. I was shopping at my apartment's mini market store in the lobby. The same Bangladeshi guy who has served me probably a hundred times, took my milk and put it in a new plastic bag, to which I quickly responded, "No plastic bag, thanks," with the same eye-rolling false patience I've had since day two. And he looked at me and smiled for the first time in over a year and said, "Oh, sorry. Save the environment!" I was so surprised I didn't know what to say. It caught me completely off guard that I tripped on my response, "Um yeah, save the environment." I repeated it just to feel the glory of the words rolling off my tongue and into understanding ears, finally. "Save the environment. Yes, exactly. Thank you." And I stood there beaming like a parent whose child finally used the potty.

Ho-ly cow. The cashier paid attention to what I had said on scores of previous occasions and he even understood why. He hadn't initiated actually saving the bag, but at least he got the concept instead of thinking I was just some annoying expat who prefers to carry his milk carton in his hands...how weird. I relayed the story as a minor triumph to Chuan. "Good for you, Hubby," was his stock response. I think he thinks maybe I should choose bigger battles.

Then a couple days later, Chuan and I were on the elevator and the same Bangladeshi cashier stepped on, pressed his button and proceeded to look down at the floor as most foreign workers do, avoiding eye contact with everyone. I thought the intersection of our lives was fortuitous — I've never see him on the lift in my building. So, I said to him with a big smile of acknowledgment, "Hey, save the environment." His bindi-ed face came alive and he responded, "Yes, yes, save the environment." And he stepped off, our short social interaction ending at the garage level. Chuan looked at me with a face of "Why are you talking to the foreign workers?" The beauty of this moment, however, was not lost on me.

Without a doubt the largest contribution I have made to Malaysia wasn't even to Malaysia as much as the world community. It was my teaching English to the Burmese kids.

I gave my last class just before Christmas, 2015. The students had decorated the room with donated tinsel and wreaths. A dirty statue of Santa Claus sat on my desk at the front of the room, its cotton balls of snow all soiled and gray.

Dim Dim wore a special bow in her hair on my last day of teaching. She showed it to me turning her head to the side, "Look teachuh!" Tamwa Oo got out the folders and put a water bottle on the desk for me. When it came time to say goodbye, the kids all came forth and hugged me like they meant it.

It's not likely I will ever see Dim Dim, Tamwa Oo, or Joel again. The other students I had over the year and a half of teaching had moved on to other schools, were resettled to other countries, or died on the street here. But wherever they are, I think a fast-fading part of me lives in them and an enduring part of them lives in me. Maybe they will remember my words of the day like forgiveness, cooperation, and respect. Did I help them with their past tense verbs and prepositions? Sure. More importantly, I saw them as human beings in a place where they are illegal and treated like rats by the government. Of all things in Malaysia, I will miss them the most.

If I look back at the reason I moved to Malaysia, I would say that I *did* achieve what I came here for — I found it in abundance in Chuan. In my time here in Malaysia, countless people have asked me, "What brings you to KL?" I've fumbled for the answer saying anything from, "I wanted to get away from the US for a while," (which always raises suspicions that I'm some sort of fugitive) to, "I came to Malaysia to find love." That's a more truthful answer and one that made no sense to anyone here and didn't make any sense to anyone in the US until I found Chuan, then everyone got it. One could say that the real reason I went to Malaysia was to find Chuan.

A mission of love, though, is the business of someone from a developed nation, a privilege of little consequence in a place that is more caught up with survival than such tender matters. And so, I abandoned revealing the truth about my intent here just as I abandoned my enthusiasm for the place a year in.

I had my fun and anguish in the 19 months of living in Malaysia, but the scales were tipped a little too much to the latter. I admitted that I simply couldn't make my life work there. True to the epiphany of the yellow bus, I found the one missing piece in my American life. I'm grateful for the handful of beautiful people I met along the way, as one always does even in the dreariest of places.

Do I have any regrets? Yeah, I shouldn't have eaten those candlenuts, and I shouldn't have scratched that guy's car. I should have wailed with Hang Thung Lia's grieving mother, and I should have tried the chocolate camel's milk. I should have picked up a few cartons of cow's urine from the grocery store as souvenirs — perhaps stocking stuffers for Christmas? Who doesn't love a carton of ruminant urine as a housewarming gift? But that's about it — there's almost nothing I miss about Kuala Lumpur except the Burmese kids and sitting with a drink overlooking the city during a monsoon.

In a few more days all the furniture will be gone, the piano will sit un-played in the store where I found it, the bed stripped of all its late-night cuddles, the yellow carpet rolled up, and the curtains on the magnificent view pulled tightly shut. The smell of Chuan's baking will be scrubbed off the walls, the oven sent to his Aunt Louise, the pots and pans to Aunt Eve. The air conditioner will be switched off and the hot, humid air will overtake the apartment. Chinese New Year fireworks will go unheard by my ears this year and Chuan's nightmares will go un-comforted when he returns to his bunk bed in his mother's apartment where he lived before our lives intersected.

My plane bound for the States leaves just after the sun casts its first orange light between the Petronas Towers onto my former home. In my 30 hours of flying I will go from being rich and exotic to being poor and ordinary, and my name ceases to be "Boss." I will return to being just another middle aged white face, but this time I won't be suffering about it...Chuan has booked his flight too and arrives in the States in just a couple of months.

Leaving Chuan behind was terribly painful but it's always harder for the one staying behind. The night before my flight, we closed the door on the last guest who came to say goodbye. The moment I clicked the door shut, Chuan melted into my arms and wept — one of the only times since we met.

"Oh Hubby," was all he could get out before his sobs echoed in the empty apartment. I took him to the bedroom and we lay on the bed while he wet my shoulder.

"Shh, shh, shh. I know. Having a bi-national relationship means long periods of separation. But we will be together in just 2 and a half months. Remember we will be together forever."

I have been amazed at Chuan's personal strength in difficult situations, but now I was leaving him with the unenviable task of closing up the apartment after my departure. It would be up to him to finish the packing and return the keys to the landlord.

He drove me to the airport early the next morning. We held hands tightly all the way — this time even in traffic — onlookers be damned. For the last time, we passed under the billboard of President Barack Obama shaking hands with the baby-faced Malaysian Prime Minister Najib Razak.

We parked at the airport, and Chuan came in with me. I checked my luggage, and we walked together to the point of departure. We had a goodbye hug more passionate than 2 men in a Muslim country should have without raising suspicion. I'm sure people thought I was his teacher or that he was my tour guide. I watched him disappear in the teeming crowd with the same spring in his step that I'd always seen.

He returned to our empty apartment and by the time I got to Tokyo, he texted me that it was just too painful to be there on his own so he invited his friends to come help. Chuan dropped off large bags of pots, pans, art supplies, and towels to the Burmese kids and David, the headmaster. They said, "Thank you. Do you have a sofa?" Chuan texted me a picture of himself with the kids and the headmaster standing on the street with all the donated items. I found it almost too painful to look at. And that was the last I heard from any of them.

Cross an ocean, start a new chapter.

CHAPTER 31
FULL CIRCLE

*M*y re-entry to the US was through Denver, Colorado. After an all-night flight from Tokyo, I wandered the Denver airport looking for something to eat and was struck by how friendly and service-oriented Americans are. "Hello, welcome! What can I get for you? How's your day going? Would you like something to drink? Cups are here if you would like water. Great. Thanks. Awesome. Have a nice day!" I was returning from a country not known for its smiling service sector or its free water. Americans aren't renowned for their deep sincerity but somehow when someone smiles and greets you and asks how you are, you feel a little less lonely. So, I'll take fluffy insincerity now after a long period of gruff sincerity, even if the good cheer really is directly linked to the tip jar.

I took my sandwich and "home baked" cookie to a table and sat near a middle-aged Jewish couple in polar fleece jumpers. They were chatting about their son's college, the coming snow storm, and whether they would get out before it arrived (things you simply don't hear about in Malaysia). I enjoyed having 100% comprehension of all chatter around me. In Asia, I drifted into public isolation as most of what was spoken around me, about me, or at me, made no sense. It became a drone of inscrutable gibberish — background noise. I had no chance of ever getting to the bottom of anything. Foreigners must accept what they get and not ask questions — a tough proposition for Americans who really want to know everything. We are a curious people, and we are generally allowed our curiosity within the confines of our own country. In the US, you can complain without fear of the dreaded "save face" whereby Asians will disappear you in a snap if you criticize them in any way. But here, a defensive American might just shoot your head off if you criticize him. That's called "shut up and save your own face."

271

Perhaps the NRA should claim that the reason Americans are so friendly is attributable to gun ownership.

I also noticed that I'm instantly invisible in America. Although almost no one is exotic in America because of its multi-ethnicity, in Asia, I savored being exoticized. It did have its perks. People usually had a little more respect for me than I get here. In Malaysia, they listened to me if they could understand me or looked at me with fascination if they couldn't. And it often got me off the hook — a white person in Asia is, in their eyes, more trustworthy than a local. Then there were the monetary expectations — it was presumed that I was rich because of the color of my skin. If only they knew that I go to half-price taco night at Rubio's and the free day at the art museum every month.

I walked in the front door of my house in Tucson, Arizona, after being away for the better part of 2 years and got my first whiff of the old place. The smell was familiar and comforting — a combination of wool rugs and linseed oil on teak furniture. The house seemed like a museum of my life — as if all had been put on hold while I was traveling the world.

The first thing I said to a housemate after I hauled my suitcases over the threshold and closed the door behind me was, "Where does one begin the task of repatriation?" The profundity of the moment was lost on him as he, a true American, didn't get up from the TV. It wasn't, however, lost on me. I had, after all, turned my back on this place, this house, this everything. None of what I walked away from had changed in my absence, and yet here I was happy to be back where I started. What had changed was me. I was returning to my old life with a new twist — a changed man. A loved man.

I've marked my piecemeal achievements of manhood at various points in my life: buying my first house, bringing my first boyfriend home to my parents, the first death of a loved one, the first time I tried to kill myself, starting a non-profit, watching it fail. Now this — becoming an expat and repatriating. Living overseas can grow you up, especially if you live in the not-so-glamorous overseas.

I cast away what billions of people would consider the winning lottery ticket of life: residency in America. I didn't revoke my citizenship, but I swore I wasn't ever going to live in the US again. A gritty 19 months in Malaysia made me rethink that. This adventure brought me to my knees, quite literally many times — on my knees before a toilet vomiting my delicate Western guts out. For all that I bitterly complained about America, Malaysia was worse, way worse. Other than a few places I visited in Europe and New Zealand, I'd say that the whole world is a lot worse off than America. Knowing this put me in the uncomfortable position of being both grateful for the bounty and stunned by the ingratitude of Americans who have never seen how the rest of the world lives with so much less.

One of the things I noticed immediately when I arrived in Tucson was the resounding quiet. Malaysia is a densely-populated country with 30 million citizens and over 2 million foreign workers, plus tourists all crammed into a country about the size of the state of New Mexico, which by the way, has a population of 2 million. There's just no way to cram that many people into a small land mass and have it be tranquil. Add to the pile 21 million motor vehicles, 9 million of which are motorcycles, half of which don't have mufflers. My ears were ringing and I didn't even know it. It was so quiet in my Arizona living room that I found it both eerie and hypnotic. I lay in bed at night with Asia still ringing in my ears — I simply couldn't get the buzzing motorcycles out of them.

Silence in the desert is a formidable presence — the quiet presses into your head. It can either seem deeply relaxing or it can drive you to distraction. Two weeks after my arrival, I'm still sitting in silence in my backyard in awe of this phenomenon of emptiness. The only buzzing here is the sound of bees and hummingbirds visiting all the flowers in my garden. I find myself enormously grateful for air I can breathe and water I can drink straight out of the tap.

Last night, something significant happened: I fell asleep and slept the entire night without the use of white noise or earplugs. In Malaysia, my white noise generator covered everything from the ungodly early call to prayer, to the midnight motorcycle-racing on the streets, to the commuter train 30 floors below that rattled the building every 2 minutes. All the unintelligible chatter of languages, the moan of mosques and machinery left 9,000 miles behind me, I now sit here in my house stunned by what was missing from my life: nothingness. Delicious nothingness. I can open the front door and it's quieter outside than inside.

Returning after being gone so long, I found myself waking up in the middle of the night not knowing where I was. I would reach for Chuan for comfort and hit the wall. I would wake up in the morning thinking I just had a very vivid dream about some strange and exotic place with people following me licking their lips, lilting languages, and squiggly things in buckets. My disorientation lasts for just about 5 seconds before I realize that I am back home. This is what it's like to be a stranger in your own bed.

Repatriating also means giving up the role of being an interloper — an observer in someone else's country. To return to your own country bestows upon you the responsibility and obligation that if there's anything in this place you don't like, it's up to you to change it. In Malaysia, I was only a bystander and a witness. There I marveled at the corruption of their prime minister and how he pulled off one of the grandest embezzlement schemes of all times, artfully crushing all resistance. Ironically, now back in America during an election year, I'm faced with the possibility of Donald Trump becoming president — someone equally corrupt and potentially *far* more dangerous than Malaysia's leader.

CHAPTER 32
HERE AND THERE

huan and I stayed in touch daily by our global chat apps. Because of the 15-hour time difference, I would tuck him in at night as I was just waking up in the morning. This went on for a couple months while he began to pack his life into 2 suitcases. He quit his job and got his paperwork in order just in case he decided to stay and get married. "Just in case," we would say with a wink.

We did a video chat from his mother's apartment the night before he left Malaysia. She wanted to speak to me directly. Uh oh. Chuan handed her the phone and her face appeared on my small iPhone. I noticed again how pretty she was and I saw her son's face in hers.

"Hello David-a. Just want to let you-a know-a…is a very hard to give up my son. Chinese mothers they don't like-a to give up son-a. I want to know he will be in good hands-a in America-a. You understand-a, David?" I could see that she was overwhelmed with emotion.

"I want you to know he'll be in good hands here. He will

have a nice home and big piano to play." I reassured her and gave her a quick visual tour of the house including a look at the 7-foot grand piano that she knew Chuan would love.

"Sank you, David-a. Oh, very nice house. You take-a good care my son, la. OK-a. Must go now." Then she handed the phone back to Chuan. For all the criticism I had leveled at his mother for trying to undermine our relationship, I got the poignancy of her plea. I appreciated that she seemed to be coming to grips with the reality that her son was unstoppable.

Before I went to bed, Chuan texted me on his way to the airport. "I'm on my way. I'll be there in 30 hours. I'm excited to be starting a new life with my Hubby," he wrote. His 2 closest friends Wai Tuck and Hao Yen drove him to the airport. He texted me a photo of them all crying, Hao Yen wearing a shirt I had given him when I was cleaning out the apartment. I somehow felt responsible for breaking up his family and his friendships.

On the day of his arrival, in April, 2016, I puttered about the house nervously putting the finishing touches on cleaning and decorating. I found a small American flag in Sebastian's box of things that he left in the closet years ago. With a sigh, I plucked it from the box and put it back into service. I put a chicken stew in the solar oven, mopped, dusted, and washed the sheets while listening to 40s housewifey music. I waited for news of his arrival at the Dallas airport. He arrived and sailed right through Customs — the American B2 visa was golden. He wasn't even asked anything about his trip or to show proof of his outbound flight.

"I'm here! I want my green card!" were his first words. I was sitting by the pool wondering why he said that. Was this all a big ploy to get a green card in America?

"Well, if that's all you want, then you can go back or stay with someone else," I angrily texted back to him.

"What? Why are you saying that?" he asked.

Sensing this chat was not going well, I called him right away. He was just teasing me and was exhausted from the flight. I had to remember that even with Chuan, some things are simply lost in translation, particularly in matters of humor. We grew up, after all, a generation apart and a world away — what's funny to him is often completely lost on me.

"Hubby, everyone is so big here! And they sell cowboy hats in the convenience stores at the airport." Big people and cowboy hats — his first impressions of America, and his first time seeing anything outside of Asia.

"I warned you that you would be arriving in Texas," I told him. "Look, you'll be in Tucson in a couple hours, and we don't wear cowboy hats here. I made a nice stew for you. We will meet you at the airport soon. I'm so excited!"

My other housemate Trish and I stopped and got some flowers for him on the way to the airport. We stood at the bottom of the escalator where arriving passengers run into the arms of their families. I was looking forward to giving him a big, juicy kiss. Then I noticed all of a sudden that I was surrounded by Muslims. Women in hijabs and men with long beards. I started to feel a little inhibited by their presence and was wondering why the Tucson airport, of all places, should suddenly be filled with Muslims. This seemed like some little poke in the face from Allah who maybe felt that I left a Muslim country without making peace with its religion. I never liked the calls to prayer interfering with my sleep, and I popped that champagne cork over a Muslim neighborhood once in Langkawi.

Chuan appeared on the TV monitor before he appeared in person. And then I had my first sight of him descending the escalator into what could be his new home. There he was, the only Asian in the crowd, in his navy blazer with a folded napkin in the breast pocket as a sartorial flourish, his bright smile making me quiver.

"Welcome to Tucson, Hubby," I said as I threw my arms around him, handing him the American flag. He seemed a little uncomfortable with the public affection, especially when surrounded, as he always has been, by Muslim people.

277

"You can kiss me here, Chuan. It's perfectly legal," I reminded him. He changed the subject.

"Hubby, the flight attendants on American Airlines are so old," was the first thing he could think to say.

Trish handed him the bouquet of flowers and welcomed him with a big hug. We collected his luggage and walked outside into the crisp, dry, desert air holding hands, a special treat we could never have in Malaysia. A 20-foot saguaro cactus towered over the parking lot.

"Oh, I saw that in the Road Runner cartoon," he said, stopping for a picture to send back to his friends of the giant cactus that looks like a headless green man with one arm akimbo.

"I feel like I need to text my Hubby in Malaysia to tell him I met this cute Asian guy at the airport. Chuan, I need to poke you to see if you're real," I told him.

It seemed hard to believe that he had finally arrived — the big, bouncy kid I met half-way around the world based on some cockamamie notion that I would find love in Kuala Lumpur. And then, here it is. Here *he* is.

Trish and I drove Chuan back to the house. We lifted his suitcases out of the trunk in the parking lot and rolled them up to the front door of our homely, 2-story brick townhouse. Coyotes yapped in the distance like crying babies. He seemed startled by the noise.

"Don't worry, they're harmless to people. Welcome home, Hubby," I told him as we stepped over the threshold. He looked around curiously at the softly lit interior. He then went right for the piano to give it a little tickle before examining the rest of the house, taking in the smells of the stew and noticing the eclectic thrift-store mix of furniture and original artwork. With its brown tile, earth-tone tapestries, and brick fireplaces, this house is the antithesis of an Asian household where the spare white box as a design concept rules. I spent too much time picking hairs off the glossy floors in Malaysia, but this house would swallow hair forever in the brocades and clashing patterns of rugs and silk wall hangings, 70s-era sofa, and dim track lighting.

We sat down at the table for a homemade dinner. "I made this stew in the solar oven. It cooked all day in the sun and didn't use any electricity," I told him spooning some into a bowl. That didn't seem to impress him, or it just befuddled him. Conservation of resources isn't really a priority in Malaysia where power is cheap and to cook with the sun would require a clear, sunny day.

"Soooo...what do you think?" I asked looking around.

"I like," was his typical slightly laconic answer.

"But you don't *love*." I felt a little disappointed that he didn't seem thrilled about the house or the piano.

"No, I like. I *like* it. It's nice...and quiet. The piano is a bit bright, don't you think?" Chuan at his core is Chinese — a people not widely known for their passionate expressions of pleasure and gratitude. I could take him to the Grand Canyon and he would say, "Is that all there is? It's a big hole." (I did do that, and he did say just that.)

I tucked him into bed for his first night of sleep and told him I would be waking him up early so we could hit the road and explore Tucson by bicycle. This would get him adjusted to the huge time difference. We folded into a cuddly little ball, making the house into a home for the first time since Sebastian left 6 years before.

I woke Chuan at 8am and presented him with a bag of gifts — his Arizona survival kit of lip balm, sunscreen, a water bottle, and most importantly, a pair of tweezers. "Everything in Arizona bites, stings, or pricks. So here, keep these tweezers in your bag and remember to stay hydrated — it's not like Asia. It's so dry here that your eyelids will stick to your eyeballs giving you the impression of being excited. Now get up, it's time to show you around. Hubby, it's your first day in America!" I think my wit was lost on him in his jetlagged state.

I saddled him up for a 15-mile bike ride and a day of

firsts. The first stop was a crosswalk. "Go ahead and push the button. Try it out," I told him. "It is where Americans will wait in their cars for you or they will be sued to kingdom come." He pushed the button and stood at the curb in wide-eyed amazement while 4 lanes of traffic came to a grinding stop, waiting for him.

"Come on," I beckoned. He stood incredulous and unsure about crossing the boulevard. He eased into the intersection and then met me on the other side with a gratified smile.

"Amazing, huh? Chuan, in Malaysia, they will run you the fuck over, but not here. Drivers live in fear of being sued and as a pedestrian, you have the right of way. That may take some getting used to, but American drivers in general are very courteous." I felt some sense of pride sharing this.

We cycled through an up-market neighborhood surrounding the University of Arizona. Old, custom-built houses sit back from the quiet, tree-lined streets. Magenta bougainvillea flowers flow over white-washed adobe walls. He took in all the sights no doubt comparing these unique homes to the barbed wire gates of nondescript homes in KL's suburbs.

"I like that one," he said pointing out a stark white 1940s Taos Pueblo style home. "And that one," pointing to a 1930s Spanish revival house with terra cotta tile roof.

"Pretty aren't they? I know Tucson isn't the most beautiful place in America, but it's not bad. And you know, Tucson is the only UNESCO City of Gastronomy in the country. I have a great lunch place in mind." His eyes lit up.

We stopped in at the University to take a peek at the music school. We ran into a friend of mine who is the head of the piano department who invited him into his office with 2 Steinway grand pianos. He asked Chuan to play something for him. Chuan sat at one of the pianos and played a very difficult Bach prelude, his untrimmed fingernails clicking like a dog's toenails on a wooden floor. Dr. Milbauer listened carefully, scratching his chin and nodding his head in approval.

"Very nice. Well, if you can play like that for an audition, you would not only be accepted to the music school, but you would most likely get a scholarship. But you're going to have to cut your nails."

Chuan was elated. Finally, something made him gush with enthusiasm. "Wow, Hubby! You really think I could get a degree in piano performance?" he asked me in utter disbelief outside the music building.

"Of course you can, but you're going to have to deal with general ed...like algebra and social studies and I know how much you *love* history." I reminded him how his eyes glazed or he fell asleep every time I even mentioned anything about history.

"Let's continue our tour of Tucson. Next stop is lunch at my favorite Mexican restaurant downtown." We cycled there with him complaining all the way about his butt on the seat. I cringed watching him drive through stop signs.

"Yo! Sweetheart, in America, stop means STOP," I yelled ahead to him. "You have to fully stop and touch down or you'll get a ticket — even on a bicycle. People in the US pay attention to signs and street lights. Oh, and your butt will adjust to the seat in time." He wasn't sure about my car-free lifestyle — no one in Malaysia gets by with just a bicycle. Not owning a car in Malaysia would be a serious mark on his status and people would take great pity upon him.

We sat down at the colorful Mexican restaurant after a forced hug from the effusive proprietor. We ordered some chicken with molé sauce and listened to the goofy, loud ranchero music.

"It's tuba and accordion. That's the legacy of Emperor Maximillian and the Austrian occupation of Mexico," I explained. His mind drifted off until the food arrived with heaping mounds of meat, beans, and tortillas. He was astonished by the portion sizes compared to the puny ones of Malaysia.

"So huge, the portions! And Hubby, why does that woman hug all the customers?"

"Yeah, that's why Americans are so giant. You're going to have to learn to order less here or soon you'll be driving around Walmart in a mobility scooter looking for stretch pants. You'll get used to the hugs."

Last stop on the way home was Trader Joe's grocery store. He had heard me speak of it before. Being as food-oriented as he is, he was fascinated by the place. It took us almost an hour to get through just a few aisles as he wanted to examine each and every package and check the prices and convert them to ringitts. He was amazed at how expensive everything was except alcohol. They had 6-packs of microbrew beers for $5.99, the price of one semi-decent beer in Malaysia.

On the way home, we nearly ran over a snake on the bike path. I freaked out, "STOP! OK, back up very slowly." I yelled, holding my hand out to alert Chuan. "They're pit vipers and they can see your heat," I explained. The 4-foot diamondback rattler was slowly crossing the pavement and not at all interested in avoiding us. If that snake had a middle finger, it would have been pointed defiantly at us. Chuan was stunned to silence to see one of the creatures he had heard about and what we had come so close to running over. Our bare ankles would have been bitten for sure had I not seen it and stopped us. "You don't want to get bitten by one, Chuan, because the treatment for a rattlesnake bite is over $150,000 plus the helicopter ride. One bottle of the anti-venom is over $10,000!"

Our lives had inverted. Since I met Chuan, he had been my trusty companion and font of wisdom for all things Malaysian. He had done his very best to keep me out of harm's way in his home country. Now I was *his* caretaker, responsible for his every need. I taught him how to fix his bicycle and where to find the best croissant and coffee. I explained blue cheese and why the moon was visible during the day, why it got so cold at night, and that a dime was smaller than a nickel. But there was no explanation for America's obsession with pumpkin spice. "Hubby, pumpkin spice deodorant?" I guided him through the land mines of health insurance as best one can. I dissected the American persona for him encounter by encounter, and I warned him of what was to come.

"Chuan, you know this is an election year. Prepare yourself for a lot of political angst. It's all people will talk about this year and anything can happen, but I think Donald Trump doesn't stand a chance of being elected." Unfortunately, there was an uprising of disenfranchised, uneducated white people who have come to resent all the progress made by women, black people, brown people, and gays. They came out of the woodwork like termites in a house fire. My country was starting to look like the same racially charged hot mess that Malaysia is.

Had I known the outcome of the election, I probably would have advised we remain overseas and wait for this political storm to blow over. Now Chuan's possible permanent residency in the US would be endangered by a president taking aim at immigrants, especially immigrants from Muslim countries. Chuan was both.

CHAPTER 33
SUMMER OF LOVE

*I*n May, we left Arizona for the summer. We jumped aboard an Amtrak train bound for Los Angeles, San Francisco, and then Portland. This journey would give Chuan a sense of the scale of America — and a chance to see life outside my little desert bubble. As the train pulled out of the station in Tucson, we sat in the dining car waiting for dinner to be served. We had been in Tucson for almost a month.

"What do you think of Tucson, Chuan? Could you make this home? Could you see yourself living here?" I asked him over a glass of wine as the train rolled through the unsightly back alleys of Tucson.

"I think so. The people are nice. There's good food. The University has a really good music program. I think I could make my life in Tucson work."

"I know Tucson isn't super fabulous. The city is great for what it *isn't* — expensive, pretentious, and competitive. But I'll take you to see fabulous and then see what you think. Fabulous comes at a high price. You'll see," I told him with a wink.

After dinner, we lay down in our bunks as we chugged through the Sonoran Desert by moonlight. Bare hills and sand dunes were outlined in the pale gray light while the train gently rocked us to sleep. In the morning, we would be in California. I prepared him for the greatest, glitziest hot mess America has to offer: Los Angeles.

We got off the train before dawn to find breakfast and have a walk around downtown before catching a mid-morning train up the coast to the Bay Area. Our walk through the grand 1920s Union Station was punctuated by the yelling of homeless people being chased out by security. This was the high price of fabulous I had warned Chuan about.

Legions of people living in their own filth, carting all their belongings in shopping carts and bags were camped out on sidewalks and in the parks. Chuan was astounded to see this.

"Oh my god, how can this happen in such a wealthy country?" he asked. Malaysia's homeless situation is minimal — almost invisible. I had worked one night for a soup kitchen in Kuala Lumpur where about 100 polite and well-scrubbed homeless people orderly lined up for a meal. By contrast, Los Angeles has an estimated homeless population of nearly 60,000.

"America's priorities are all about the military and preservation of wealth. If there's anything seriously wrong in this country, you can almost always trace it back to greed," I explained as we stepped over mangled, gangrened legs laying across the sidewalk.

We returned to the station to continue our journey north. An upright piano sits in the lobby near the ticket kiosk inviting passersby to play. A homeless woman sat at the piano playing the same gospel tune over and over shaking her head like Stevie Wonder. I approached and asked her if we could share the piano so that Chuan could play. She reluctantly gave up the keyboard and Chuan took a seat to play Beethoven's Pathétique sonata. People stopped to listen while I stood by looking at their amazed faces. For a few moments on that hectic weekday morning, Chuan was calming a city on the verge of a nervous breakdown.

We continued our train ride up the Pacific coast and through the wine country toward San Francisco, disembarking after 2 days of train, in Emeryville. We spent a month house sitting in Marin County, having daily picnics by the Bay, at the beach in our down coats, or in parks in San Francisco trying to stay upwind of the homeless camps. We spent a couple of days in Monterey and at day at Esalen in Big Sur, his first time at a nude hot springs. I gave him a massage overlooking the Pacific with whales breaching below us.

"Chuan, sit up — there's a mama whale with its baby swimming by. You don't see that in KL, do you!?" We leaned on the railing looking out over the lapis lazuli Pacific checked with the gleaming white spouts of whales.

"What do you think of Esalen, Hubby? Isn't this the most beautiful place on earth?" I asked.

"It's nice. But the people are so self-absorbed. Everyone is like, me, me, me."

"Oh, you mean like that woman Spirit who talked endlessly about herself and then asked me for a cigarette?" I laughed.

Our tour continued on to Northern California and a one-day stop at Saratoga Springs, a rural resort in Lake County, for the Generate gathering. Generate is a spin-off of the Radical Faeries, kind of spiritual men's gathering that, "Invites you to soar high, dive deep, sit quietly, and dance joyously in exploration of what harmony is for you." What better way to immerse him in the last remaining vestiges of the California hippie culture than to take him to this gathering? The gathering was also a chance for him to let his hair down and experience something he'd never experience in Asia.

We walked into the verdant retreat center from the parking lot to join the group for lunch at the main lodge. We were greeted by a huge circle of men in various states of undress holding hands to give thanks for the food and the people who prepared it. I looked around the circle and made eye contact with many men I'd known for decades. They were eager to meet Chuan as they had read about him on my blog and welcomed him with big, naked, sweaty hugs.

Chuan checked the roster of "playshops" and decided to take the sacred spanking session at 3. I decided to take the self-guided nap workshop, until the drumming circle punched holes in my bliss and I went to the pool to sun my buns. Chuan emerged from his session invigorated. "Hubby, the teacher is a famous author and I met some really nice people — it was great!"

"Yeah, but did you get spanked? Let me see your red marks," I playfully demanded.

"No, the workshop was not really about spanking. It was about achieving altered states and connection. Breath and spaciousness," he said to me half mocking, half serious.

What? I couldn't believe my ears. It shocked me that he would be so brave to take that class, that he would actually enjoy the experience, and relay it to me in new age speak. He was starting to seem more American, more Californian than I was.

In advance of our arrival at the gathering, I had asked Chuan if he would work on a performance piece with me for the talent show. He very reluctantly agreed. My vision was that we would write a story, each in our own words, about how we met and fell in love in Malaysia. I wanted him to have the chance to appear in front of everyone and be seen, heard, and appreciated. I wanted our story to be known. What I didn't tell him was that there was going to be a big surprise ending.

We diligently worked on our performance, writing, editing, and rehearsing it several times before we left for the gathering. Before the show, I spoke to Seth, the master of ceremonies.

"Seth, Chuan doesn't know but I'm going to propose

marriage at the end of the piece. I know we are going to go over the time limit…"

He cut me off mid-sentence, "Take as much time as you want. This is a special moment and we're honored to have it in the show." I was thrilled and nervous and hoped Chuan didn't suspect something was up when he saw me talking to Seth.

The audience slowly poured in. Hundreds of alternative guys — guys in dresses, guys with beards, drag queens, naked guys. It was the Generate talent show — the highlight of the gathering and we were going to rock the show with a great story of love complete with a happy ending.

Seth introduced us and we took to the stage with our scripts. The audience silently waited for us to begin. Our friend Charlie played the piano as accompaniment and I began our story:

"This is the story of finding love in strange places, against all odds. I'm finally over my broken heart from my ex, Sebastian. When romantic loneliness becomes unbearable, where can a middle-aged white guy still turn heads? Asia!"

"Hello, hi, my name is Chuan. I'm Malaysian-born Chinese. I speak English, Malay, Cantonese, and Mandarin. I'm a hairdresser, classical pianist and I live with my mother and brother in our condo in Kuala Lumpur…"

We go on to tell how we met and began our relationship. I end the piece:

"We've been on an extraordinary journey against the odds of society and geography but here we are today — a personal triumph for us both — a shimmering example of the endurance of the human heart on its tireless journey for companionship here on our lonely little planet."

The audience applauds and cheers for us as we hug and kiss for the crowd. Chuan thinks the performance is over and begins packing up his script to leave the stage when I go into the audience and grab a pillow for my knee. He pauses and looks at me as I drop it to the floor before him. With one knee on the pillow, I take the scripts out of his hand and take his hands in mine. I say his name and then I lose my composure and am barely able to speak. Then he loses his. I look up at him and tears are streaming down his quivering face.

"You've been a wonderful boyfriend for almost 2 years now. I've waited most of my life for this moment and I want to bring this ship into the shore and ask you to marry me." I couldn't resist that cheesy REO Speedwagon line.

Chuan looks to the audience and says, "What do you think I should say?" Someone yells, "Think about it!" There's scattered laughter and some sobs.

"Of course, I'm gonna marry you," he says, lifting me off my knee pillow and into an embrace. The audience goes wild with a standing ovation. The whole thing was caught on film and posted to YouTube so our friends and family could enjoy it.

I was told later that some guys in the audience said, "I'm going to Malaysia on my next vacation." Seth came up to tell me how touching it was for everyone and that there wasn't a dry eye in the house. We were officially engaged that night in May, 2016. If only the wedding would have gone as smoothly.

CHAPTER 34
IN SICKNESS AND IN HEALTH

*C*huan and I were busy with our friend Jean at her house in Marin folding paper cranes, making starry crowns, and shopping for bling rings and party favors for the upcoming wedding. The ceremony would be conducted before 6 witnesses in the ornate rotunda of San Francisco's city hall, a place we chose as a nod to the birthplace of same sex marriage in America. We spent the preceding days shopping for a wedding cake and planning a menu for the reception to be held afterwards at some friends' house in San Francisco. That's when everything went wrong. Very wrong.

Really, no wedding is complete without a visit to the emergency room the day before. We were to be married on an ordinary Tuesday in August — 2 years to the day of our first meeting in Malaysia. Two days before the wedding, I began feeling a little feverish. Surely, I thought, this must be wedding jitters, just like the jitters I had before my first choral performance with the University of Arizona that gave me a giant sty in my eye. I went on stage that afternoon with one eye swollen shut, trying to sing Haydn's *Lord Nelson Mass* looking like a pop-eyed goldfish. Or like my debut performance singing with the Tucson Symphony Orchestra chorus when I got bronchitis and wheezed on stage like an old pump organ. The fever must be nerve-related and all I had to do was calm myself down and I'd be fine. Then the abdominal pain began. Maybe it was something I ate and nothing that a little Rolaids and a Benadryl couldn't cure, right?

I put myself to bed early that night leaving Chuan and Jean to make the party favor packets alone. In the morning, I would surely feel fine and we would begin putting together the reception menu. I woke with a high fever and lay in bed thinking, please god, don't let me be sick — in the course of a man's life, this is *the worst possible time to be sick*. This cannot be happening. My teeth chattered, my chest tightened and I pulled up the covers to stay warm in the guest room but I couldn't calm the shakes which had now become violent. The nausea became overwhelming so I stumbled downstairs to seek help from Chuan and Jean who were busy preparing deviled eggs.

Appearing at the kitchen door a pale and shaking ghost, I croaked out, "I'm really sick you guys and I don't know what to do." I ran to the sink and bent over. I felt Chuan's arm wrap around me as I was heaving something yellow down the drain.

"Oh dear! Hubby, I'm here," Chuan comforted me.

"Let's get you to the hospital right away," Jean said. I

protested because I wasn't sure my new health insurance plan would cover me in California.

"Wait! That could cost me thousands of dollars." I was feeling terribly helpless, perhaps about to become a casualty in America's health care crisis. Between the dry heaves and shaking, Chuan stuck a thermometer in my mouth and it came out at 103. This is not the jitters. This is *serious*.

"Chuan, can you get on the phone and call Blue Cross and ask them if I'm covered out of Arizona and which hospital I can go to if I can even *go* to a hospital?" He ran off and started dialing and handed me the phone. I sat on the sofa dealing with abdominal pain and what felt like death rattles coming in waves. I rushed the operator for an answer. "Hurry up! Don't ask me for my policy number again, I already gave it to you twice. This is an emergency! I think I have appendicitis."

"I'm sorry, sir, for purposes of security we need your home address and date of birth." I started yelling, taking out years of frustration with the train wreck of the American medical system on her. I could tell the operator was concerned that someone might die while she was asking me for the last four of my social security number.

After 2 transfers, they confirmed that I could go to any hospital in an emergency and that I would be covered. Chuan immediately ran upstairs and got my backpack stuffed with things in case I would need an overnight stay in the hospital.

Jean clicked the garage door opener and within minutes we were on the way to the Marin General emergency room at rush hour which meant being stuck in heinous Bay Area traffic. My fever shakes got violent for a few minutes and then settled down. In a calm moment, I called our friend Lawrence in San Francisco to tell him that the wedding might be off and to contact everyone on e-vite to let them know that there might not be a wedding reception after all.

By the time we arrived at the hospital, my shakes had strangely stopped. After the usual questions in triage, the nurses guessed it was appendicitis and so I was admitted to a room — my first time in a hospital in America — and thus began the questions, the poking, prodding, sampling, and waiting. There was some discussion about a CT scan to determine if I was indeed suffering from appendicitis but the doctor ruled it out after probing my belly. I curiously had no pain when he pressed and released quickly on my abdomen.

Chuan sat by my side holding my hand. Tears kept pouring out of my eyes. The vows that we might be saying tomorrow were unfolding before me now, "...in sickness and in health." I felt so embarrassed to be taking up this much attention on the day when we should be celebrating and having our own little double bachelor party. Instead I'm in a hospital with an unexplained fever and tubes in my arm. If I had ever questioned Chuan's devotion, I wasn't now.

"Chuan, thank you so much for being with me and taking such good care of me. You know, I am so lucky to have you," I told him.

"Hubby, we're gonna get married tomorrow and we'll be together forever," he assured me.

I noticed a woman playing a hand-held harp outside the room. Code blue announcements were being made in the hall. I wondered how many people died in this ward and the last thing they heard was that harp, thinking it was the angels coming to get them. I was in desperate need of a pee and asked the nurse's station where the bathroom was. They pointed it out to me.

"Hey, while you're at it, give us a sample, OK?" They handed me a container for a urine sample. I returned the jar to them with a nice cloudy sample of stinky pee. I guess I should have known. They looked at it with raised eyebrows and within 15 minutes, the doc came in to tell me that it tested positive for infection. They quickly put me on Levofloxacin and suggested that this was probably an acute prostate-related urinary tract infection — not a sexually transmitted one. A UTI is apparently not that uncommon in men of my age.

"I heard you're getting married tomorrow," the doc told me with a little chuckle as he sat down on his rolling chair to write notes in my folder.

"Yeah, some way to spend the day before, huh? I should be out at a titty bar." He noticed me holding Chuan's hand from the bed.

"Well, we're gonna get you patched up and at that altar tomorrow. The antibiotics should work quickly," he assured me. "And now for the hardest part. Tearing off the IV tape." Mother of god that *was* the hardest part of the day! I gripped the bed rail while Nurse Diesel yanked a 6-square inch patch of my fur off.

Four hours and $7,250 later, on the eve of my wedding day, I emerged from the hospital with a bald spot on my right arm and a sheet of paper that said, "No sex. No alcohol. Side effects of medication may include depression, anxiety, irritability, and suicidal thoughts." With a little side trip to the emergency room down a path of chastity, sobriety, and suicidal ideation, we were off to the altar to see about getting married after all.

We got home and my inbox was swamped with emails from people wondering what the hell had happened. I had to quickly respond to everyone that the wedding was on but we didn't get the chance to cook: "I'm fine. Just a UTI. Nothing to worry about. See you tomorrow. Bring pizza."

Feeling enormously grateful for health insurance and Sir Alexander Fleming, I fell into bed and set the alarm for 7 to get us to the city hall rotunda on time. Chuan was busy composing a group text message to his entire extended family in Malaysia and Hong Kong to tell them that not only is he gay but that he is marrying his boyfriend in San Francisco in the morning. He asked me to proof it before he sent it.

"It all looks good. That's pretty courageous of you to come out to everyone — even your grandparents," I said, encouraging him to hit send. He stayed up to wait for some of the responses. His brother gave his tacit acceptance: "If you feel that it's the right thing to do, then go ahead." Then his aunts and uncles and cousins all started sending their congratulations. He came to bed relieved and gratified. His mother had pretty much given up on trying to dissuade us from our marriage — what she had once called "that thing you're going to do next week." A week before, she was reminding Chuan of all the unhappy marriages in the family and cautioning him about getting into one himself. A little cold war ensued between mother and son, but a couple days before the wedding she finally waved her white flag and gave us her blessing. She did continue to send little texts of advice like, "Son don't always wear shorts. It's just not that pleasant," and "Son, read the paper so that you have something to talk about," and, "Son, think of your future."

In the morning, my fever was just over 100 and I was still feeling weak but not enough to cancel the wedding.

"Chuan wake up, today's your wedding day," I said, shaking him and throwing off the covers.

"You're feeling better, huh?" he groused.

We got dressed quickly to try and beat rush hour on the way into the city. I wore a vintage bow tie, vest with 7 brass buttons, and a brandy-colored pork pie hat. Chuan also wore a bow tie and his signature navy blazer with white napkin for a pocket square. We looked like eccentric thrift store queens. We sat in the back of Jean's little blue car as she raced us across the Golden Gate Bridge through the fog bank toward city hall. I was still feeling slightly dizzy and nauseous from the car ride when we parked and made our way through the homeless encampments in the plaza across from city hall.

As you push the gilded doors of city hall open, you enter what appears to be an inside-out wedding cake. It is a Beaux-Arts fantasy in marble swirls and cream plaster friezes that you just want to eat.

For a gay couple, getting married is not just a grand declaration of love, it is a political triumph. For us to walk up

295

the marble steps of city hall that morning with the expectation that we would be married was the culmination of decades of court battles, countless relationships shattered by beady-eyed bureaucrats who turned their backs on us refusing to issue marriage licenses. Entering this hallowed hall, holding hands and bearing wedding rings was no small feat, both politically and personally.

Beams of filtered sunlight stream in from the rotunda windows shedding light on a rich and dark history. San Francisco's city hall witnessed Marilyn Monroe and Joe DiMaggio's wedding in 1954. Years later, City Supervisor Harvey Milk and Mayor George Moscone were gunned down here in 1978 in an angry rage. Milk's bronze bust sits at the top of the stairs watching over all those who come to be hitched, gay and straight.

We made our way to the back corner of the hall to register with the clerk. A heterosexual black couple was all dressed up with corsages and bouquets, waiting to be married. Two young gay guys in ripped jeans, boots, and leather jackets sat waiting for their marriage license. We signed various papers and met with the woman who would be our officiant to perform the ceremony. She seemed incompetent and bumbling with a very thick Philippine accent with over-pronounced B's and P's. She looked like she was related to the Star Wars character, Yoda, and so we called her "Mrs. Yoda" but we had not yet seen her standing.

While she processed our paperwork, the guests were still arriving and looking radiant. A handful of friends came to bear witness to the occasion and we all proceeded to the top of the stairs under the rotunda awaiting our Justice of the Peace. Finally, she arrived, and behold, there she was — all 4½ feet of her — Mrs. Yoda, our pint-sized piece of Justice and trusty guide through the gates of holy matrimony. She started looking around and calling, "David...David?" I got all panicky and my fever surged before I realized that the couple to be wed before us also had a David in their party.

While we waited for the other couple to be married, our singer songwriter friend Lawrence unpacked his guitar and sang *Can't Help Lovin' Dat Man of Mine* for us. His sweet tenor voice echoing in the rotunda calmed our nerves and drew the attention of Chinese tourists who starting gathering around, snapping pictures and filming. Chuan and I stood clasping each other's cold, clammy hands. I was holding on to his hand half out of affection and half to keep from keeling over from residual fever and exhaustion. I kept checking my watch.

Finally, our time came and Mrs. Yoda beckoned us to the top of the stairs to get married, fittingly, in full view of the bronze bust of Harvey Milk. Chuan and I stood facing each other in front of the Justice and she began her ceremony softly and almost inaudibly. It sounded something like this:

...nurture your love carefully and watch your love grow, for mutual love between 2 people is the greatest gift of all...

At least I saw her mouth moving and her admiring eyes reading as she looked each of us in the eye, but I could barely hear her. With the ambient sound of the rotunda's live acoustics, the elevator bells dinging, and the murmur of the Chinese tourists who were watching, I simply had to go on memory of what she was saying from having seen this on YouTube previously. We leaned in closer to her and the nearer we drew, the fainter her voice became. Our circle tightened around her to the point that we were almost in a group hug hanging on Mrs. Yoda's every word. She was practically whispering in our ears.

Jean produced the handmade silver rings we had found in a craft shop in North Beach. We said our vows to each other and placed the rings on each other's fingers. The hardest part was to keep from bursting into tears about the whole process.

Mrs. Yoda went on amid the din of the rotunda:

...may you strive all of your lives to meet this commitment with the same love and devotion as you have on this day.... ding, ding....commitment....murmur, murmur....delight in each other's company, and never take the other for granted... murmur, murmur...greatest gift to share...ding, ding...by virtue of the authority vested in me by the State of California, I now pronounce you partners for life.

There was nothing about kissing the bride, so I spoke up, "Excuse me! Do I get to kiss the bride?" We all laughed, Chuan and I kissed and placed flower leis, sent by my cousin from Connecticut, on each other.

Chuan read some talking points from his iPhone, half laughing and half crying, and I stumbled, in a slightly delirious way, through some proclamations of love for Chuan. I had planned on writing something more formal beforehand but instead I had spent the day in the hospital, so I improvised. Sweat was running down my arms and pant legs. I felt I could pass out from the combination of nerves and fever. Looking into Chuan's wet eyes only made it more difficult to speak. I said something about not deserving Chuan. As a finishing touch, and to give credit where credit is due, Chuan and I posed for pictures kissing the bronze cheeks of Harvey Milk on either side of his bust.

For the Chinese tourists circulating around us, our wedding was a bonanza of WeChat posts: they got to film a same sex, Caucasian-Asian, age-divergent marriage in ground zero for the gays that surely, they had read about. And so, on the 2nd year anniversary, on the opposite side of the planet from where Chuan and I had met in Kuala Lumpur, we were wed. No one from either of our families attended. No one had believed the yellow bus epiphany would actually materialize. My family had their unexpressed doubts about the credibility of this marriage of a 52-year old to some 29-year old from Malaysia.

As we descended the massive marble staircase to go to the reception, Chuan's words summed up the whole morning, "Hubby, we got married. *Shit!*" I think he meant, "Wow!"

There were 2 wedding receptions — one in San Francisco where we uncorked a stockpile of champagne we had been accumulating all summer. I didn't get to have any of it because of my antibiotics and the possible side effect that I might get depressed and commit suicide in the middle of the reception. Our Arizona friends held another reception a couple weeks later in Tucson. This time I got to partake in champagne toasts.

Chuan's mother's texts continued flowing in seamlessly but now took on a different tenor with her realization that her son was married and irretrievably installed in America. "Son, don't forget to clean the house," she texted, and, "Watch out, you'll get fat in America." She also inquired if cactus juice was on sale — in her own way and on her own terms, she had accepted our marriage.

CHAPTER 35
HOME AT LAST

*O*ur honeymoon was an unglamorous return to Tucson in the middle of summer to begin the immigration process that would hopefully grant Chuan permanent residency. Applying for an American green card is an unenviably tedious task for anyone, especially for someone coming from a Muslim country, and for me being of meager income. We gathered all our paperwork, our financial statements, birth certificates, affidavits of friendship, pictures, etc., and contacted an immigration attorney. After several hours of counseling from our attorney, medical exams, and just over $5,500 in fees, we were ready to present our briefcase full of information to the US Department of Homeland Security. The certified checks were cut, the applications were filled out and mailed in and then we waited for our appointment to be interviewed.

In the intervening months, Donald Trump assumed the presidency, possibly putting Chuan's application in peril. The new president had not yet singled out Malaysia as one of his targeted Muslim countries, but I began losing sleep over the issue.

In some ways Chuan is like a child. He moves through life relatively unconcerned about most of the details that torment the rest of us, so I do the worrying for both of us. At 3 am I would wake up feeling like a tiny speck caught in a massive bureaucracy that could take away the gentle being sleeping next to me.

I imagined a Customs agent with guns and dogs separating us and asking Chuan questions like: "Why did you tell the Customs agent in Malaysia that you were 'just friends' in your tourist visa interview? Why didn't you have a return flight booked when you entered the US? You intended to get married, didn't you? You abused your tourist visa by getting married!"

In my nightmares, I could see Chuan cowering like a child and wetting his pants when the agent handcuffs him and takes him to a detention center for deportation. I worried that I had gotten him into something he couldn't manage himself and without me or our attorney to defend him, he would be smashed like a little bug.

The months clicked by and I checked the mailbox each day for notice of our interview. Finally, one afternoon, it arrived. I ran into the house tearing the envelope open. I yelled upstairs, "Chuan, we have our immigration interview date in 3 weeks!" He ran down and read the letter. We called our attorney and arranged to meet her for a preparatory session. Some friends sent in their notarized letters affirming our relationship and we printed out 82 photographs of us together for the past 2½ years — pictures of us in Bali, Borneo, Thailand, and all over the American West. We had pictures of us singing in the Tucson Symphony Chorus together and of Chuan cutting my parents' hair in Florida. There was really no way this relationship could be deemed fraudulent.

The morning of our interview we put on our suit jackets and gathered all our paperwork. I sat in the car with my pulse slightly accelerated wondering if I should have taken a Xanax. Considering that drooling in a stupor in the lobby wouldn't really make a good case for a reliable husband, I guess I made the right decision to not partake. I ran through all the scenarios in my head, reviewed all the potential questions they can ask you to prove the marriage is a sham.

"Chuan sleeps on the right side of the bed. His favorite food is everything. He likes to watch *House, MD* and listens to Beethoven," I muttered to myself in the car.

Before the interview, I sent out a notice to all our neighbors and friends that we would commemorate or commiserate the decision at a nearby restaurant that evening as we expected to know immediately whether or not he would be approved for his green card. I said we would be wearing green scarves if he got to stay and black if he had to leave.

Then we waited in the sterile lobby of the US Customs and Immigration Service surrounded mostly by Mexicans who were there for similar reasons. I was heartened not to have to see a photo of Donald Trump's frowning face in the lobby, perhaps they hadn't yet arrived since he had only been in office 3 weeks. Our attorney, Claudia, was late causing me no small amount of distress. I called her office and they said she was on her way. I paced around a bit trying to make light conversation. Claudia finally arrived looking radiant and giving us both hugs and encouragement.

Chuan's name was called by a woman in a blue satin blouse and beige skirt. It was not an officer's uniform with a gun and Taser as I had expected. Was *she* the officer we were assigned or the assistant? Claudia was behind us as we walked to meet the agent and whispered, "You're lucky, she's nice." I felt some sense of dread lifting off my shoulders.

She was indeed our officer and had lived in San Francisco years ago. In the 10 minutes of previewing our case she saw we were married in San Francisco's city hall. She saw we were first time married, gay, no criminal records, or violations of visas. All this added up to the extreme unlikelihood that we were faking this marriage.

We dumped on her desk the pile of pictures of the past years of our relationship, along with our sworn statements from friends. Then we pulled out a stack of wedding cards, top of the pile being the handmade bicycle wheel watercolor made by our friends Thom and Alex from the Tucson Village Farm.

It was all enough that the officer said to us, "You got your green card the minute you walked in the door, but I have to go through some formalities. Your green card will arrive in a couple weeks. But you are officially a permanent resident of the United States as of today."

Oh. My. God. It happened. It was *that* easy? This officer in the blue satin blouse just made our lives enormously better. We finished the rest of the interview and she didn't separate us to ask us things like what side of the bed we sleep on and does he have any distinctive moles or birthmarks?

We walked out of the office back to the lobby within a half hour of entering and flashed Trish, our housemate, the thumbs up. A big smile came over her face. What a RELIEF! I no longer have to have my bank accounts scrutinized, I don't have to have a million we-fies on my blog to prove our relationship. It's over, done, finished. Glory hallelujah, justice is, on rare occasions, done in America. We went home feeling exultant and exhausted and ready to party.

We got to the restaurant a little ahead of schedule wearing our green scarves. Some of the friends coming texted for a peek and a clue but we didn't tell anyone. At the stroke of 6, Alex came running up the stairs with a single green balloon and a look of worry on her face as she rushed to us. I heard her say, "Are they wearing green? Oh, thank god!" The look of fear turned to relief and she threw her arms around Chuan. Practically the whole neighborhood came with cards, gifts, some edible greens as a symbolic gesture, and a chocolate fudge cake (not sure what that symbolized). We put a bunch of tables together to accommodate everyone and bought a round of drinks for everyone. All our neighbors and friends

303

have grown fond of Chuan — his kindness, his generosity, his piano playing, his curry — and perhaps seeing me not lonely and miserable anymore.

Chuan and I stood up and offered a toast to everyone, thanking them for their support and telling the story of the officer in the blue satin blouse. We drank to the triumph of love and law.

That night I lay in bed thinking about all the struggles of gay relationships over the decades that made this marriage possible for us. In my lifetime, I have gone from visiting shadowy gay bars where we had to park in the back so no one would see or vandalize our cars, to the age of AIDS when plenty of Americans were happy to see us dying. We went from serving in the military in secrecy to serving openly. We went through several rounds of being granted the right to marry and then having it reversed.

I myself lost a relationship because of the previous inability to welcome my partner to live in the US. And now I have the full federal right to be married and rights of immigration for my spouse. Never in this bureaucratic process was I ever judged or looked at in a cross way. Never were we denied any of our rights or our dignity by anyone in any of the many governmental agencies we dealt with from California to Arizona to the federal government.

I thought about the enormously long process finding a husband has been from packing up and moving to Malaysia, to falling in love with Chuan, to falling out of love with Malaysia. Then there was the tourist visa application, closing up the apartment, the separation, the repatriation, the reunion, the hospital, the marriage, and finally immigration. It was a dizzying 2½ years and absolutely worth it.

A few months ago, while on a visit to see my family in Florida, I watched my husband cut my parents' hair on their back porch amid my father's orchid collection. Chuan spoke gently with my 80-year old mother while spraying her hair with a cool mist of water. He separated sections of fine gray strands and combed them out in preparation for cutting. I watched him gently adjusting her head. Tufts of wet, gray hair landed on the black drape. Then I watched Chuan cut my father's hair with delicate precision. He stands behind the 86-year old gently combing and silently snipping. Hardly a word is spoken as my parents both seem to surrender to the moment. They can feel the care that he is taking with them and it calms them. I sat watching and thinking, how can you *not* love this guy? My parents couldn't resist, just as Chuan's fragile grandparents can't when he leads them by the hand, steadying them through the chaotic markets of Malaysia.

My parents abandoned their concerns about him being a suitable partner for me and melted into the tender kindness that is so very rarely found anywhere, and yet is so very Chuan. They knew shortly after experiencing his warmth and devotion that I found a great guy. They gave us their blessing. "Listen," my mother said, "Here's the deal, no more calling me 'Mrs. Gilmore.' From now on you call me 'Mom.'"

Although our relationship has an internationally intriguing component to it, it's not perfect. I'm a Neatnik, and Chuan's a bit sloppy. I'm perennially melancholy, and he's sometimes frustratingly cheerful. I pick up his socks and grumble about it and he tries to cheer me up with a video that I don't find funny. I'm a reader. He's a watcher. The biggest problem, though, is the one with the balloon payment down the road. There's just no escaping the fact that I'm 23 years older. That means if we live and die with a typical life-expectancy, I will time out well before he does, leaving him stranded in his middle age. It's heartbreaking for me to even think of this, but when some wonderful guy sweeps you off your feet, do you tell him, "Umm, excuse me young man, stop the music and put me down. Yes, put me down! I'm too old for you and one day, years from now, you'll be at my bedside holding my icy old hand and we will have a teary farewell and then you'll be alone the rest of your life."

In a quiet moment, late at night Chuan will address this concern, "Hubby, you won't leave me alone in my old age, we'll both die together." He even has the nerve to say it cheerfully. This is not exactly settling news for me just before going to bed, or at any time. I don't know what sort of fate *that* vision holds for both of us, but it is his solution to this ultimately intractable problem. Perhaps what's more realistic is that I will become so cranky and irascible in my old age that when I die, he'll be deeply relieved to see me go and will have Hubby v.2 waiting in the wings. This scenario somehow gives me a bit more peace of mind.

On the other hand, one of the benefits of a May-December relationship is that I qualify as the voice of age and experience in the relationship. Having already exhausted 2/3 of my life, I am able to appreciate the preciousness of each moment we have together, and I let my younger husband know of my gratitude almost unfailingly, each day.

"Chuan, how lucky are we to have found each other. You know, nothing is forever, and I'm so grateful for you in my life," I whisper in his ear first thing in the morning, my stale morning breath curling his hair. My existential ponderings are mostly lost on his young mind. And then he fulfills *his* part of our arrangement adding some youthful sparkle.

"Yes, Hubby, me too. Hey, I just had a dream that we filled up the backyard with water and got a pair of pet dolphins. We called them Sissy and Chad," and he goes back to sleep satisfied for having shattered my solemn moment into laughable little bits complete with magical dolphins in the desert.

Life is full of impracticalities and mysteries. Closing up my life in America to chase a dream of love was anything but practical and sane. Following that yellow bus vision to the ends of the earth made no real sense to anyone with his feet on the ground, no less to me. But I did it anyway, and here, snoring away while I write at dawn, is the living, breathing proof that sometimes life just can't be linear and predictable. Well, it could have been. I could have stayed home sitting in my backyard hoping for some small joy to scribble in my sad little book of happiness. Instead I went on a fantastic journey across the oceans and came back with a wonderful guy — a really good one. And that *is* a happy ending indeed.

AFTERWORD

A year after Chuan had been in the US, his mother and all his aunts were in dire need of a good cut and color. His entire family was missing their star hairdresser. So, he made the journey back to Malaysia, without me, to spend a month with them. Returning to his mother's apartment in the Chinese housing projects outside of Kuala Lumpur, Chuan was greeted by his mother, "Oh, you've gotten fat!" Her cool greeting set the tone for a bumpy transition from West to East.

Chuan's first text to me when he arrived in KL was, "I'm back. Have an ugh feeling. Hubby, they're not so civilized here." I had to laugh because American politics seemed to be at an all-time low in 2017 with the ascendancy of Donald Trump to the White House. In the coming days, Chuan relayed back to me how no one in his family had any interest in him or his new life as a gay married man in the States. Questions to him were all about money and financial security.

"All my mother talks about is her dumpling business," he wrote to me. "I'm back to being the houseboy and hairdresser. They don't care anything about my life in the US or about my marriage."

"Well, I'm not surprised, Chuan. When did they *ever* ask

about the inner workings of your life? Your grandfather thought I was a CIA spy and your mother said to watch out for white people because they're selfish. All they want to know about me is if my business is prospering. I think they love you but they just don't know how to express it in any warm and fuzzy way that you're now accustomed to in the States. Here our friends will look you in the eye and ask you how you are and wait for an answer. Americans will ask you all the questions about your life that your own family wouldn't dare to ask."

Still, the human heart must find a way to express itself. Even the Chinese, not known for their overt outpourings of love find a way to express their care for loved ones. You just have to know where to look to find them. In Chinese culture, affection is doled out in "ang pow," small red packets of money customarily exchanged with family members at Chinese New Year, weddings, and special occasions. They are usually given from the older to younger generations or to the sick. Every year, Chuan would receive a red packet from each of his uncles, aunts, his mother, and his grandparents. Customarily, when the gifts are given to a couple, there would be 2 envelopes — one for the husband and one for the wife.

This year when Chuan arrived back in Malaysia, a pile of red packets was waiting for him at his mother's apartment as he had been in the States for Chinese New Year. When he sorted through the packets he saw that he had double the number of packets this year but the name David was on half the envelopes. Being that Chuan's brother's name is also David, he assumed they were to be given to his brother. They weren't. Every member of the family had acknowledged our marriage by including a packet for me as Chuan's spouse. This seemingly small event meant that I had been welcomed into the family.

Chuan snapped a photo of the pile of little red envelopes and texted it to me. I pinch-zoomed in on the photo to see that my name was indeed written on the packets. I stared dumbstruck at the screen. It wasn't a California-style embrace. It wasn't with any grand professions of love or promises for the future, but it was a clear statement. Chuan is certain that they don't talk about our relationship. Even though they aren't Muslim Malaysians, they still have led sheltered lives from government censorship of all things gay. In this regard, all Malaysians who haven't found a way over the internet firewall remain generations behind the West. Still, someone in the family must have put the word out that Chuan is now married, and even if it's to a dude, he deserves to be included in the family.

"Chuan, I can't believe my eyes! Was there any discussion about this?" I asked in shock at this gesture, and wanting to give credit where credit was due.

"Nope. I don't think they talk about us over the dinner table."

"But how did they know to include me? Your grandparents don't have smart phones and so they didn't get your text when you announced last year that you were marrying your boyfriend. *Someone* in your family has been championing our relationship to the older generations. Who do you think it was? Maybe they think I'm old and sick and it was a pity gift?" Chuan didn't seem to appreciate my prying and my looking the gift horse in the mouth. Getting to the bottom of things is so very American. Maybe I just needed to accept the trans-Pacific hug. Quietly. Humbly. But still, I wanted to know who in his family had been good-mouthing us.

The night before Chuan was to leave Malaysia and return back to me in the States, he asked if I would do a quick video chat with his mother to reassure her once again that I would take care of him in America. Even though conversations with his mother are always awkward, I agreed. His mother's round and wet face appeared on my phone.

"Hello Mrs. Choy," I said.

"Hello David," she seemed barely able to speak.

"I want you to know that I will take good care of your son. Please don't worry. He has a good life in America. He will get a good education and he has a nice home here." She nodded her head with appreciation, tears filling her narrow eyes.

"Thank you, David," she said trying not to lose her composure. So, I lost mine.

"Oh, you're so welcome. Chuan is a wonderful guy and I'm sure it's hard to say goodbye to him." We looked into each other's eyes via our small screens for just one second, nothing more. But in that second it was clear that we have one thing in common — our love of a wonderful young man. Saying goodbye to Chuan, no matter which side of the planet we're on, is never going to be easy.

I had my answer as to who could possibly be promoting welcoming a Caucasian, gay, American into the family. It was someone I would never have thought would be up for the task and the very person who loses the most every time her son leaves to be with me. Then we simultaneously pressed the red "end" button.

And Chuan folded space.

ABOUT THE AUTHOR

David Gilmore is a free lance writer, photographer, and filmmaker living in Tucson, Arizona. He was the host and producer of the Edward R. Murrow Award winning radio show *Outright Radio,* featured nationally on Public Radio International from 1998-2004. He is a NEA and CPB grantee and has contributed essays to the *Gay & Lesbian Review Worldwide, The Advocate,* and was a contributing author in *Johns, Marks, Tricks, and Chickenhawks.* He is the author of the book *HomoSteading at the 19th Parallel — one man's adventure building his nightmare dream house on the Big Island of Hawaii.*

Accompanying photos for this book can be seen on Instagram at justawanderingeye and videos on YouTube at the channel MisterThistleFlower. The author can be reached at davidgdesigns@gmail.com.

Cover design and most photography in this book are by the author with a little help from Sebastian Bock, Tom Truss, Scott Simmons, and Trish Haines.

Made in the USA
San Bernardino, CA
24 November 2017